HYMNS FOR
SIGNING

AMERICAN SIGN LANGUAGE

HYMNS FOR SIGNING

ABINGDON PRESS
Nashville

HYMNS FOR SIGNING
Copyright © 1995 by Abingdon Press

This book is printed on recycled, acid-free paper.

ISBN 0-687-43180-8

02 03 04 — 10 9 8 7

MANUFACTURED IN THE UNITED STATES OF AMERICA

EDITOR'S PREFACE

A work like *Hymns for Signing* is probably never a completed project, as sign language, like all languages, is fluid. However, LaVerle Carrington, head translator, and I are very excited about the finished project. We hope that you can use *Hymns for Signing* as a tool to help make worship services accessible to those persons who depend upon American Sign Language. We realize that persons may have preferred that we translate some of the hymns differently. Remember that this is a tool for you to use, so feel free to write changes or notes in your copy in order to best serve your needs. I believe that the best way for an interpreter to use this book would be to look at the worship bulletin before the service and look over the hymns to be sung to be sure that he/she is familiar with the meaning and flow of each hymn. Section numbers correspond with hymn selections in *The United Methodist Hymnal.*

Much work went into producing this hymnal. I would like to thank LaVerle and Wendy Carrington, who headed up the translation team and did the bulk of the translating as well as entering the hymns into the computer. Those who volunteered to help with the translation are: Lee and Janet Painter, Jean Miller, the Reverend Tom A. Summey, Jr., Angie Liston, and Barbara Clark. Several interpreters for the deaf looked over the hymnal and tried out the hymns, giving us some comments. These interpreters included: Debbie Johnson, Gerri Wellman, Teresa Wilson, Diane Peterson, Lori McKenzie, and Ronda Hewlitt. Recognition needs to be given to the United Methodist Congress of the Deaf, out of which this project was born. I also want to thank the United Methodist Board of Discipleship and the Scarritt Foundation for their financial support in funding the project. Finally, I want to thank Gary Alan Smith for his help, and the United Methodist Publishing House for agreeing to publish this work.

Curt D. Keller, Editor

INSTRUCTIONS TO SIGNERS

Personal pronouns are signed with the "index" finger. The locations are decided by the interpreter as to being present or not being present.

Possessive pronouns are signed with an "open palm" hand shape and are signed the same as personal pronouns. The direction is signed toward the owner.

The Agent suffix is signed to change verbs to nouns making a person. An example, Maker (make + agent).

Adjectives can appear either before or after the noun, depending on which emphasis the writer placed on the description.

Classifiers are used to describe a place or thing and represent sizes and shapes. Some of the hand shapes that are used are "F hand shape," R and L bent "L" hand shapes, "C" hand shape, both "C" hand shapes, "B" hand shape, both "B" hand shapes, etc.

Negative words are signed with a head shake and eyebrows squeezed together.

Positive words are signed with a nod of the head.

The sign "finish" is used in many of the songs to show action has already been accomplished. Sometimes "finish" will appear before or after the verb.

Directional verbs should be signed in the direction of the subject or object location. Some of these words in the hymns are "show," "give," "look," "ask," "help," "send," "tell," and so forth.

"Itself," "himself," "yourself," etc., should be all signed in place of the "who" question sign. Move the right "10" toward the left "index." The "place" sign should be signed for the "where" question sign. The sign for "happen" should be signed for the "when" question sign. "Reason" should be signed for the "why" question sign. These changes are made when questions are not being asked.

When a noun and a verb represent the same sign, the verb will always be the larger sign; the noun will be the smaller sign and often repeated.

"Here" is indicated by pointing to the location; "there" is indicating by pointing to the location off to the side to show difference between "here" and "there."

"This" and "that" used in the hymns are often signed in the location of the object or thing, rather than signed into the left palm.

When indicating a noun meaning "many" or "mass," the sign "plenty" will be signed at the end of the sentence.

American Sign Language: A Comprehensive Dictionary by Martin L. A. Sternberg, Ed.D. (New York: Harper and Row, 1981), has been the resource book used for this hymnal.

Numbers in parentheses refer to the meaning of the word found in the above dictionary. Some words have several concepts associated with them and this numbering system is used to help clarify which concept if one has questions, i.e. (#2).

1. O, one thousand languages sing my
   great(#3) Redeemer(#1) praise, glory my
   God, King, triumph(#1) God grace (#1).

2. My gracious ruler(#1), my God, assist me
   proclaim, spread through-out all
   world, honor, your name.

3. Jesus, name help fade our fears,
   bids(#1) our sorrows stop; True music, for
   sinner ears, true life, health, peace.

4. Jesus destroy power that control(#1) sin,
   Jesus free prisoner, Jesus blood can make
   sinner clean; Jesus blood finish save me.

5. Jesus speak, listen his voice, new
   life after death finish receive; sorrow,
   broken hearts rejoice, humble poor believe.

6. Listen, Jesus, you deaf; his praise, you quiet,
   your free talk use; you blind, look-up
   your Savior come, leap, you crippled, now joy.

7. Through Jesus, your Lord, you will(#1)
   know, will(#1) feel your sins finish forgive,
   look-forward-to[1] your heaven coming, know love,
   heaven same.

[1]Look-forward-to: R and L "V" hand positions, palms down, right in front of the left. Move both hands out and back several times.

I'll Praise My Maker While I've Breath

1. I praise God while I still(#1) breath;
   happen my voice is(#1) lost because death,
   praise will take-up my noble power(#1). My
   day praise will continue, while life, belief,
   life continues, living forever endure(#2).

2. Happy are(#1) people hope depend Israel
   God, himself made heaven, earth, ocean with
   all plans; his truth forever strong support,
   he saves burdened, feeds poor, no one will
   find God promise vain.

3. Lord gives blind new sight; Lord help
   improve weak mind, give hurting heart peace.
   God helps stranger[1] sorrow, woman without
   husband, children without father,
   gives prisoner free release.

4. I praise my God himself gives me breath;
   happen my voice lost because death,
   praise will take-up my noble power(#1).
   My day praise will continue, while life,
   belief, life continues,
   living forever endure(#2).

[1]Stranger: Sign "strange" (#1) then add the person ending sign.

Come, Thou Almighty King

1. Come, almighty King,
   Help us sing your name, help us praise!
   Father all glory, over-all victory(#1),
   come reign over us, Lord God!

2. Come, show your Word,
   Unite your mighty(#2), our prayer attend!
   Come, bless your people give your word success;
   Holy Spirit, come-upon us!

3. Come, Holy Spirit,
   Your holy witness accept this happy hour.
   God is(#1) mighty(#2), rule(#1) every person,
   never leave(#1) us, Spirit Power(#1)!

4. You, great(#3) One-in-Three,
   eternity(#1) praises give God,
   from-then-on, God control(#1) best,
   May we see God glory, eternity(#1) love, praise!

All Creatures of Our God and King

1. All people our God, King, rise(#3) your
   voice with us sing, O praise you! Alleluia!
   See sunrise gold shine, see moon bright shine!

Refrain:
   O praise you! O praise you!
   Alleluia! Alleluia! Alleluia!

2. O wind, clouds, rain, through which
   all people live, O praise you! Alleluia!
   Your sunrise every-morning,[1] praise rejoice,
   bright night,[2] find voice!

Refrain

3. O river(#2) clean, make signs (or music)
   for Lord look-down (or hear) Alleluia!
   Alleluia! O fire become bright night,
   give warmth, please look-around.

Refrain

4. O earth, every-day open new bless
   on our way. Alleluia! Alleluia!
   You let flowers, fruit grow,
   let God glory show also!

Refrain

5. All you have tender-heart(#1), forgive other
   people, accept responsibility, O praise you!
   Alleluia! You ever-since accept pain sorrow,
   praise God, give God your burden, take-care-of!

Refrain

6. Our peace death, wait finish
   our last(#1) breath, Alleluia! Alleluia!
   You lead home child God, same way
   Jesus, our Lord, finish walk.

Refrain

7. Let God bless all things, worship God
   humble(#1), O praise God! Alleluia!
   Praise, praise, Father, Praise Son,
   Praise Spirit, Three-in-One.

Refrain

[1]Every-morning: Begin morning from the left and move all the way to the right.
[2]Night: Use the sign for "all night."

Blessed Be the Name   63

Bless be(#1) name!
Bless be(#1) name!
Bless be(#1) name Lord!

Bless be(#1) name!
Bless be(#1) name!
Bless be(#1) name Lord!

64   Holy, Holy, Holy! Lord God Almighty

1. Holy, holy, holy! Lord God Mighty(#2)!
   Early morning our song praise you.
   Holy, holy, holy! Mercy(#2), mighty(#2), God,
   three persons, blessed Trinity!

2. Holy, holy, holy! All angels love you,
   cast off golden crowns around shine[1] sea;
   Angels kneeling before(#3) you, God, same
   past, true now, will(#1) always be(#1).

3. Holy, holy, holy! No matter dark hide
   you, no matter eye sinner your glory may(#1)
   not see, only you holy; no other equal you,
   God perfect, power, love, purity(#1).

4. Holy, holy, holy! Lord God Mighty(#2)! All
   your work praise your name, earth, sky(#2),
   sea. Holy, holy, holy! Mercy(#2), mighty(#2),
   God, three persons, blessed Trinity.

[1]Shine: Should be signed coming off the back of the left hand, indicating sea surface is shining.

Praise, My Soul, the King of Heaven

66

1. Praise my soul, King heaven, thanks bring
   your throne;[1] save, health, make new, forgive,
   always God praise sing, Alleluia!
   Alleluia! Praise everlasting(#2) King.

2. Praise Lord for grace, favor, all people
   trouble; praise God, still same always, slow
   anger, quick bless. Alleluia! Alleluia!
   Glory now God faithful (#2).

3. As father, God, takes-care, saves us;
   make our weak body well(#2), God true knows;
   as mother, God kind accept us, save from all
   enemies. Alleluia! Alleluia!
   More, more, God mercy(#1) spreads.

4. Angels heaven above, worship, you see
   God, face-to-face; angels victory(#1), now
   worship, gather(#2) from every group.
   Alleluia! Alleluia! Praise with us
   God grace.

[1]Throne: R and L "C" hand positions, palms facing down and separated, move both hands back toward the body in an arc motion, representing the arms of a large chair.

We, Thy People, Praise Thee

Refrain:
> We, your people, praise you, God every
> nation! We, your people, praise you,
> praise you, Lord All eternal!

1. Day wonder(#2), day beauty, day joy
   filled with light(#1), tell your good, tell
   your mercy(#1), tell your glory mighty(#2).
   We, your people, praise you, praise you,
   praise you always-still.

Refrain

2. For your bless, for your good, we
   sing joy song you, song glory, song
   triumph(#1) our God, King. We, your
   people praise you, praise you, praise
   you always-still.

Refrain

When in Our Music God Is Glorified

1. Happen during our music, God glory(#2),
   praise leave(#2) no place for pride,
   seems all world shout Alleluia!

2. Happen often, during music, we finish
   find new opportunity(#3) world sound, as
   worship change us more inspire,[1] Alleluia!

3. Church has worship, song, faith, love,
   through generations wrong, begin
   witness truth every language, Alleluia!

4. Remember Jesus sang psalm that night,
   happen awful evil against his teach.
   Then(#1) let us sing, Jesus, himself won
   battle, Alleluia!

5. Let every person ready praise! Let all
   rejoice with signs offer! May God give us
   faith sing always, Alleluia!

[1]Inspire: R and L flat "O" hand positions, palms facing body at the heart, fingers pointing up, move both hands up opening into "5" hand positions.

Glory Be to the Father

Glory be(#1) Father,
Son, Holy Spirit;
as was, begin, is(#1)
now, future, world
continue. Amen. Amen.

O Worship the King

1. O worship King, all glory above,
   O thank sing God power(#1), God love;
   our support, Defender, Lord God Almighty,
   surround with honor, full praise offer.

2. O tell God might(#1), O sing God grace,
   God life is(#1) bright(#1), God heaven
   all-over(#1), God path anger, like(#2) black
   clouds above, dark is(#1) God path on
   move disturb.

3. Earth with all secrets wonder(#2) not
   yet told, Mighty(#2) God your power(#1) began
   long-ago, finish established through law
   not changed, sea around earth finish form
   like(#2) coat.

4. Your love take-care, what word can use?
   Breathes air, shines bright; shines from hills,
   comes flat-all-over, sweet becomes like(#2) dew,[1]
   rain.

5. Weak children on earth, humble(#1) and weak,
   we trust you, find you never fail; your
   mercy(#1) true tender(#1), true strong(#1)
   continue, our God, Defender, Redeemer, Friend.

[1]Dew: sign "water" then the sign for "wet," moving in a clockwise circle, indicating dew all over.

All People That on Earth Do Dwell

1. All people here on earth, sing Lord
   with cheerful word, Lord serve with
   happy his praise announce; come
   before(#3) Lord, rejoice.

2. Know Lord is(#1) God indeed; without
   our help God finish make us; we his people,
   God feed us, God take-care his people.

3. O enter his gate with praise; approach with
   joy, enter his place; praise, glory, bless
   his name always, for is(#1) right do.

4. Reason, Lord our God is(#1) good; God
   mercy(#1) is(#1) forever sure; God truth always
   strong(#1) show, will continue from generation, generation.

How Great Thou Art

1. O Lord my God! Happen, I inspire[1]
   wonder(#1) consider(#1) all worlds your
   hands finish made, I see stars, I hear
   continue thunder, your power(#1) through-out
   world display.

Refrain:

   Then(#1) sings my soul, my Savior God you;
   very wonder(#2) you are(#1), very
   wonder(#2) you are(#1)! Then sings my
   soul, my Savior God you, very wonder(#2)
   you are(#1), very wonder(#2) you are(#1)!

2. Happen, through woods, open place forest
   I wander(#2), see birds sing sweet trees,
   happen I look-down from high mountain
   wonder(#2), see river, feel pleasant breeze;

Refrain

3. Happen I think, that God, his Son not
   save, sent(#1) Jesus die, I difficult
   control(#2); that on cross, my sin glad bear(#4),
   Jesus bled, died, take away my sin;

Refrain

4. Happen, Jesus will come with shouts
   acclamation, bring me home, true joy will
   fill my heart. Then(#1) I will kneel humble adore,
   proclaim, my God, very wonder(#2) you are(#1)!

Refrain

[1]Inspire: R and L flat "O" hand positions, palms facing body at the heart, fingers pointing up, move both hands up changing into "5" hand positions.

Holy God, We Praise Thy Name

1. Holy God, we praise your name; Lord all, we kneel before(#3) you; all on earth your rod demands; all heaven above love you. Continue your world control(#1); forever your reign.

2. Pay attention, glad heaven hymn, angel group(#1) sing above, Angel join angel continue sing praises, fill heaven with sweet cooperate: Holy, holy, holy Lord.

3. See, believers line-up join your holy name hallowed(#2); prophet swell(#1) glad music, white-robed angels follow. From morning till sunset, through church song continue.

4. Holy Father, Holy Son, Holy Spirit: three name we call you, although essential only one; not divided, God we demand you, worship kneel, while we have faith.

5. Jesus, you are(#1) glory King, Son God, throne[1] splendid(#3); but deliver bring you all honors finish surrender, was born Virgin-Mary on humble(#1) bless morning.

[1]Throne: R and L "C" hand positions, palms facing down and separated, move both hands back toward the body in an arc motion, representing the arms of a large chair.

Stanzas 1–4 ASL translation © 1995 The United Methodist Publishing House
Stanza 5 ASL translation © 1995 Church Hymnal Corporation

¡Canta, Débora, Canta!

1. Sing, "D" girl, Sing! Sing, "D" girl, Sing!
   Mother Israel, leader nation army, sing
   hymn victory(#2) our God.

Refrain:
   Because our God is(#1) good! God is(#1)
   good, finish choose people themselves
   are(#1) humble. Because our God is(#1)
   good! God is(#1) good, will(#1) strength
   people with might(#1)!

2. Sing, "D" girl, Sing! Sing, "D" girl, sing!
   We rise(#3)-up our voice, all people
   together, sing triumph(#2) our God.

Refrain

Gloria in Excelsis

Glory be(#1) God on high, on earth,
peace, good will(#2), all. We praise
you, we bless you, we worship you,
we glory you, we give thanks you for
your great(#3) glory: O Lord God,
heavenly King, God Father Mighty.
O Lord, your only Son, Jesus Christ;
O Lord God, Son God, Son Father,
take-away sins world, give us mercy(#1).
You take-away sins world, receive our
prayer. You sit right hand God Father,
have mercy(#2) upon us. Because you only
holy; you only are(#1) Lord; you only,
O Jesus, with Holy Spirit, are(#1)
most high, glory God Father. Amen.

Thank You, Lord

Thank you, Lord.
Thank you, Lord.
Thank you, Lord.
I only want
thank you, Lord.

85   We Believe in One True God

1. We believe one true God, Father, Son,
   Holy Spirit, always with us, help, need,
   praise through-out all heavenly group(#1)
   group(#1); through your mighty-power(#1)
   alone, all is(#1) finished made.

2. We believe Jesus Christ, Son God,
   Virgin-Mary Son, Jesus come-down from
   heaven, win(#1) salvation for us; through
   cross, death we are(#1) save from sin
   terrible suffering.

3. We confess Holy Spirit, himself from God,
   both continue; himself always support,
   comfort us all pain, fears, needs.
   Bless Holy Trinity,
   praise forever, be(#1) you.

86   Mountains Are All Aglow

1. Mountains are (#1) bright with autumn(#1)
   color(#2) bright; rivers are(#1) fill water,
   giving life our days. Golden field(#2)
   grow-grow wave(#1), praise God plenty harvest;
   thankful, grow tall, pay-attention our
   happy songs praise!

Refrain:
> Grow far as eyes can see far, grow far as
> humble(#1) hands can work, every harvest is(#1)
> from our Lord; every blessing is(#1) from our God.
> Praise for harvest, thanks our God.
> Praise for harvest, praise, praise God.

2. Every land[1] plenty rich harvest for all;
   every tree is(#1) fill with delicious grow
   new fruit. Sun, rain through Lord plan will(#1)
   come proper time. Work hard, God finish
   give-us reason for deep-in-heart thank-thank.

Refrain

3. Early spring is(#1) time sow all God
   seed(#3) life. Work hard plow God earth;
   make plans. Look-forward(#1)[2] God give
   harvest true plenty; promise bless will(#1)
   become ours each display.

Refrain

4. Praise Lord as we accept God word
   deep-in-heart. God finish[3] send sunshine, rain,
   for seed(#3) may grow. Dry area which seem empty,
   flowers still(#1) may bloom; trust God promise,
   we will show our thanks God!

Refrain

[1]Land: Sign for "dirt," then sign "spread."
[2]Look-forward: Sign "look"(#1) with both "V" hand positions, palms facing down, fingers point out, move out and back several times.
[3]Send: "Send" #2 in the opposite direction, coming from God.

What Gift Can We Bring

1. What[1] gift can we bring, what offer,
   what can show, what words can convey,
   joy this day? When grateful we come,
   remember, rejoice, what song
   can we offer, honor, praise?

2. Give thanks for past, for people with
   vision, finish planted, watered,
   dreams can become true. Give thanks for
   now, for study, for worship, for mission(#1)
   that calls(#1) us change prayer into work.

3. Give thanks for tomorrow, full surprises,
   because know no matter tomorrow may happen,
   God word is(#1) our promise always, forever;
   we rest God take-care live unite God love.

4. Now we bring this gift, this offer, this
   show, this word can convey, joy this day!
   Happen grateful we come, remember, rejoice,
   this song now we offer honor, praise.

[1]What: First stanza "what" should be signed as "where"(#2).

Maker, in Whom We Live

1. Maker, yourself we live, united you allow
   us move, you receive glory, power, praise for
   your create love. Let all angel group(#1),
   group, give thanks God high, while earth
   again joy song, sounds through heaven.

2. God, Jesus let all save people
   give people lives through thanks you for
   you redeem(#1) grace. Heaven sing group(#1)
   proclaim your grace you show sinner, proclaim,
   "Salvation our God, Salvation Jesus."

3. Holy Spirit, let all your angels love
   your holy might(#1), bless your power(#1) make
   new heart. No angel speech can tell your
   love happy height(#2), glory joy cannot(#1)
   be(#1) spoken, happy sight.

4. Eternity(#1), Trinity God, let all
   group(#1), group, above, let all people earth,
   remember live unite your love. Happen Heaven
   earth disappear before(#3) your glory
   face, all angels sing your love, finish
   make your everlasting praise.

Joyful, Joyful, We Adore Thee

1. Joy, joy, we love you, God Glory, Lord
   love; hearts open like flower before(#3)
   you, flower-open sun above. Melt dark sin
   sad; remove(#1) dark doubt(#1). You give
   glad always, inspire[1] us everyday.

2. You make all beautiful surround you,
   earth, heaven show your beauty, stars,
   angels sing around you, center continue
   praise. Field(#2), woods, vale, mountain
   flowers all-over, shining sea, birds singing,
   water run-over, call(#1) us rejoice you.

3. You give, forgive, continue bless,
   always bless, you give-us joy for live(#1)
   deep-in-heart happy rest! You our Father,
   Jesus our brother, all people live(#1) in
   love are(#1) yours, teach us love
   each-other, inspire us joy divine.

4. People, join mighty sing group(#1),
   which morning stars began, love divine is(#1)
   reign over us, bind all people in time.
   Always sing, we march(#1) onward, victory
   among struggle; joy music leads us heaven,
   triumph(#1) song life.

[1]Inspire: R and L flat "O" hand positions, palms facing body at the heart, fingers pointing up, move both hands up opening into "5" hand positions.

Ye Watchers and Ye Holy Ones

90

1. You watchers(#1), you holy people, rejoice
   angels, heaven, inspire¹ happy music,
   Alleluia! Shout, kingdoms, prince control(#1),
   good, high angels, angels singing:

Refrain:
   Alleluia! Alleluia! Alleluia! Alleluia! Alleluia!

2. Heavenly angels class, more glorious
   angels class, lead angels praises,
   Alleluia! You give Holy Word,
   most merciful(#1), praise Lord.

Refrain

3. Answer you people, continue rest, you
   long-ago fathers, prophets bless,
   Alleluia! Alleluia! You holy followers,
   you, people suffer strong(#1), all angels
   victorious(#2), inspire song.

Refrain

4. O friends, let sing joy, heaven
   music repeat, Alleluia! Alleluia! God
   Father, God Son, God Spirit, Three-become-One.

Refrain

¹Inspire: R and L flat "O" hand positions, palms facing body at the heart, fingers pointing up, move both hands up opening into "5" hand positions.

Canticle of Praise to God

1. O come, let us sing unto Lord; let us
   sincere(#2) rejoice strength our salvation.

2. Let us come before(#3) Jesus with
   thanksgiving; show ourselves glad in
   Jesus with psalms.

3. Because Lord is(#1) great(#3) God,
   great(#3) King above all gods.

4. God hand all control(#1) world; strength
   hills is(#1) God control(#1) also.

5. Sea is(#1) God, He finish made sea;
   God hand prepare dry[1] land.

6. O come let us worship, bow-down(#2),
   kneel before Lord our Maker.

7. Because God is(#1) Lord our God; we
   are(#1) people his kingdom, people his hand.

8. O worship Lord, beauty holy; let
   all world stand surprise God.

9. Because God comes, because God comes
   judge world; with righteous(#2) judge
   world, people with God truth.

10. Glory Father, Son, Holy Spirit; As was
    begin, is(#1) now, future, world continue. A-men.

[1]Land: The sign for "dirt," then sign "spread."

For the Beauty of the Earth

1. For beauty earth, for glory sky(#1),
   for love you give us since our birth,
   over around us rest(#1);

Refrain: *(for Communion Day)*
   Lord all, you we offer our   Jesus, our God, you we offer
   song with grateful praise.   our sacrifice praise.

2. For beauty each hour, day,
   night, hill, vale, tree, flower,
   sun, moon, stars bright;

Refrain

3. For joy, listen, see, for heart,
   mind delight, for inspire[1] cooperate,
   join(#3) feel, listen, see;

Refrain

4. For joy people love, brother, sister,
   mother-father, child, friends on earth,
   friends above, for all gentle(#1) thought calm;

Refrain

5. For your church, ever(#3) rise(#3)
   holy hands above, offer-up ever(#2)
   support church pure(#2) sacrifice love;

Refrain
   6. God himself, best Gift Divine,
      world free give, for your great(#3),
      great(#3) love, peace earth, joy heaven;

Refrain

[1]Inspire: R and L flat "O" hand positions, palms facing body at the heart, fingers pointing up, move both hands up opening into "5" hand positions.

93   Let All the World in Every Corner Sing

Antiphon:
    Let all world every place sing:
    my God, King!

1. Heavens are(#1) not too-high,
   God praise may go that place;
   earth is(#1) not too-low,
   God praises there may grow.
   Let all world every place sing:
   my God, King!

Antiphon

2. Church with songs must shout,
   no door can forbid sing.
   But, more than all,
   heart my bear(#4) longest part.

Antiphon

94   Praise God, From Whom All Blessings Flow

Praise God, from whom all bless come,
praise God, all people here below:
Alleluia! Alleluia! Praise God, begin
all our gifts! Praise Jesus Christ, whose
power(#1) rise(#)! Praise Spirit, Holy Spirit!

Praise God, From Whom All Blessings Flow   95

Praise God, from whom all bless come:
praise God, all people here below; praise
God above, you heaven group(#1); praise Father
Son, Holy Spirit. Amen.

Praise the Lord Who Reigns Above   96

1. Praise Lord, himself reigns above,
   take-care followers earth; praise holy
   God love, all his great(#3) show; praise
   him for noble deed. Praise him for special
   power(#1); all good come from God,
   let earth heaven adore.

2. Celebrate eternity(#1) God with harp,
   songs, soft bell(#2), loud ring(#2) high
   praise sing; praise every music sound;
   all arrive heaven skill, all power(#1)
   music bring, music heart.

3. God, himself inspire[1] people live, let
   every person sing, people give glory God,
   people honor King, Holy(#1) be(#1) your
   name beneath, as heaven, earth adore;
   praise Lord every spoken word, let all
   things praise Lord.

[1]Inspire: R and L flat "O" hand positions, palms facing body at the heart, fingers pointing
up, move both hands up opening into "5" hand positions.

97   For the Fruits of This Creation

1. For harvest(#2) this world, thank
   God; for good gifts every country, thank
   God; for plow, sow, harvest(#2), silent
   grow while we sleep, future needs earth
   take-care, thank God.

2. Only award work, God will(#2)
   done(#2); we give help our neighbor
   God will(#2) done(#2); our world
   task take-care hungry, sorrow, we share
   harvest(#2), God will(#2) done(#2).

3. For Spirit harvest(#2), thank God;
   for good we all receive, thank God;
   for wonder(#2) that surprise us, for truth
   continue confuse us, important,
   love finish find us, thank God.

To God Be the Glory

1. Give God glory, great(#3) things God
   done(#2)! True, God loved world,
   God gave-us Son, himself yield his life,
   forgive sin, open heaven all people enter.

Refrain:

   Praise Lord, praise Lord, let people hear
   his voice! Praise Lord, praise Lord,
   let people rejoice! O come Father through
   Jesus Son, give him glory,
   great(#3) things he done(#2)!

2. O perfect redeem, accept life, every
   believer, promise God; sinner himself truly
   believes, that moment from Jesus
   forgive received.

Refrain

3. Great(#3) things he finish taught us,
   great(#3) things he done(#2),
   great(#3) our rejoicing through Jesus Son;
   but pure(#2), higher, great(#3) will(#1) become
   our wonder(#2), our joy, happen we see Jesus.

Refrain

99 My Tribute

99

God be(#1) glory, God be(#1) glory,
God be(#1) glory,
for things God done(#2).
With Jesus blood
he finish saved me;
with his power(#1)
he finish rise(#1) me;
God be(#1) glory,
for things he done(#2).

This ASL translation © 1995 Communique Music, Inc.

100 God, Whose Love Is Reigning O'er Us

1. God, himself love reign over us,
   begin all, end(#1) true; hear
   universal sing group(#3) sing joyful
   praise you: Alleluia, Alleluia, worship long-ago, worship new.

2. Word God from nature coming spring
   green, autumn gold; mountain river
   like(#2) children sing, ocean like(#2)
   hear-thunder strong(#1): Alleluia, Alleluia,
   as create world story is(#1) told.

3. Long-ago glory, Holy God choose man, woman
   too; Abraham faith, Sarah[1] story, teach
   people faithful(#2) you. Alleluia, Alleluia,
   your promise keep us true.

4. Agree, new again Jesus, child born
   free us; send(#2)[2] heal[3] us, sent teach us how
   we may become children love. Alleluia,
   Alleluia, rise(#1) Jesus, our Savior!

5. Rise(#3) our voices song faith
   will(#1) show; live our choices,
   people same our music, sing, Alleluia,
   Alleluia, join(#3) love, our praises ring(#2)!

[1]Sarah: Right "S" hand position at the right cheek, palm facing left.
[2]Send: "Send"(#2) except in the opposite direction, coming from God.
[3]Heal: Sign for "make," then the sign for "well"(#2).

This ASL translation © 1995 William Boyd Grove

From All That Dwell Below the Skies   101

1. All people live here on earth,
   let God praise rise(#3); let
   Redeemer(#1) name sing,
   through world, through every person.

2. Eternal[1] are(#1) your mercies(#2), Lord;
   eternal truth continue your word.
   Your praise will heard every where,
   till our life earth finished.

3. Your wonderful story, your people,
   bring songs praise, divine sing;
   great(#3) salvation proclaim loud,
   shout for joy Savior name.

4. In every land[2] begin song;
   every land music belong(#1);
   cheerful sounds all people sing,
   fill world with loud praise.

[1]Eternal: Sign "eternity"(#1).
[2]Land: Sign for "dirt," then sign "spread."

This ASL translation © 1995 The United Methodist Publishing House

102 Now Thank We All Our God

1. Now let us thank our God, with heart,
   hands, signs, himself done wonderful things,
   whom this world rejoices; from our mother
   arm finished bless us, on our way with many
   gift love, still is(#1) ours today.

2. O may this generous(#2) God through all
   our life be(#1) near us, with ever(#3) joyful
   heart bless peace cheer us; keep us ever(#2),
   grace, guide us happen trouble with doubt;
   free us from all evil, now world here, future.

3. All praise thanks God, Father now
   give; Son, Spirit reigns with God, highest
   heaven; one eternal God, earth heaven adore;
   as long ago, now, will(#1) always continue.

103 Immortal, Invisible, God Only Wise

1. God live always, can't see, God himself wise,
   bright we can't see hid from our eyes, most bless,
   most glory, Lord God Almighty, victory(#1),
   your great(#3) name we praise.

2. Never rest, never hurry, silent(#1) as light, not want,
   not waste, you reign might(#1); your justice(#1)
   like(#2) mountains high above your clouds
   which are(#1) begin, good, love.

3. You give life all, both great(#1) small; all life
   you up-there, true give life all; we grow,
   grow-grow like green grows tree,
   become old, die but you never change.

4. You reign glory; you live bright;
   your angels adore you, all hiding angels
   sight; all praise we will(#1) give; O help
   us see, only great(#3) bright hide you.

God of Many Names   105

1. God many names, sum-up become One,
   your glory come, meet us, inspiring,
   continue become; God protect
   arms, begin time, joy we sing
   your praises, breath life every people.

Refrain:
   Hush, hush, hallelujah, hallelujah! Shout, shout,
   hallelujah, hallelujah! Sing, sing, hallelujah,
   hallelujah! Sing God is(#1) love, God(#1) love.

2. God Jewish faith, depart, law, your glory came,
   met us, joy sister, Moses; God Jesus Christ,
   rabbi for poor, joy we sing your praises,
   crucified, alive forever.

Refrain

3. God wound hands, begin love, your glory came,
   met us, carpenter new world; God many names,
   sum-up become one, joy we sing your praises,
   inspiring continue become.

Refrain

107 Righteous and Just is the Word of Our Lord

Refrain:
Righteous, equal, is(#1) word our Lord;
faithful(#2), wonder(#2) are(#1) Lord work.
Justice(#1), right what God love, people
sit throne God right. From Lord love kind,
all earth fill with mercy(#1), from Lord
love kind, all earth filled with mercy(#1).

1. Through divine word from heaven,
   that way heavens were finish made;
   then(#1) from God came great(#2) breath,
   made stars night. God gather(#1) all
   water became ocean. God made dry land,
   made valleys from rivers.

Refrain

2. Fear God, all earth, all people!
   Bow-down(#2) God, all countries(#1)!
   Great(#3) skill work, grand(#2) wonder(#2),
   God command, life began. But people evil
   habit, find God plan frustrate. Only God
   judgment, God plans made certain,
   proclaim forever.

Refrain

108 God Hath Spoken by the Prophets

1. God finish speaking through prophets,
   speak never change Word, each from
   generation-generation proclaim, God only,
   righteous Lord! Center world loss hope,
   turmoil, strong belief support, God eternal
   reign forever, God first, God last.

2. God finish speaking through Jesus,
   Jesus everlasting Son, bright Father
   glory, with Father ever one; spoken
   through Word show, God only, before
   world began, Light, only, shine
   on-earth, Jesus, as God became man.

3. God still(#1) speak through Spirit, speak
   our heart again, long-ago Word inspire,[1]
   God himself Word, now as past. Through
   rise(#3), collapse, country(#1), One sure
   faith still(#1) believe strong, God continue,
   Word never changing, God first, God last.

[1]Inspire: R and L flat "O" hand positions, palms facing body at the heart, fingers pointing up, move both hands up opening into "5" hand positions.

Creating God, Your Fingers Trace   109

1. God, himself create, your hand shape
   clear plan far space, let sun, moon, stars,
   bright, no-matter hide, praise your might(#1).

2. Sustain God, your hands provide earth
   secrets known, not-yet told; let water
   mix with wind, make able life,
   proclaim your care.

3. Redeem(#1) God, your arms hug all now
   despise(#1) for belief, people; let peace,
   come like(#2) small bird, make known
   your heal[1] love.

4. Living God, your teaching interest one
   family with many, many names; let every
   person be(#1) touch-heart through grace till
   we praise you face-to-face.

[1]Heal: Sign for "make," then the sign for "well"(#2).

110   A Mighty Fortress Is Our God

1. Mighty(#2) defender is(#1) our God,
   defense never fail; our help, God among
   people, but much evil succeed. For our
   old enemy still seeks give us trouble;
   devil skill, power(#1) are(#1) great(#2),
   provide cruel(#1) hate(#1), on earth is(#1)
   no(#1) equal enemy-person.

2. Happen we our strength trust, our
   struggle fail, if not right man support
   us, man God himself choose. Ask (quote)
   "who that?" Answer is(#1) Christ Jesus,
   Lord worship his name, from
   generation, generation same,
   God must win battle.

3. In-spite-of here world fill with devils,
   should try hurt us, we will not fear,
   because God finish decide his truth
   triumph(#2) through us. Devil Dark show no
   mercy(#2), we don't fear devil because devil
   anger we can endure(#1), because look,
   devil ruin sure; one word from God can
   collapse devil.

4. That word above all earth power(#1),
   no(#1) thank people, accept;
   Spirit, gifts are(#1) ours, through God
   himself support us. Abandon(#1) things,
   family, abandon(#1) this life also;
   people can kill body; God truth continue
   still(#1); his kingdom forever.

How Can We Name a Love   111

1. How can we name Love that inspire[1]
   heart, mind, live all we know, think, do,
   seek, find? Within our daily world, every
   person face, Love is(#1) show, God
   is(#1) found, hid in everyday place.

2. If we know life, built on strength
   care, that ask no great(#1) award but
   strong, make certain, was simple(#2) there,
   with mother-father name we can explain,
   that way respect, love continue, father
   kind, mother strong, sure.

3. Happen people share task, strength,
   skills unite old-new activity, make-do
   with shared joy, our Friend, Helper
   will(#2) is(#1) better understood, that
   all should share, create, care,
   know that life is(#1) good.

4. True, many people name, everyday we all
   can meet now, feel, show work, home,
   street. Yet[2] every person name we see,
   shines as bright sun; Jesus alone is(#1)
   Love full grown, life, hope begun.

[1]Inspire: R and L flat "O" hand positions, palms facing body at the heart, fingers pointing up, move both hands up opening into "5" hand positions.
[2]Yet: In ASL this meaning is signed "but."

113   Source and Sovereign, Rock and Cloud

1. Begin, Ruler(#1), Support, Sky, Defend,
   Beginning, protect from danger, Bright,
   Judge, Defender, Mercy(#2), Might(#1), Life
   ever-since give life:

Refrain:
   May church, prayer, remember no(#1) one holy
   name, but truth past name all is(#1) God whom
   we proclaim.

2. Word, Wisdom, Strong(#2), Spread, Shepherd,
   Savior, Servant Jesus, Well(#3), Water, Bread,
   Wine, Way Himself leads us God.

Refrain

3. Storm, Still(#2), Breath, Holy Spirit, Thunder,
   Wind, Fire, Comfort, Counselor,
   Now Love, Enthusiasm never becomes tired.

Refrain

Many Gifts, One Spirit 114

1. God change glory, God time space, happen
   we fear future, give-us your grace. In
   middle change ways, give us grace praise.

Refrain:
   Many gift, one Spirit, one love known many
   ways. Our difference, is(#1) bless, from
   diversity(#2), we praise one Giver(#1), one
   Lord, one Spirit, one Word known many ways,
   hallowed(#1) our days. For Giver(#1), for
   gift, praise, praise, praise!

2. God many colors, God many show, you
   finish make us different, bless many same
   group(#1). As old way disappear, let your
   love fade our fear.

Refrain

3. Fresh(#1) morning, new every-night, you
   still(#1) create continue love, light.
   This we see, as dark fade, many gift
   from one great(#3) heart.

Refrain

How Like a Gentle Spirit

1. Happen like(#2) gentle(#1) spirit
   deep-within God reins our warm feel,
   everyday, gives us strength challenge,
   win(#1) in-spite-of danger, our chosen way.

2. Let God be(#1) God, no-matter life
   found; let every person accept call(#1)
   witness; all people become one through
   God decree(#2); let God be(#1) God,
   let God be(#1) God for all.

3. God like(#2) mother eagle, wait
   near, might(#3) arm, power(#1) clear;
   God like(#2) gentle(#1) shepherd still(#2) our
   fear, comforts us against peace chest(#1).

4. Happen our vain right(#1) we plan shape
   God image as we see ourself, pay attention voice
   above our basic(#2) desire(#1); God is(#1)
   maker, we broken stone.

5. Through all our worry, demand right(#1)
   of boy-girl relationship(#1), group(#1)
   people, same-all-over[1] love God shines
   through, for God is(#1) love, beyond
   way, place, all freedom(#2) choice we follow.

[1]Same-all-over: R and L "Y" hand positions, palms down, hands separated, move both "Y" together, counterclockwise several times.

The God of Abraham Praise

1. God Abraham praise, himself reign[1] throne
   above; Lord God Almighty, God love; God,
   great(#3) God! through earth, heaven confess;
   I bow, bless holy name, forever bless.

2. Great(#3) God finish sworn; I this oath
   depend. I will(#1), like(#2) eagle, ascend
   heaven. I will(#1), see God face; I will(#1)
   worship God power(#1), sing wonder(#2)
   God grace forever.

3. Heaven land[2] I see, with peace, plenty
   bless, land bless liberation, continue
   rest. Land plenty, milk, honey,[3] oil, wine,
   tree life forever grow with mercy(#1) crowned.

4. God, himself reigns above, great(#3)
   angels sing, "Holy, holy, holy!" cry(#3),
   "Almighty King! Himself was, now is(#1),
   forever continue; God, Lord, great(#3),
   God, we worship you."

[1]Throne: R and L "C" hand positions, palms facing down and separated, move both hands back toward the body in an arc motion, representing the arms of a large chair.
[2]Land: The sign for "dirt," then the sign for "spread."
[3]Honey: Make the sign for "syrup," with this exception: use the Right "H" hand position, palm facing the body.

117   O God, Our Help In Ages Past

1. O God, our help years past, our hope
   for years future, our protect from
   strong(#1) rough(#1) force, our heaven home!

2. Under dark your throne,[1] your people
   still(#1) live safe; sufficient is(#1) your arm
   alone, our defense is(#1) sure.

3. Before(#3) hill order(#3) founded,
   before(#1) earth became form, from everlasting,
   you are(#1) God, continue years same.

4. One thousand years, before(#3) your eyes,
   like(#2) evening fade; short as fade night,
   before(#1) sun-rise.

5. Time, like(#2) continue river, like(#2)
   all people who breathe; people move forgot,
   as dream fade, begin day.

6. O God, our help years past, our hope for
   years future; you become our guide while life
   continue, our heaven home!

[1]Throne: R and L "C" hand positions, palms facing down and separated, move both hands back toward the body in an arc motion, representing the arms of a large chair.

The Care the Eagle Gives Her Young   118

1. Mother eagle take-care young, safe
   eagle high home, is(#1) like(#2)
   tender[1] love God, for us made clear.

2. Happen time travel comes, mother
   eagle push young birds fly, same we
   encourage bold try, for courage height.

3. If we go-back-and-forth without help,
   as young eagle fall(#4), we same, beneath(#2)
   us God mighty(#2) arm carry us, one, all.

[1]Tender: To be signed at the heart with one sign only, "soft."

O God in Heaven   119

1. O God heaven, give your children mercy(#1),
   bless, songs never stop, love unite
   us, grace redeem(#1) us, O God heaven,
   precious Lord, our God.

2. Jesus, Redeemer(#1), may we remember your
   gracious strong(#1) feel, your resurrection.
   Worship we bring you, praise we will(#1) sing
   you, Jesus, Redeemer(#1), Jesus, our Lord.

3. Spirit come-down, himself is(#1) bless,
   strength for tired, help for needy; protect
   our concern, your be(#1) our worship, Spirit
   come-down, Spirit love.

Your Love, O God

1. Your Love, O God, is(#1) broad like(#2)
   land,[1] field(#2), wide as wind, our home heaven.
   You leave us free seek you, reject you, you
   give us freedom, answer yes, no.

Refrain:
   Your love, O God, is(#1) broad like(#2) land,
   field(#2), wide as wind, our home heaven.

2. We long(#2) for freedom where(#2) our true
   life receive hope, courage progress. We seek
   free, space, understanding for dream,
   look for ground where(#2) trees can grow.

Refrain

3. But there wall(#1), keep us divided;
   we block each other with hate, war. Fear
   is(#1) like(#2) stone our hearts, our pride
   self, same we have hard hearts.

Refrain

4. O judge us, Lord, your judgment free us,
   found our feet in free open space; carry us
   as far as your compassion wander(#1), among
   children living people.

Refrain

[1]Land: Sign for "dirt," then the sign for "spread."

This ASL translation © 1995 Hope Publishing Company

There's a Wideness in God's Mercy 121

1. True lot God mercy(#1), like(#2) big
   sea; true kind God justice(#1), which
   is(#1) more than liberation.

2. True welcome for sinner, more grace
   for good people! True mercy(#1) with Savior;
   true heal[1] with Jesus blood.

3. For love God more broad than
   measure our mind; heart God is(#1) most
   wonder(#2) kind.

4. If our love were but more simple(#1),
   we should depend God word; our lives will(#1)
   be(#1) bright through presence our Lord.

[1]Heal: Make the sign for "make," then the sign for "well"(#2).

This ASL translation © 1995 The United Methodist Publishing House

God of the Sparrow God of the Whale 122

1. God little bird, God big fish ocean,
   God scatter stars, How people say inspire[1] respect?
   How can people Praise?

2. God earth-quake, God storm, God thunder,
   How people cry(#3) Pain? How people cry(#3) Save?

3. God rainbow,[2] God cross, God empty grave,
   How people say Grace? How can people Thank?

4. God hungry, God sick, God lost son,
   How people say Take-care? How people
   say Life?

5. God neighbor, God enemy, God separates
   bad from good, How people say Love?
   How people say Peace?

6. God generations, God near help, God loving
   heart, How your children say Joy?
   How your children say Home?

[1]Inspire: R and L flat "O" hand positions, palms facing body at the heart, fingers pointing
up, move both hands up opening into "5" hand positions.
[2]Rainbow: Sign for "color." Then R and L "5" hand positions, palms facing body on the left
side, move right "5" up and arc to the right.

This ASL translation © 1995 Jaroslav J. Vajda

123   El Shaddai

God Almighty, God Almighty,
most high(#1) God, O Lord
generation, generation you
still(#1) same, through power
name. God Almighty, God Almighty
We will(#1) love you, O Lord
we will(#1) praise ascend you high(#1),
God Almighty.

This ASL translation © 1995 The Sparrow Corp.

124   Seek the Lord

1. Seek Lord himself now before(#3),
   pray Lord himself before(#3). Let
   sinner stop sin, wrong doers change
   mind. People themselves sin, God has
   pity; people change, God forgive. Same as Lord
   say world that disbelieve.

2. "Don't(#1) judge me through people rules(#2)!
   As heaven safe high above earth,
   true high are(#1) my thoughts ways than yours.
   See how rain, snow from heaven make
   earth flower, grow fruit, give you,
   before(#1) return, seed sow, bread eat.

3. "True my word return not empty;
   not from work stop, till word finish
   achieve(#1) my purpose, world joy, peace."
   God is(#1) love. How close prophet, important
   Bible word? Prophet inspire,[1]
   is(#1) Jesus, we finish know!

[1]Inspire: R and L flat "O" hand positions, palms facing body at the heart, fingers pointing up, move both hands up opening into "5" hand positions.

Sing Praise to God Who Reigns Above   126

1. Sing praise God himself reigns above,
   God all world, God power(#1), God love, God
   our salvation. With heal[1] comfort my soul,
   full, every false talk still(#1):
   God all praise, glory.

2. Lord never far, but through all
   grief(#2) pain, always now help, support,
   our peace, joy, bless. As with mother
   tender hand, God gentle(#1) leads chosen
   group(#1): God all praise, glory.

3. That way all my work ever since,
   I sing your praises, that world may hear
   grateful song my voice not tired praise.
   Joy, in Lord, my heart, both soul, body,
   bear(#4) your part: Give God all praise, glory.

4. Let all people name Jesus holy name,
   give God all praise, glory; let all people
   want Jesus power proclaim, wonder(#2) story!
   Cast-out each false idol, for Jesus is(#1)
   Lord, Jesus only: God all praise, glory.

[1]Heal: Sign for "make," then the sign for "well"(#2).

127 Guide Me, O Thou Great Jehovah

1. Lead me, great(#3) God, my-self travel
   through this bare(#2) land.[1] I weak, but
   you mighty(#2); support me with your
   power(#1) hand. Bread heaven, bread heaven,
   feed(#2) me till I want no more; feed(#2)
   me till I want no more.

2. Open now clear begin, where(#2) heal[2]
   change happens, let fire lead through night,
   cloud lead through day. Strong(#1) deliverer(#1),
   strong(#1) deliverer(#1), you still(#1) my strength,
   shield(#1), you still(#1) my strength, shield(#1).

3. Happen I walk near "J"-river, bid(#1) my
   fears fade; death, hell(#1) destroy,
   let me arrive safe heaven. Songs praises,
   songs praises, I will(#1) always give you,
   I will(#1) always give you.

[1]Land: Sign for "dirt," then the sign for "spread."
[2]Heal: Sign for "make," then the sign for "well"(#2).

1. Jesus lead me: O bless thought!
   Words with heaven comfort fill!
   No-matter I do, no-matter I go,
   still(#1) God hand lead me.

Refrain:
   Jesus lead me, Jesus lead me, through his own
   hand, he lead me; his faithful(#2)
   follower I will(#1) become, for through
   his hand he lead me.

2. Sometimes, during time deep gloom,
   sometimes where(#2) beauty place bloom,
   through water still(#2), over(#2) troubled
   sea, still(#1) God hand that lead me.

Refrain

3. Lord, I will(#1) place my hand yours,
   I will(#1) never speak low voice; no
   complain; content, no-matter choice I
   see, since my God that lead me.

Refrain

4. Happen my work on earth done(#2),
   happen through your grace victory(#1) finish,
   strange death cold feeling, I will not flee,
   because God through "J"-country(#1) lead me.

Refrain

129   Give to the Winds Thy Fears

1. Give wind your fears; hope be(#1) not
   trouble. God hear your cry, count your
   tears, God will(#1) ascend your head.

2. Through wave(#1), clouds, storm, God
   gentle(#1) clears your way; you wait God
   time; true night will(#1) finish, become happy day.

3. Leave(#2) God mighty(#2) control(#1),
   choose, command; true will(#1), you wonder(#1),
   that way, how wise, how strong God hand?

4. Let us in life, in death, your last(#3)
   truth declare with our last(#1)
   breath your love, Father care.

130   God Will Take Care of You

1. Don't(#1) worry no matter happens, God will[1]
   take-care you; beneath(#1) God arms, love
   continue. God will take-care you.

Refrain:
    God will take-care you, through everyday
    over(#1) all way; God will take-care you
    God will take-care you.

2. During days work, when heart become weak,
   God will take-care you; happen danger(#1) danger(#2)
   attack your way, God will take-care you.

Refrain

3. All you need, God will provide, God will
   take-care you; nothing(#1) you ask will deny(#1),
   God will take-care you.

Refrain

4. No matter may be(#1) test, God will
   take-care you; depend God love, strength,
   God will take-care you.

Refrain

¹Will: Use "the will"(#1).

We Gather Together   131

1. We gather(#2) together ask(#1) Lord
   blessing; Jesus correct, hurry his will(#2)
   make known. Sinner burden now stop from
   pain. Sing praise Jesus name; Jesus
   never forgets his people.

2. Near us guide us, our God with us
   join(#3), appoint, maintain(#1), his
   kingdom divine; true from begin, fight we
   were win(#2);
   You Lord were near us,
   all glory be(#1) yours.

3. We all true praise you, you lead
   triumph(#1), pray that you still(#1) our
   defender. Let your people escape trouble;
   your name be(#1) ever(#3) praised!
   O Lord, make us free.

132   All My Hope Is Firmly Grounded

1. My hope is(#1) strong(#1) support, great(#3)
   living Lord; himself, no matter I need Lord, himself
   never fails keep his word. God I must full
   trust, God ever(#3) good, just(#1).

2. Tell me, who can trust our character(#1), people
   weak, not safe? Which open house can endure(#2)
   strong wind succeed? Built weak dirt, nothing(#1)
   can support through our own wisdom plan.

3. But every time, every season, out love
   abundant store(#2), God provided all world,
   begin life continue. We share earth, air
   breath depend God never fail take-care.

4. Thank, O thank, our great(#3) Creator, through
   God only Son Jesus; God only, heaven maker,
   mold us from earth. Quick pay attention,
   strong(#1) work, God will(#1) feed(#2) all people.

133   Leaning on the Everlasting Arms

1. Wonder(#2) fellowship, wonder(#2) joy
   divine, depend Jesus protect; wonder(#2)
   blessing, wonder(#2) peace mind,
   depend Jesus protect.

Refrain:
Depend, depend, safe, protect from
all danger; depend, depend, depend
Jesus protect.

2. O how sweet walk here on holy
   way, depend Jesus protect; O how bright
   path becomes everyday,
   depend Jesus protect.

Refrain

3. What[1] have I dread? What have I fear(#1)?
   Depend Jesus protect; I have bless peace
   with my Lord true near, depend Jesus protect.

Refrain

[1]What: R and L "5" hand positions, palms facing up in front of the body, move back and forth, right to right, left to the left several times.

O Mary, Don't You Weep   134

Refrain:
   O Virgin-Mary, don't(#2) you weep(#1), don't(#2)
   you mourn, O Virgin-Mary, don't(#2) you weep(#1),
   don't(#2) you mourn; Egypt army drowned,
   O Virgin-Mary, don't(#2) you weep(#1).

1. One morning, bright-fair, I will(#1)
   arise(#2), enter heaven; Egypt army drowned,
   O Virgin-Mary, don't(#2) you weep(#1).

Refrain
2. Happen I arrive heaven, I will(#1) sing,
   shout, not person heaven keep me out; Egypt
   army drowned, O Virgin-Mary, don't(#2) you weep(#1).

Refrain

3. Happen I arrive heaven, I will(#1) wear(#2)
   shoes, will(#1) go around announce gospel(#2);
   Egypt army drowned, O Virgin-Mary, don't(#2)
   you weep(#1).

Refrain

136   The Lord's My Shepherd, I'll Not Want

1. Lord my shepherd, I not want.
   He make me lie-down grow green field(#2);
   he lead me near quiet water.

2. Lord make new my soul, I will walk
   paths righteous(#2), for
   his own name.

3. Yes, I walk through valley
   dark death, I fear no evil; because you
   are(#1) with me, your rod-staff comfort me.

4. You prepare food for me, before(#3) my
   enemies; my head anoint(#1) with oil(#2),
   my cup run-over.

5. Good, mercy(#2) will sure follow me all
   my life; I will live God
   house forever.

1. King love my shepherd is(#1), his good
   never fail. I need nothing(#1) if I am(#1)
   his, he is(#1) mine forever.

2. Place living water, my
   save self he lead; place green grass
   grow, with spiritual food provided.

3. Contradict, foolish, often I stray,
   yet with love he sought me; his shoulder[1]
   gently brought me home rejoice.

4. Death dark valley I fear no evil with
   you, precious Lord, near me; your rod-staff
   my comfort continue, your cross
   before(#3) guides me.

5. You spread(#1) table(#1) before(#3) me, your
   anoint(#2) grace give; what carry delight from your
   pure(#2) cup pour?

6. True through all long days, your good
   never fail; Good Shepherd, may I sing your
   praise in your house forever.

[1]Shoulder: A "right angle" hand position, palm facing body. Tap on right shoulder several times.

Praise to the Lord, the Almighty

1. Praise offer Lord, Almighty, King
   world! O my soul, praise him, because
   Jesus is(#1) your health, salvation! All
   you can sing, now his church come near;
   join me, glad worship.

2. Praise offer Lord, himself over all
   things wonder(#2) reign, same eagle Jesus
   protect, yes Jesus keep protect. God
   care(#1) surrounds all, himself true good
   he supports. Ask(#2) you not
   know his sustain?

3. Praise offer Lord, himself prosper your
   work, defends you, sure his good, mercy(#1)
   here daily care you. Ponder new what[1]
   Almighty can do, himself with his
   love your friend.

4. Praise offer Lord, himself care(#1)
   your life, bring you back, prepare you
   well(#1) for task that ever(#3) before(#3)
   you. Then(#2) your need God as mother
   true hurry; spreading continue
   grace over you.

5. Praise offer Lord! O let all that
   is(#1) me worship him! All things that
   live, breathe, come now with praises
   before(#3) him! Let "amen" from his
   people sound again, gladly forever
   love him.

[1]What: Right and Left "5" hand positions, palms facing up in front of the body. Move both hands back and forth, right to the right, left to the left.

1. Great(#3) your faithful(#2), O God
   my Father; there no possibility turn
   with you; you change not, your compassion
   never fail; you same past, you
   will be(#1) same forever.

Refrain:
   Great(#3) your faithful(#2)! Great(#3)
   your faithful(#2)! Morning tomorrow
   morning new mercy(#1) I see; all things I
   have need your hand finish provide;
   great(#3) your faithful, Lord, give me.

2. Summer, winter, spring, harvest, sun,
   moon, stars above, join(#3) all nature, many,
   many witness your great(#3) faithful(#2),
   mercy(#1), love.

Refrain

3. Pardon for sin, peace that endure(#2),
   your own presence cheer, guide; strength for
   today, bright hope for tomorrow, bless all
   mine, with many, many more bless.

Refrain

141   Children of the Heavenly Father

1. Children heaven Father safe his care(#1)
   keep us near; like (#2) baby bird, like (#2) star
   heaven, same protect never was give.

2. God himself, take-care, protect, his
   holy meeting room, children grow; from
   all evil things he saves children; his
   mighty(#2) arms he carry children.

3. Not life, not death, will(#1) Lord ever
   separate his children; unto children, he
   show his grace, all sorrow God knows.

4. No matter God give, no matter God take,
   God never leave(#2) his children; God love
   purpose only save children pure, holy.

This ASL translation © 1995 Augsburg Fortress

142   If Thou But Suffer God to Guide Thee

1. If you let God guide you, hope God
   through all your ways, God will give
   strength(#1), no matter happens you, you
   endure(#2) through evil days. Himself
   trusts God love that never changes, build
   foundation that nothing(#1) can move.

2. Only be(#1) still(#2), wait God comfort,
   cheerful hope, with heart content, accept
   no matter your Maker pleasure, all know love
   finish sent; we know our wants are(#1)
   known, for we call(#1) become God people.

3. Sing, pray, keep God ways not differ;
   true do your part faithful(#2), trust God
   word; no matter nor worthy, you will(#1)
   will(#1) find true for you. God never
   gave-up need person that trust God indeed.

On Eagle's Wings 143

God will rise(#3) you like wings
eagle, carry you early sunrise
make you shine like(#2) sunshine,
God will take-care(#3) you.

This Is My Father's World 144

1. Here my Father world, my listening
   ears, all nature sings, surround me rings,
   music sphere.[1] Here my Father world:
   I satisfy with thought about, rocks, trees,
   skies, seas; God hand wonders(#2) made.

2. Here my Father world, birds singing
   sounds, morning light, flower white, declare
   maker praise. Here is(#1) my Father world:
   God shines all that beautiful, through green
   grow, I hear God pass;[2] God shows me every place.

3. Here my Father world. O let me
never forget that no matter wrong seem often
strong(#1), God rule(#1) still(#1). Here
my Father world: Why should my heart
be(#1) sad? Lord is(#1) King; let heavens
ring(#2), God rule(#1); let earth be(#1) glad!

[1]Sphere: Can also be signed "area."
[2]Pass: L "index" hand position, palm facing out, finger tip pointing up. R "index" hand position, palm facing body, finger tip pointing up. Move R hand from right to left in front of the L.

145   Morning Has Broken

1. Morning finish bright, like(#2) first
morning; blackbird finished singing,
like(#2) first bird sing. Praise for sing!
Praise for morning! Praise for people,
begin new from Word!

2. Beautiful new rain, through sunlight from
heaven, like(#2) first dew[1] on first grass.
Praise for beauty wet garden,
began complete(#1) where(#2) Jesus feet walk.

3. Mine is(#1) sunlight! Mine is(#1) morning
began one light, first garden saw play!
Praise with happy,[2] praise every morning,
God enjoy[3] new day!

[1]Dew: Sign "water," then sign for "wet," starting from the left moving to the right, indicating wet all over.
[2]Happy: Is signed with both open palms, brushing upwards at the heart several times.
[3]Enjoy: Is signed with both open palms, moving in circles in opposite directions at the heart several times.

All Things Bright and Beautiful

Refrain:
   All things bright, beautiful, all people
   big(#2), small(#2), all things wise, wonderful(#2):
   Lord God made all world.

1. Each little(#1) flower opens,[1] each little
   bird sings, God made various colors,
   God made smallest wings.

Refrain

2. High purple color mountains,
   river-running near, sunset, morning,
   brightens-up sky.

Refrain

3. Cold winter wind, pleasant summer
   sun, grow fruit garden: God made
   all world.

Refrain

4. God gave us eyes see beauty, lip-read,
   we may tell, how great(#3) is(#1) God
   Almighty, himself finish make
   all things well(#1).

Refrain

[1]Open: R and L "cupped" hand positions, palms facing each other, finger tips touching.
Open and close fingers several times, leaving heels of hands together (natural opening of a
flower).

148   Many and Great, O God

1. O God many your things great(#3),
   Maker earth, heaven. Your hands
   finish scatter heaven with stars;
   your hands spread mountains, land. Look,
   your word, waters formed; deep
   seas obey your voice.

2. Give us fellowship with you, your star
   continue still(#1); come unto us, live with
   us; with you are(#1) found gifts life.
   Bless us with continue life, eternal
   life with you.

149   Let's Sing Unto the Lord

1. Let sing unto Lord, hymn rejoice.
   Let sing-hymn love, begin new day.
   God made sky above, stars, sun,
   oceans; God saw everything good(#1),
   because his work filled with
   beauty. Alleluia! Alleluia! Let
   sing unto Lord. Alleluia!

2. Let sing unto Lord, hymn adore,
   which show our love, faith, hope all
   world. Through all that finish made,
   Lord be(#1) praised for great(#3), true
   we sing God, himself, gives beauty
   bless. Alleluia! Alleluia!
   Let sing unto the Lord. Alleluia!

1. God, himself scatter stars heaven,
   continue time, place, made sun bright-shine,
   through silent space, we your children, same
   you, share active power(#1) with you. Great(#3)
   Creator, still(#1) create, show us what we
   still(#1) can do.

2. Proud, found our new cities, worthy
   buildings, row-on-row[1], yet windows[2] blank,[3]
   no feeling, look-down street below, where(#2)
   lonely people walk not noticed, forget city
   worse, lost purpose(#2), mean(#2), not much
   care where people go.

3. We finish challenge real world since
   grow-up our class; known joy make able
   through not known large space; probe(#1)
   secrets very small(#1), give real power(#1),
   face-to-face with life destruction,
   our most triumph(#2) time.

4. As each far horizon call(#1), can
   challenge us new, children create purpose(#1)
   serve others, honor you. May our dreams
   prove best with promise, each activity
   well(#1) begun. Great(#3) Creator, give us
   guide till our goals, your goals same.

---

[1]Row-on-row: R and L "bent 5" hand positions, palms facing down, move both hands forward, then repeat the sign.
[2]Yet: In ASL this meaning is signed "but."
[3]Blank: Right "5" hand position, palm facing out, middle finger point out, other fingers point up. Starting on left, move to the right.

151   God Created Heaven and Earth

1. God create heaven, earth, all things
   perfect began live; God great(#3)
   power(#1) made night, day,
   earth change day, night.

2. Let us praise God great(#3) mercy(#1);
   All our needs love wait; God, himself
   made all that lives, God gives
   every person bless.

3. God himself only one, will ever(#2)
   be(#1); idols are(#1) worthless(#2);
   idol hand-made wood, clay, can't help us
   happen we pray.

4. But beyond compare God grace saves
   us from death tragedy; people on earth
   small(#2), big(#2), give thanks for
   bless belief.

This ASL translation © 1995 Boris and Clare Anderson

152   I Sing the Almighty Power of God

1. I sing almighty-power(#1) God, himself,
   made mountains, spread flowing[1] seas far,
   made high sky. I sing wisdom that plan
   sun rule(#1) day; moon shines full God
   command, all stars obey.

2. I sing good Lord, himself filled earth
   with food, himself, form people through Word,
   finish, announce people good. Lord, your
   wonders(#2) show, no matter I look-around(#1),
   I look-over[2] ground I walk, I gaze sky.

3. True every plant, every flower here,
   show your glory, clouds appear(#3),
   storms-wind, through your plan from throne;[3]
   while all that accepts life from you is(#1)
   ever(#3) your care; every place we can go,
   God, himself always there.

[1]Flowing: Sign "wave"(#1).
[2]Look-over: Use the sign for "look for."
[3]Throne: R and L "C" hand positions, palms facing down and separated, move both hands back toward the body in an arc motion, representing the arms of a large chair.

Thou Hidden Source of Calm Repose   153

1. Your hidden begin calm rest(#1), your
   all-sufficient love divine, my help,
   protect from my enemies, I am(#1) safe if
   you mine; look(#1), from sin, grief, shame,
   Jesus I hide me, your name.

2. Salvation is(#1) your might(#1) name, keep
   my happy soul above; brings comfort, power(#1),
   peace, joy, everlasting(#2) love; with your
   loving name are(#1) given forgive,
   holiness, heaven.

3. Jesus, you true my all, my rest(#1) toil,
   my fade pain, make well(#2) my broken heart,
   in war my peace, in loss my profit, my smile
   beneath(#1) influence cruel ruler, in shame my
   glory, my crown.

4. My want plenty provide, in weak my
   mighty-power(#1), bind my perfect liberation,
   my light Satan dark hour, in grief my joy
   silence, my life death, my heaven in hell(#1).

All Hail the Power of Jesus' Name

1. All praise power(#1) Jesus name! Let angels kneel; bring forward heavenly crown, crown him Lord all. Bring forward heavenly crown, crown him Lord all.

2. You chosen people Israel class, you saved from fall, welcome Jesus himself saves you through his grace, crown him Lord all. Welcome Jesus himself saves you through his grace, crown him Lord all.

3. Sinners, whose love can never forget, bitter, hate, go spread your memory victory(#1) his feet, crown him Lord all. Go spread your memory victory(#1) his feet, crown him Lord all.

4. Let every person, every class on this earth, Jesus all power(#1) shows, crown him Lord all. Jesus all power shows, crown him Lord all.

5. Crown Jesus, you people your God, himself from his altar(#1) call(#1), praise name Jesus, crown him Lord all. Praise name Jesus, crown him Lord all.

6. O with far holy crowd we may kneel Jesus feet! We will join everlasting(#2) song, crown him Lord all. We will join everlasting(#2) song crown him Lord all.

All Hail the Power of Jesus' Name

1. All praise mighty(#1) Jesus name! Let
   angels kneel, let angels kneel, bring
   forward heaven crown, crown him, crown
   him, crown him, crown him,
   crown him Lord all.

2. You chosen people Israel class, you
   saved from ruin, you saved from ruin,
   welcome him who saves you through his
   grace, crown him, crown him, crown
   him, crown him, crown him Lord all.

3. Sinners, whose love can never forget,
   bitter, hate, go spread your memory
   victory(#1) his feet, crown him, crown
   him, crown him, crown him,
   crown him Lord all.

4. Let every person, every class on this
   earth, on this earth, Jesus all mighty(#2)
   shows, crown him, crown him, crown him,
   crown him, crown him Lord all.

5. Crown him, you people your God, himself
   from altar(#1) call(#1), himself from altar(#1)
   call(#1); praise name Jesus, crown him,
   crown him, crown him, crown him,
   crown him Lord all.

6. O with far holy crowd we may kneel Jesus
   feet we may kneel Jesus feet, we will
   join everlasting(#2) song, crown him, crown
   him, crown him, crown him Lord all.

This ASL translation © 1995 The United Methodist Publishing House

I Love to Tell the Story

1. I love tell story, hidden things above,
   Jesus, his glory, Jesus, his love. I love
   tell story, because I know story true;
   story satisfy my long(#2) like (#2) nothing(#1) else
   can satisfy.

Refrain:
   I love tell story, will be(#1) my story
   glory, tell old, old story, Jesus, his love.

2. I love tell story; more wonder(#2) story
   seems, than all golden fancy(#2), all golden
   dreams. I love tell story, story inspire[1]
   me; that only reason, I tell story now you.

Refrain

3. I love tell story; story pleasant tell
   again, seems each time I tell story, more
   wonder(#2) sweet. I love tell story,
   because some people never heard meaning
   salvation, from God own holy Word.

Refrain

4. I love tell story, for people know
   story best, seem hunger, thirst, hear
   story same others. Happen places glory, I
   sing new, new song, will(#1) be(#1), old, old
   story, I have loved ever since.

Refrain

[1]Inspire: R and L flat "O" hand positions, palms facing body at the heart, fingers pointing up, move both hands up opening into "5" hand positions.

Jesus Shall Reign

1. Jesus will(#1) reign where (#2) sun continue
   shine all over; Jesus kingdom spread
   from east ocean, west ocean, till
   moon become full, fade no more.

2. Jesus continue pray, continue
   praises, crown Jesus; Jesus name, like(#2)
   sweet perfume, will(#1) rise(#3) with every
   morning offer.

3. People, area every language, live on
   Jesus love with sweet song; baby
   voices will(#1) proclaim, baby early
   bless on Jesus name.

4. Bless plenty where(#2) Jesus reign;
   all prisoners leap, detach chains; weak
   find ever(#2) rest(#1), all who suffer
   become bless.

5. Let every person rise(#1), bring honors
   special our King; angels come-down
   with songs again, people say again loud amen!

This ASL translation © 1995 The United Methodist Publishing House

Come, Christians, Join to Sing

1. Come, Christians, join(#3) sing: Alleluia!
   A-men! loud praise Jesus our King: Alleluia!
   A-men! Let all, with heart, voice,
   before(#3) his throne[1] rejoice; praise
   his gracious choice. Alleluia! Amen.

2. Come, arise(#1) your heart high(#1):
   Alleluia! A-men! Let praises fill sky;
   Alleluia! A-men! Jesus is(#1) our guide,
   friend; Jesus come us; Jesus love continue;
   Alleluia! A-men!

3. Again praise Lord yet(#1); Alleluia!
   A-men! Life will(#1) not end(#1) burden; Alleluia!
   A-Men! On heaven happy foundation, his
   good we will(#1) love, singing forever,
   Alleluia! A-men.

¹Throne: R and L "C" hand positions, palms facing down and separated, move both hands back toward the body, in an arc motion, representing the arms of a large chair.

159   Lift High the Cross

Refrain:
   Arise(#1) high cross, love Jesus proclaim
   till all world worship his bless name.

1. Come, Christians, follow this triumph(#2)
   show. Group(#1) God unity join(#3) together.

Refrain

2. Each new-born servant of crucified
   Jesus, bear(#3) on calvary-cross(#1)
   seal(#1) Jesus himself died.

Refrain

3. Jesus, himself past arise(#1) cross,
   as you finish promised, lead world you.

Refrain

4. Our song triumph(#2) will(#1) always be(#1):
   Praise crucified Jesus for victory(#1)!

Refrain

Rejoice, Ye Pure in Heart 160

1. Rejoice, you pure heart; rejoice,
   give thanks, sing; your glory
   banner-wave high, cross
   Jesus your King. Rejoice, rejoice,
   rejoice, give thanks, sing.

2. Your clear praise inspire, alleluia
   loud; while answer sound high over(#1),
   like(#2) wreath smoke cloud. Rejoice, rejoice
   rejoice, give thanks, sing.

3. Yes, through life long path, still(#1)
   singing as you go; from youth become old,
   through night, day, glad, sorrow.
   Rejoice, rejoice, rejoice, give thanks
   sing.

4. Last(#1), march will end(#3); weary people
   will(#1) rest(#1); traveler find heaven home,
   Jerusalem bless. Rejoice, rejoice,
   rejoice, give thanks, sing.

5. Praise God, himself reign heaven,
   Lord himself we love, Father, Son, Holy
   Spirit, one God forever. Rejoice,
   rejoice, rejoice, give thanks, sing.

Rejoice, Ye Pure in Heart

1. Rejoice, you pure heart; rejoice, give
   thanks, sing, your glory banner-wave high,
   cross Jesus your King.

Refrain:
   Praise God! Praise God! Rejoice,
   give thanks, sing.

2. Your clear praise rise(#3) God sing,
   alleluia loud; while answer sounds
   high-over(#1), like(#2) wreath smoke cloud.

Refrain

3. Yes, through life long(#1) path, still(#1)
   singing as you go; from youth become old,
   through night, day, glad, sorrow.

Refrain

4. Last(#1), march will(#1) end(#3); weary
   people will(#1) rest(#1); traveling people
   find heaven home, Jerusalem bless.

Refrain

5. Praise God himself reign heaven, Lord
   himself we love, Father, Son, Holy Spirit,
   one God forever.

Refrain

Refrain:
    Alleluia, alleluia! Give thanks rise(#1)
    Lord. Alleluia, alleluia! Give praise
    Jesus name.

1. Jesus is(#1) Lord all earth. Jesus
    is(#1) King world

Refrain

2. Spread good story over(#1) all earth
    Jesus finish died, finish rise(#1).

Refrain

3. We finish crucified with Jesus.
    Now we will live forever.

Refrain

4. Come, let us praise living God,
    joy sing our Savior.

Refrain

163   Ask Ye What Great Thing I Know

1. Ask(#1) you what(#2) great(#3) thing I know,
   that delights inspire[1] me true? What
   high honor I win(#1)? Whose name
   I glory? Jesus Christ, crucified.

2. Who defeats my fierce enemy? Who
   comfort my saddest sorrow? Who revive
   my faint(#1) heart, make well(#2) heart
   hidden pain? Jesus Christ, crucified.

3. Who is(#1) life in life me? Who will
   be(#1) death? Who will place me on
   Jesus right, with many group(#1)
   light? Jesus Christ, crucified.

4. This great(#3) thing I know; this
   delights, inspires me true; faith Jesus,
   himself died save, Jesus, himself triumph(#2)
   conquer grave: Jesus Christ, crucified.

[1]Inspire: R and L flat "O" hand positions, palms facing body at the heart, fingers pointing up, move both hands up opening into "5" hand positions.

164   Come, My Way, My Truth, My Life

1. Come, my Way, my Truth, my Life:
   same way as gives us breath, same
   truth as ends(#3) all struggle, same
   life as kill death.

2. Come, my Light, my Feast, my
   Strength: same light as shows feast,
   same feast as mend(#1) long, same
   strength as make Jesus visitor.

3. Come, my Joy, my Love, my Heart:
   same joy as none can inspire,[1] same
   love as none can separate, same heart
   as joy, love.

[1]Inspire: R and L flat "O" hand positions, palms facing body at the heart, fingers pointing up, move both hands up opening into "5" hand positions.

Hallelujah! What a Savior   165

1. Man Sorrow! wonder(#2) name for Son
   God, himself came save poor(#3) sinner.
   Hallelujah! How wonder(#2) Savior!

2. Bear(#4) shame, mock rude(#2), my place
   Jesus stood blamed, promise my forgive
   with his blood. Hallelujah!
   How wonder(#2) Savior!

3. We guilty, sinful, weak; Jesus Son
   God clean, full suffer for people sin.
   Hallelujah! How wonder(#2) Savior!

4. Jesus rise(#3) cross die; Jesus cry,
   "True finished!" now heaven high praise.
   Hallelujah! How wonder(#2) Savior.

5. Happen Jesus comes, our glory King,
   take all Jesus saved people heaven,
   again we will sing this song; Hallelujah!
   How wonder(#2) Savior!

166   All Praise to Thee, for Thou, O King Divine

1. All praise you, for you, O King
   divine, finish give up glory that
   right was your, that our dark heart,
   your grace might(#2) shine:

Refrain:

   Alleluia! Alleluia!
2. You came us, humble thought;
   you seek people without friends poor(#1),
   through your death was God
   salvation made:

Refrain

3. Let Jesus mind be(#1) in us, which
   was in you, himself, was servant, that
   we might(#2) be(#1) free, humble yourself
   death Calvary(#1):

Refrain

4. For where(#2) reason(#1) through God
   eternal purpose, you are(#1) wonder(#2)
   over all people now, given name which
   all people will(#1) bow:

Refrain

5. Let every person confess with one
   agree in heaven, earth that Jesus
   Christ is(#1) Lord; all people
   love God Father.

At the Name of Jesus

1. Name Jesus every person will(#1) bow, every
   person confess Jesus King glory now; true
   Father pleasure, we should called Jesus Lord,
   himself, from begin was mighty(#2) Word.

2. Humble for time, receive name from
   sinners, unto whom Jesus came, faithful(#2)
   Jesus endure(#2), clean till last(#1), brought
   again victory(#1), no matter from death
   Jesus rise(#1).

3. Endure(#1) triumph(#2) with person
   light, through all class people center
   high, God rule(#1), Father protect; fill
   with glory, perfect rest.

4. Make Jesus King your heart; there let
   Jesus conquer all that not holy, all that
   not true. Crown Jesus as your captain,
   during temptation; let Jesus will(#2),
   embrace you, light, power.

In Thee Is Gladness

1. You true glad, among all sadness, Jesus
   sunshine my heart. Through you
   give gifts heaven, you true Redeemer. Our
   heart you make, our bonds you break; which
   person trust you sure, finish build
   dependable, endure(#2) forever. Alleluia!
   Our hearts desire(#1) see you shining;
   dying, living, you are(#1) faithful(#2),
   nothing can separate us. Alleluia!

2. If God be(#1) ours, we fear no power(#1),
   not earth, sin, death. God see, bless, worse
   sorrow, can change sorrows quick same breath.
   For which reason story told God glory with
   heart, voices; all heaven rejoice, singing
   forever: Alleluia! We shout for glad,
   triumph(#2) over(#2) sadness, loving,
   praising, voices still(#1) singing
   glad hymn(#1) forever: Alleluia!

170   O How I Love Jesus

1. True name I love hear, I love
   sing name worth; name sounds like(#2) music
   my ear, sweetest name on earth.

Refrain:
>   O how I love Jesus, O how I love Jesus,
>   O how I love Jesus, because he first
>   loved me!

2. Name tells me Savior love, himself died
   free me; name tells me Jesus precious blood,
   sinner perfect plea.

Refrain

3. Name tells Jesus, himself love heart
   can feel my deep grief; himself each sorrow
   bear(#4) part that none can bear(#3) below.

Refrain

There's Something About That Name

Jesus, Jesus, Jesus! There
something about that name! Manager,
Savior, Jesus! Like(#2) fragrant after rain.
Jesus, Jesus, Jesus! Let all-heaven
earth, proclaim: Kings, kingdoms will(#1)
all fade, but there something
about that name.

My Jesus, I Love Thee

1. My Jesus, I love you, I know you are(#1)
   mine; for you all foolish sin I give up.
   My gracious Redeemer, you are(#1) my Savior;
   I ever(#3) love you, my Jesus love now.

2. I love you because you first love me,
   receive my pardon on Calvary; I love you
   for wear(#2) crown on your head; I ever(#3)
   love you, my Jesus love now.

3. In houses glory, continue delight,
   I ever(#3) love you heaven true bright;
   I ever(#3) sing with glisten crown on my head;
   I ever(#3) love you, my Jesus love now.

173   Christ, Whose Glory Fills the Skies

1. Jesus, himself glory fill sky(#1),
   Jesus true, only light, Son, Righteousness,
   rise(#1), triumph(#2) over(#2) dark night; Sunrise
   from high be(#1) near; light my heart appear.

2. Dark, gloomy is(#1) morning, without you;
   sad is(#1) day return, until your mercy(#1)
   I see; till shine inward bright provide,
   cheer my eyes, warm my heart.

3. Then visit my soul; pierce gloom sin,
   grief; fill me, bright divine; scatter
   all my disbelief; more, more yourself
   show, shine perfect day.

174   His Name is Wonderful

His name is(#1) wonder(#2), his name is(#1)
wonder(#2), his name is(#1) wonder(#2), Jesus
my Lord. He is(#1) mighty(#2) king, Rule(#1)
everything, his name is(#1) wonder(#2),
Jesus my Lord.

He great(#3) Shepherd, Support all
generation, mighty(#2) God is(#1) he;
bow-down before(#3) him, love adore
him, his name is(#1) wonder(#2),
Jesus my Lord.

Jesus, the Very Thought of Thee

1. Jesus, true though you, with kind fill
   my heart; but, your face delight see,
   before(#3) you rest(#1).

2. O hope every sorry heart, O joy all
   humble, people who fall, true you kind!
   How good people who seek!

3. But what people who find? Yes, this
   nor speech, nor pen can show; what
   is(#1) love Jesus? None, but people
   who love Jesus know.

4. Jesus, you true our only joy, as you
   will(#1) become our award; Jesus, you true
   our glory now, through eternity.

Majesty, Worship His Majesty

Ruler(#1), worship your ruler(#1);
unto Jesus be(#1) all glory, honor, praise.
Ruler(#1), kingdom authority, move
from his throne[1] unto his own;
sing his hymn. True praise, rise(#3)
on high name Jesus. Inspire[2] come glory,
Christ Jesus, King.
Ruler(#1), worship your ruler(#1),
Jesus, himself died, now glory, King all kings.

[1]Throne: R and L "C" hand positions, palms facing down and separated, move both hands back toward the body in an arc motion, representing the arms of a large chair.
[2]Inspire: R and L flat "O" hand positions, palms facing body at the heart, fingers pointing up, move both hands up opening into "5" hand positions.

177   He Is Lord

He is(#1) Lord, he is(#1)
Lord! He is(#1) rise(#1) from
dead, He is(#1) Lord! Every
person will bow, every person
confess that Jesus Christ is(#1) Lord.

178   Hope of the World

1. Hope world, you Jesus great(#3)
   compassion, speak our broken fear heart
   through struggle. Save us, your people,
   from consume(#2) passion(#2), himself
   through our own false hopes,
   aim are(#1) tired.

2. Hope world, God gift from high heaven,
   bring hungry people, bread life,
   still(#1) give your spirit us make well(#2)
   wound world, end(#3) all bitter struggle.

3. Hope world, walk dirty roads, showing
   wander(#2) people, path light, you walk
   near us, because tempting ways,
   attract us from you continue night.

4. Hope world, himself through your cross
   finish save us from death, dark sorrow, from
   sin, guilt, we give again, love your mercy(#1)
   gave us; you accept our lives,
   use us as you will(#2).

5. Hope world, O Jesus conquer death
victory(#1), himself through that victory(#1)
finish conquer grief, pain, we will(#1)
faithful(#2) your good news glory; you
are(#1) our Lord! You reign forever.

O Sing a Song of Bethlehem   179

1. O sing Bethlehem, shepherds watching,
   information came shepherds, from angels
   heaven. Bright shine-on Bethlehem, fills
   all world today; Jesus birth,
   peace on earth, angels sing always.

2. O sing "N"-town, sunshine days joy;
   O sing fragrant flowers breath, Boy without
   sin. Because now flowers "N"-town, every
   heart may grow; now spread fame his
   precious name, all winds-blow.

3. O sing "G"-country(#1), water, woods, hill,
   Jesus, himself walked-on sea, order wave
   calm. Save wave "G"-sea, plenty dark
   trouble move, when faith finish hear Jesus
   word, come peace upon soul.

4. O sing Calvary, cross glory, dread
   Jesus, himself crucified-on cross, take-away
   our sins. Because Jesus himself died cross,
   is(#1) rise(#1) from grave, Jesus, our Lord,
   through heaven adore, is(#1) mighty(#2)
   now save.

180   O Jesus, My King and My Sovereign

1. O Jesus, my King, my Rule(#1), my joy
   is(#1) sing him my praise. He is(#1)
   king, still(#1) he comfort me like(#2) family,
   he is(#1) king, still(#1) Jesus shares all his
   love. He leave(#2) all his glory heaven,
   come rise(#3) my life from remainder. I true
   happy today, life joy came stay through him.

2. O Jesus, my friend, my desires, darkness,
   light always near; Jesus walks near me,
   patient, humble, gives me his comfort, cheer.
   That why I will faithful(#2) follow,
   because he is(#1) my King, guide. I am(#1)
   happy today, life joy came stay through Jesus.

3. O Lord, tell me what can I give you for
   all your great(#3) good me? Can this be(#1)
   enough; serve, love you, promise all my life
   you? If true, then accept my faithful(#2),
   you only I surrender. I happy
   today, life joy came stay through you.

181   Ye Servants of God

1. You servants God, your Rule(#1) proclaim,
   make known wide his wonder(#2) name;
   name all victory(#1) Jesus praise, his
   kingdom is(#1) glory, rule(#1) over(#1) all.

2. God rule(#1) on high, mighty(#2) save,
   still(#1) He is(#1) near, his life we have;
   great(#3) crowd his triumph(#2) will(#1) sing,
   appoint salvation Jesus, our King.

3. Salvation God, himself sits on throne[1]
   Let all cry(#3) loud, honor Son; praises
   Jesus angels proclaim, fall-down-on-faces[2]
   worship Jesus.

4. Then let us adore, give Jesus his right,
   all glory, power, all wisdom, might(#1),
   all honor, bless with angels above,
   thanks never cease, infinite love.

[1]Throne: R and L "C" hand positions, palms facing down and separated, move both hands back toward the body, in an arc motion, representing the arms of a large chair.
[2]Fall-down-on-faces: Use the sign for "fall for."

Word of God, Come Down on Earth   182

1. Word God, come-down earth, living rain
   from heaven come-down; touch-our-hearts,
   give us faith, hope, love continue. Word
   almighty, we love you; Word made alive,
   we long(#2) pay attention you.

2. Jesus eternity(#1) throne[1] high, Jesus
   himself gave life world, Jesus came from
   heaven die, crucified for our salvation,
   saving Jesus, world make new, speak us,
   your love overflowing.

3. Jesus heal blind able see, speak, heal
living blind; we are(#1) deaf: our
Jesus; free our speech tell your kindness.
Be(#1) our Jesus pity spoken; heal world,
through our sin broken.

4. Jesus speak your Father love, Jesus
with God beyond all tell, Jesus send(#1)
us from above God Spirit, live with us,
Jesus truth, all truth lead us; life
with one Love care(#3) us.

¹Throne: R and L "C" hand positions, palms facing down and separated, move both hands
back toward the body, in an arc motion, representing the arms of a large chair.

184   Of the Father's Love Begotten

1. God Father love, before(#1) world
began, God is(#1) First, Last, God,
begin, end(#1), he things that are(#1),
things past, things future years
will(#1) see, everlasting, everlasting.

2. O high heaven, adore him; angel
group(#1), his praise sing; power(#1), kingdoms,
bow before(#3) him, praise our God,
King; let no language earth be(#1) silent,
every voice, cooperation ring,
everlasting, everlasting.

3. Jesus, yourself with God Father, O
Holy Spirit, yourself singing, high thank
give, not tired praises continue: honor,
glory, power, eternal victory(#1),
everlasting, everlasting.

When Morning Gilds the Skies

1. Happen morning bright gold sky,
   my heart express:[1] May Jesus Christ be(#1)
   praised! Like(#2) work, prayer, Jesus I
   improve: May Jesus Christ be(#1) praised!

2. Night becomes like(#2) day, happens from
   heart we say: May Jesus Christ be(#1)
   praised! Power dark fear happen plenty
   singing people hear: May Jesus Christ
   be(#1) praised!

3. Let all earth around ring with joy
   sound: May Jesus Christ be(#1) praised!
   Heavens eternal joy, beautiful music is(#1)
   this: May Jesus Christ be(#1) praised!

4. Divine is(#1) my song, while life is(#1)
   mine: May Jesus Christ be(#1) praised! This
   eternal song, through all generations
   since: May Jesus Christ be(#1) praised!

[1]Express: R and L "S" hand positions at the heart, palms facing body. Move both "S" hands up and out opening into "5."

This ASL translation © 1995 The United Methodist Publishing House

186 Alleluia

1. Alleluia, alleluia, alleluia, alleluia,
   alleluia, alleluia, alleluia, alleluia.

2. He is(#1) my Savior. He is(#1) my Savior.
   He is(#1) my Savior. He is(#1) my Savior.
   He is(#1) my Savior. He is(#1) my Savior.
   He is(#1) my Savior. He is(#1) my Savior.

3. I will[1] praise Him. I will praise Him.
   I will praise Him. I will praise Him.
   I will praise Him. I will praise Him.
   I will praise Him. I will praise Him.

[1]Will: Use "the will"(#1).

This ASL translation © 1995 Manna Music, Inc.

187 Rise, Shine, You People

1. Rise(#1), shine, you people! Jesus Lord
   finish enter our individual story; God
   him is(#1) center. Jesus comes us,
   through death, sin surround,
   with grace no limits.

2. See how Jesus send(#1) power evil turmoil,
   give us freedom, light, life, healing.
   All men, women, themselves through guilt
   are(#1) compel(#1), are now(#1) forgiven.

3. Come, celebrate, your banner high,
   your songs, prayers against dark send(#1).
   All world go tell story Jesus glory.

4. Tell how Father send(#2)[1] Son save us.
   Tell Son, himself life, freedom gave us.
   Tell how Spirit calls from every nation
   God new world.

[1]Send: Use the "send" #2 sign but in the opposite direction, coming from the Father.

Christ Is the World's Light   188

1. Jesus is(#1) world light, Jesus no
   other; born our dark, Jesus became our
   brother. If we finish see Jesus, we
   finish see Father: Glory God on high!

2. Jesus is(#1) world peace, Jesus no
   other; no one can serve Jesus, hate
   another. Who else join(#1) us God
   Father? Glory God on high!

3. Jesus is(#1) world life, Jesus no
   other; sold past for money, crucified
   cross, our brother; Jesus, himself
   save us, rule(#1) with God Father:
   Glory God on high!

4. Give God glory, God no other;
   give God glory, Spirit, Son, Father;
   give God glory, God with us, my
   brother: Glory God on high!

Fairest Lord Jesus

1. Fair(#1) Lord Jesus, rule(#1) all
world, O you, God, man, Son, you will(#1) I
worship, you will(#1) I honor, you, my
heart glory, joy, crown.

2. Fair(#1) are(#1) field(#2), fair(#1)
still(#1) woods, spread-all-over flower
bloom-spring: Jesus is(#1) fair(#1), Jesus
is(#1) pure, himself makes sorrow heart sing.

3. Fair(#1) is(#1) sunshine, fair(#1)
still(#1) moonlight all shining star group:
Jesus shines bright, Jesus shines
pure than all angels heaven can boast.

4. Beautiful Savior! Lord all world!
Son God, Son Man! Glory, honor,
praise, adore, now forever your.

Who Is He in Yonder Stall

1. Who is(#1) he far house, himself feet
shepherds kneel?

Refrain:
True Lord, O wonder(#2) story!
True Lord, King glory; Jesus feet
we humbly kneel, crown Jesus,
crown Jesus, crown Jesus Lord all!

2. See, midnight, who person
prays dark garden?

3. Who he, Calvary pains asks
   for bless Jesus enemies?

Refrain

4. Who he, from grave comes
   heal,[1] help, save?

Refrain

5. Who he, from far throne[2]
   rule(#1) world light alone?

Refrain

[1]Heal: Sign for "make," then the sign for "well"(#2).
[2]Throne: R and L "C" hand positions, palms facing down and separated, move both hands
back toward the body, in an arc motion, representing the arms of a large chair.

Jesus Loves Me   191

1. Jesus loves me! This I know, because
   Bible tells me true. Little children
   him belong; children weak, but
   he strong.

Refrain:
   Yes, Jesus love me! Yes, Jesus love me
   Yes, Jesus love me! Bible tells me true.

2. Jesus love me! This I know, as he
   loved long ago, bring children sit
   Jesus, saying, "Let children come me."

Refrain

3. Jesus love me still(#1) today, walking
   with me on my way, want as friend give
   light, love all who live.

Refrain

192   There's a Spirit in the Air

1, 7 True Spirit air, tell Christians
     every place: Praise love that Jesus
     show, living, working, our world.

2. Let your shy, find your language; tell
   world what God finish doing. God, Jesus
   finish come stay. Live tomorrow life today!

3. Happy believers break bread, happen
   hungry child fed, praise love that
   Jesus show, living, working, our world.

4. Still(#1) Spirit leads fight, see wrong
   change right: God, Christ finish come
   stay. Live tomorrow life today!

5. Happen stranger(#1) not alone, happen
   people no home, find home, praise love
   that Christ show, living working, our world.

6. May Spirit fill our praise, guide our
   thought, change our ways: God, Christ
   finish come stay! Live tomorrow life today!

Jesus! The Name High Over All

1. Jesus! name over(#1) all, hell(#1)
   earth, sky; angels, persons fall-flat-on-face,[1]
   devils fear, depart.

2. Jesus! name sinner precious, name sinner
   given; name scatters all sinner guilt
   fear, name change sinner hell(#1) become heaven.

3. O that world might(#2) experience, see plenty
   Jesus grace. Arm love that surround
   me, will(#1) all world embrace.

4. You I will(#1) continue proclaim, no matter
   earth, hell(#1) oppose; free confess your
   glorious name, before(#3) world enemies.

5. Jesus only righteous I show, Jesus
   save truth proclaim; true all my business
   here below(#1) cry-out(#3), see Jesus.

6. Happy, if with my last(#1) breath, I may
   whisper Jesus name, preach Jesus all, cry-out(#3)
   death, "Look, see Jesus!"

[1]Fall-flat-on-face: Use the phrase sign "fall for."

194   Morning Glory, Starlit Sky

1. Morning glory, star shine[1] sky,
   music above, teacher truth, birds
   travel, autumn leaf(#1), memory gift,
   grace(#1) youth.

2. Open are(#1) gift God, gift love
   mind-sense(#1); hid is(#1) love agony,
   love endeavor, love worth.

3. Love that give, give ever(#2) more,
   give with zeal, with eager hands; save not,
   keep not, all satisfy, all endeavor,
   gives all.

4. Love take-away is(#1) made full, determine
   free others, poor make many rich,
   weak give power(#1) become.

5. Jesus, himself shows us God, without
   power hang(#1) cross, nail, crown-thorns(#1),
   tell what God love must mean.

6. Here is(#1) God; no king, power(#1) easy
   desire(#1) reign; here is(#1) God, himself
   arm love, ache, tired, world sustain.

[1]Shine: Use the directional "shine" coming from the sky.

195   Send Your Word

1. Send(#2)[1] your Word, O Lord, same
   rain-falling earth. Send(#2) your Word.
   We seek your continue grace(#1), with
   hearts that hunger, thirst, sorrow, agony.
   We will all be(#1) lost dark without your
   guide light(#1).

2. Send(#2) your Word, O Lord, same
   wind-blowing earth. Send(#2) your Word.
   We seek your wonder(#2) power(#1), pure(#2)
   that reject all sin, no matter sin
   continue-remain. Bring us complete(#2)
   victory(#1); free us all indeed.

3. Send(#2) your Word, O Lord, same dew[2]
   over hill. Send your Word. We seek your
   continue love. Because life that suffer(#2)
   struggle with sorrow, hurt, send(#2) your
   heal[3] power(#1) love; we long(#2)
   for your new world.

[1]Send: This is a directional sign coming from God, not the person.
[2]Dew: Use the sign for "water," then the sign for "wet," followed by all-over sign.
[3]Heal: Use the sign for "make," then the sign for "well"(#2).

Come, Thou Long-Expected Jesus   196

1. After long time, final(#1) Jesus came, born
   free your people; from our fears sin, free us,
   let us find our rest you. Israel strength
   comfort, you are(#1) hope, all world;
   precious desire(#1), every nation,
   joy, every desire(#1) person.

2. Born deliver(#1) your people, born
   baby, yet[1] King, born reign in us forever,
   now your gracious kingdom come.
   Through your own eternal spirit rule(#1)
   all our hearts alone; through your
   sufficient merit, rise(#3) us your glory throne[2].

[1]Yet: In ASL this meaning is signed "but."
[2]Throne: R and L "C" hand positions, palms facing down and separated, move both hands
back toward the body in an arc motion, representing the arms of a large chair.

Ye Who Claim the Faith of Jesus

1. You yourself demand faith Jesus, sing
   bless that done, happen love
   God Father overcome sin, victory(#1) win(#2),
   happen God asked Virgin-Mary become mother
   his only Son.

2. Finish bless choose(#1) people Lord himself
   finish come; Finish bless land[1] promise plan
   for Jesus home earth; but more bless
   mother, herself born Jesus.

3. Therefore(#3) let all faithful(#2) people
   sing honor Virgin-Mary name; let church,
   share thanksgiving belief; song
   gladness Jesus mother sang, let
   Christian, sing same:

4. "Praise my soul, God great(#3); my
   Savior I rejoice; all generation call[2] me
   bless, God praise I sing my voice; God
   finish feel sorry all might(#1), humble
   are(#1) God choice."

[1]Land: Sign "dirt," then the sign for "spread."
[2]Call: Sign called #3 as a verb.

My Soul Gives Glory to My God

1. My soul offer(#1) glory my God. My
   heart overflow[1] praise. God inspires[2] my
   depressed, many wonder(#2) ways.

2. My God finished great(#3) things for
   me: yes, holy his name. All people will(#1)
   declare me bless, bless people will(#1) share.

3. From generation generation, all people
   fear, like(#2) mercy(#2), love give,[3] provide(#2)
   justice(#2) far, near, forgive selfish hearts.

4. Love cast-out mighty(#2) from self(#1)
   throne,[4] encourage weak, leave(#2) hungry
   spirits satisfied, rich seem become poor.

5. Praise God, himself love promise
   support people grief(#1), remember past
   promise with present(#3) faithful(#2).

[1]Overflow: To be signed at the heart.
[2]Inspires: R and L flat "O" hand positions, palms facing body at the heart, fingers pointing up, move both hands up opening into "5" hand positions.
[3]Give: Directional verb coming from God.
[4]Throne: R and L "C" hand positions, palms facing down and separated, move both hands back toward the body in an arc motion, representing the arms of a large chair.

Tell Out, My Soul

1. Tell, my soul, great(#3) Lord!
   Many, many bless, give my spirit
   voice; give[1] me promise God word; in
   God my Savior will(#1) my heart rejoice.

2. Tell, my soul, great(#3) God name!
   Make known God might(#1), himself wonder(#2)
   work finish; God mercy(#1) sure, from
   generation, generation same; God holy
   name, Lord, mighty(#2) God.

3. Tell my soul, great(#3) God might(#1)!
   Power(#1), kingdoms place glory near;
   proud hearts, stubborn will(#2) start fade
   away, hungry fed, humble rise(#3) high.

4. Tell, my soul, glory God word!
   Strong is(#1) promise, God mercy(#1) sure.
   Tell, my soul, great(#3) Lord
   children, children, forever more!

[1]Give: Directional verb coming from God.

People, Look East

1. People, look(#1)-east. Time near
   begin year. Make your house clean as you
   able, beautiful fire place, set-up[1] table
   People, look(#1)-east: Love, Visitor on way.

2. Plow be(#1) glad. No matter earth is(#1)
   bare(#2), one more seed-planted(#2) earth.
   Give-up your strength seed grow, that in time
   flower may bloom,.[2] People, look(#1)-east: Love
   Rose,[3] on way.

3. Stars, keep watch. Happen, night
   dark, one more night moon will(#1) full,
   shining[4] beyond freeze cold, bright as sun
   moon together. People, look(#1)-east: Love,
   Star, on way.

4. Angels announce with shout joy Jesus,
   himself brings new life earth. Arrange
   every hill, valley with continue sound word,
   Lord is(#1) coming. People look(#1)-east: Love,
   Lord, on way.

[1]Set-up: Sign "establish" or "found."
[2]Bloom: May be signed with R and L "cupped" hands, palms together, opening and closing,
moving from left to right.
[3]Rose: Sign "flower" with an "R" hand position.
[4]Shining: Is signed off the back of the hand.

Hail to the Lord's Anointed

1. Welcome Lord anoint(#2), David[1] great(#3)
   Son! Welcome time begin, Jesus rule(#1) on
   earth! Jesus came break burden, free
   prisoner; take away sin, rule(#1) equal.

2. Jesus comes with quick help, people themselves
   suffer wrong; help poor, needy, call(#1) weak
   become strong; give people songs for
   content, people dark change light, whose soul,
   guilty, dying, are(#1) precious Jesus sight.

3. Jesus will(#1) come-down like(#2) rain on green
   earth; love, joy, hope, like(#2) flowers, began
   grow Jesus path. Before(#3) Jesus on-mountain,
   will(#1) peace, announce, go, righteous(#2),
   begin, from hill into valley continue.

4. Jesus will(#1) continue prayer, daily vow
   ascend; Jesus kingdom still(#1) increasing,
   kingdom continue. Begin time Jesus will(#1)
   never remove covenant;[2] Jesus name will(#1) continue
   forever; that name for us is(#1) love.

[1]David: Right "D" hand, palm facing body at the right temple, tap several times.
[2]Covenant: Sign "agree" or some may sign "promise."

Jesus, Jesus, his name
called Jesus. God with
us, show us, his name
called Jesus.

Note: There is no ASL sign for "Emmanuel:" however, some have signed Emmanuel the
same as Lord, except with an "E." We have chosen to use "Jesus" in place of "Emmanuel"
here. If you use a sign for "Emmanuel," simply use it in place of "Jesus."

This ASL translation © 1995 Music Services

I Want to Walk as a Child of the Light   206

1. I want walk as child Jesus. I want
    follow Jesus. God spread stars give
    bright(#1) world. Star my life, is(#1) Jesus.

Refrain:
    Jesus, there is(#1) no dark. Night, day
    both like(#2). Jesus is(#1) light city
    God. Shine[1] my heart, Lord Jesus.

2. I want see bright God. I want look-at
    Jesus. Clear Son God, shine-on my path,
    show me way Father.

Refrain

3. I look(#1) for coming Jesus. I want be(#1)
    with Jesus. Happen we finish run race
    with patience, we will(#1) know joy Jesus.

Refrain

[1]Shine: This should be signed directionally, coming from God.

This ASL translation © 1995 Maranatha! Music

207   Prepare the Way of the Lord

1. Prepare way Lord. Prepare way Lord,
   all people will(#1) see, salvation our God.

2. Prepare way Lord, all people will(#1) see
   salvation of our God. Prepare way Lord.

209   Blessed Be the God of Israel

1. Bless God Israel, himself comes
   free us, himself visits, saves us, gives
   us freedom. Prophet speak mercy(#2), freedom,
   relief; God will(#1) fill promise bring
   our people peace.

2. Now from house David,[1] child grace(#1)
   given; Savior comes among us, rise(#1) us
   heaven. Before(#3) God goes announce,
   shows way, prophet salvation, announce day.

3. On prisoner darkness, sun-rise begin,
   begin forgive sinner eyes, guide feet,
   traveling people on path peace; O bless
   our God, Savior with songs that never cease.

[1]David: Right "D" hand position, palm facing body at the temple, tap several times.

1. All world wait see Promised Jesus,
   open plow, Lord sowing.[1] All world, bound,
   struggle, seek true liberation; cries-out(#3)
   for justice search for truth.

2. Like(#2) prophet say Israel people,
   "Virgin-Mary mother will(#1) born Jesus," because
   his name means "God with us," our brother will(#1)
   be(#1), with Jesus hope will(#1) grow again
   within our hearts.

3. Mountains, valleys will(#1) become flat-over;
   open new roads, new way(#1) for Lord.
   He now come closer, all come see,
   open door as wide as can.

4. Humble house Promised Jesus appear(#2),
   yet,[2] feel his presence throughout world
   today, because Jesus lives all Christians,
   with us now; again, with Jesus coming
   brings us liberation.

[1]Sowing: R and L flat "O" hand positions, palms down and separated. Move both hands forward, several times, with thumbs gliding across fingertips, indicating sprinkling seeds.
[2]Yet: In ASL this meaning is signed "but."

O Come, O Come, Emmanuel 211

1. O come, O come, Emmanuel,[1] save people
   Israel, that sorrow lonely wander(#2) here,
   until Son God appear.

Refrain:
   Rejoice! Rejoice! Emmanuel will(#1) come
   you, O Israel.

2. O come your wisdom from high, prepare
   all things far, near, show us path
   knowledge make us follow your way.

Refrain

3. O come, O come, great(#3) Lord might(#1),
   yourself, your people Mountain height, long
   ago, gave law, through cloud,
   power(#1) inspire.[2]

Refrain

4. O come, you Begin Jesus grandfather,
   represent your people; before(#3) you
   rulers(#1) silent collapse; all people your
   mercy(#2) call(#1).

[1]Emmanuel: There is no ASL sign for "Emmanuel"; however, some have signed Emmanuel the same as "Lord", except with an "E." We have chosen to use "Jesus" in place of "Emmanuel" here. If you use a sign for "Emmanuel," simply use it in place of "Jesus."
[2]Inspire: R and L flat "O" hand positions, palms facing body at the heart, fingers pointing up, move both hands up opening into "5" hand positions.

St. 1, 3 ASL translation © 1995 Church Hymnal Corporation;
St. 4 ASL translation © 1995 The United Methodist Publishing House

213   Lift Up Your Head, Ye Mighty Gates

1. Lift-up[1] your heads, you strong(#1) gate;
   look(#1) King glory waits; King, kings is(#1)
   coming near; Savior world here!

2. Open door your heart; make your heart same
   house God, prepare your heart for use
   heaven separate from daily use, beautiful
   with prayer, love, joy.

3. Redeemer(#1), come, live with us; we
   open our hearts you let us feel your inner
   life; show us your grace(#1), love.

4. Your Holy Spirit leads us until our glory
   goal won(#1); eternal praise, eternal fame
   offer, Savior, your name!

[1]Lift-up: R and L "S" hand positions, palms facing down, bend both wrists up, palms facing out.
Note: Stanzas 2 and 3 should all be signed at the heart with emphasis.

Savior of the Nations, Come   214

1. Savior world, come; Virgin-Mary Son, here
   make your home! Marvel now, O heaven,
   earth, that Lord choose(#1) birth like(#2) happen.

2. Not happen through people blood, body;
   through Spirit our God, Word God became
   person, woman baby made pure(#2), healthy.

3. Wonder(#2) birth, O wonder(#2) Baby
   Virgin-Mary, clean! Person, divine become
   one, eager now Jesus work accomplish!

4. God Father is(#1) Jesus begin, again
   God himself work his plan; crucified dead,
   hell fade, God high throne Jesus rise(#1).

5. Now your manger[1] shine bright night with
   new born baby; let no night light fade, let
   our faith ever(#3) shine new.

[1]Manger: R and L "5" hand positions, palms facing each other, fingers interlocked pointing down.

To a Maid Engaged to Joseph

1. Young girl engaged Joseph,[1] angel Gabriel[2]
   came. "Fear not," angel told Virgin-Mary, "I
   come bring good news, good news I come tell
   you, good news, I say, good news.

2. "Because you high favor God Lord all,
   himself with you. You
   most bless on earth, you most bless,
   most bless, God choose(#1) you,
   you bless!"

3. But Virgin-Mary very trouble hear
   angel word. What was angel saying?
   Hear voice trouble Virgin-Mary, hear angel
   words, hear voice trouble Virgin-Mary hear.

4. "Fear not, because God with you,
   you born baby. His name will(#1)
   called Jesus, God baby from on high. Jesus
   will(#1) reign forever, forever reign on high."

5. "How this happen?" said
   Virgin-Mary, "I not yet wife." Angel
   answered quick, "Power, God will(#1)
   come on you short time, your baby will(#1)
   be(#1) God baby."

6. As Virgin-Mary hear angel, Virgin-Mary
   wonder(#1) angel words. "Look-me,[3] I your
   servant," Virgin-Mary said God. "True
   let happen; I ready accept your word."

[1]Joseph: Right "J" hand position at the left shoulder, palm facing the body making the "J" on left shoulder several times.
[2]Gabriel: Sign "G" then the sign for "angel."
[3]"Look" in stanza 6 should be signed in reverse toward the body.

Lo, How a Rose E'er Blooming

1. Look(#1), how Rose[1] always bloom from young
   plant finish growing! Jesus past generation
   coming, as people past finish sing. Rose
   grew, flower bright, middle cold, happen
   night almost finish.

2. Past Isaiah[2] foretell birth, Baby I have mind;
   with Virgin-Mary we see, Virgin-Mary kind(#2).[3]
   Shows God love right, Virgin-Mary gave us
   Savior, happen night almost finish.

3. O Flower, itself[4] fragrance soft, sweetness
   fill air, scatter glory bright through
   darkness all-over(#1). True Jesus may yet[5]
   God, Jesus save us from sin, death,
   share our every burden.

[1]Rose: Sign "flower" with a "R" hand position.
[2]Isaiah: Right "I" hand position, palm facing out. Then sign "prophet."
[3]Kind: This means "same quality" or "class."
[4]Itself: Left "index" hand position, palm facing right. Right "A" hand position, palm facing
body, move right "A" toward left index.
[5]Yet: In ASL this is signed "but."

Away in a Manger

1. Away manger, no place for bed, little(#1)
   Lord Jesus lie-down(#3) his sweet head.
   Stars[1] sky look-down where(#2) Jesus lie(#3),
   little(#1) Lord Jesus, asleep on hay.[2]

2. Animals make low sound, baby awakes,
   but little(#1) Lord Jesus make no crying sound;
   I love you, Lord Jesus, look-down from sky,
   stay near my bed till morning here.

3. Be(#1) near me,[3] Lord Jesus, I ask you stay
   close me forever, love me, I pray;
   bless all precious children your loving care(#1),
   prepare us for heaven live with you there.

[1]Stars: Should be signed from the left to right.
[2]Hay: Right bent "5" hand position, palm up under the chin, brush upward with the heel of the right hand against the chin several times.
[3]Me: This is signed with R and L "cupped" hand positions, palms facing body. Bring both hands toward the body, fingertips touching, then move both hands downward.

218   It Came Upon the Midnight Clear

1. Came upon midnight clear, that
   glory song past, from angels bow near
   earth, touch angels harp gold: "Peace
   earth, good will(#2) men, from heaven
   all gracious King." World earnest
   still(#2), hear angel sing.

2. Still(#1), through divided sky angels
   came, with peace wings open, still(#1)
   angels heaven music sounds over-all(#1)
   weary world; above world sad, humble(#1) land[1]
   over, angels stay bow one place, ever(#3)
   over(#2) sounds, bless angels sing.

3. You, beneath(#1) life(#1) heavy burden,
   people body kneel low(#2), people work
   hard(#1) way(#1) pain walk slow,
   Now look!(#1) because glad, wonder(#2) time
   come quick on way. O rest(#1) next(#4)
   weary road, hear angels sing.

4. For look(#1)! days fade quick,
   through prophet see past, happen with
   ever(#3) years, years, will(#1) come time
   forecast, happen peace will(#1) over(#1)
   all earth, bright spread quick, all world
   send[2] again song, which now angels sing.

[1]Land: Sign for "dirt," then the sign for "spread."
[2]"Send"(#2) in the opposite direction, coming from God.

What Child Is This   219

1. What child is(#1) this, himself,
   lie-down(#3) rest(#1), Virgin-Mary-lap
   sleep? Whom angels meet with music
   sweet, while shepherds watch(#1)
   take-care-of(#3)?

Refrain:
   This, this is(#1) Christ King, whom
   shepherds watch, angels sing; hurry,
   hurry, bring him praise, baby,
   son Virgin-Mary.

2. Why Jesus lie(#3), same humble house
   where cows, donkey feed(#2)?
   Good Christians, fear, for sinners here
   silent Word plead.

Refrain

3. True, bring Jesus perfume, gold,
   perfume, come, farmer, king,
   receives Jesus; King, kings salvation
   brings, let love people place Jesus throne.[1]

[1]Throne: R and L "C" hand positions, palms facing down and separated, move both hands
back toward the body in an arc motion, representing the arms of a large chair.

Angels From the Realms of Glory

1. Angels from kingdom glory, come
   over(#1) all earth; you yourself sing
   create world story now proclaim Jesus birth:

Refrain:
   Come, worship, come, worship, worship
   Christ, newborn King.

2. Shepherds, out-field(#2) last(#3)
   watch-over(#1) your sheep through night,[1]
   God with us now living; light baby
   Jesus shine far:

Refrain

3. Wise man, leave(#2) your wonder(#1),
   brighter vision(#2) shine afar; seek
   great(#3) Desire(#1) world; you finish
   see Jesus star:

Refrain

4. Angels, before(#3) altar[2] bow, watch(#2)
   long(#2), hope, fear; quick Lord, coming
   form baby will(#1) appear:

Refrain

[1]Night: Use the sign for "all night."
[2]Altar: R and L "A" hand positions, palm facing down, thumbs touch, separate move both hands down. (Indicating the building of a rock table for altar.)

In the Bleak Midwinter

1. Bare(#2) middle winter(#1), freeze
   wind make quiet sounds, earth hard like(#2)
   metal(#2), water like(#2) stone(#1); finish
   snow-fall, snow,[1] snow, snow, bare(#2)
   middle winter(#1) long ago.

2. Our God, heaven cannot hold him, neither
   earth sustain; heaven, earth will(#1) fade
   away happen Jesus comes reign. Bare(#2)
   middle winter(#1), house for cow enough
   Lord God Almighty, Jesus Christ.

3. Angels, highest angels may finish meet,
   angels, highest angels fill heaven;
   but Jesus mother only, her[2] young girl joy,
   worship Jesus with kiss.

4. What[3] can I give Jesus, poor as I?
   If I were shepherd, I will(#1) bring sheep;
   If I were Wise Man, I will(#1) do my part;
   yet[4] what I can give Jesus: I give my heart.

[1]Snow: Sign "snow" alternating right on left, left on right, etc.
[2]Her: Point off to the side.
[3]What: Use the sign "where"(#2).
[4]Yet: In ASL this is signed as "but."

Child So Lovely

Refrain:
> Child true beautiful, here I kneel before(#3) you,
> child true beautiful, you are(#1) Christ my God.
> Child true beautiful, here I kneel before(#3) you,
> child true beautiful, you are(#1) Jesus our Lord.

1. You finished heaven beautiful, God pure(#2),
   melt my devotion, melt my tender[1] feel,
   melt all my soul.

Refrain

2. All my life, my love, my soul, same;
   this what I offer, offer joy,
   kneel your feet.

Refrain

3. Goodbye, tender baby, goodbye, child,
   goodbye; goodbye, sweet beloved, goodbye,
   sweet beloved; goodbye, child, goodbye.

Refrain

[1]Tender: "Tender" can be signed either "soft" or "warm."

Break Forth, O Beauteous Heavenly Light   223

1. Bright(#1), O beautiful heaven light,
   conduct(#2) morning; O shepherds, don't
   fear, but hear angel warning.
   This child, now weak as baby, our confidence,
   joy will(#1) be(#1), power(#1) block devil from
   our make peace eternal.

2. This night wonder(#2), night joy,
   born Jesus, our brother; Jesus comes not
   mighty(#2) destroy, call(#1) us love each
   other. How could Jesus quit as king
   position(#3), exchange for world greedy(#1),
   hate? What[1] deep low pride made certain
   world salvation?

3. Come, precious child, into our hearts,
   leave(#2) your bed behind you! Let this be(#1)
   where(#2) new life starts for all who seek,
   find you. We honor you, offer thanks, praise,
   for all your gifts this time grace(#1); come,
   conquer, deliver us, this world, forever.

[1]What: Use the sign for "where"(#2).

Good Christian Friends, Rejoice

Refrain:
>   Good Christians friends, rejoice
>   with heart, soul, voice;

1. pay attention what we say: News,
   news! Jesus Christ born today! Cow,
   donkey before(#3) Jesus bow, Jesus
   in manger[1] now. Jesus born today,
   Jesus born today.

Refrain

2. now you hear continue joy: News, news!
   Jesus Christ was born for this! Jesus
   finish open heaven door, you bless
   forever. Jesus was born for this,
   Jesus was born for this.

Refrain

3. now you need not fear grave: News,
   news! Jesus Christ was born save! Call(#1)
   you one, call(#1) you all enter Jesus
   everlasting room. Jesus was born save,
   Jesus was born save.

Refrain

[1]Manger: R and L "5" hand positions, fingers pointing down and interlocking, palms facing each other.

My Master, See, the Time Has Come   226

1. My Ruler(#1), see, time finish come
   give your servant leave(#1), go peace, long
   wait for, your promise now fill.

2. Because I finish see salvation,
   Lord. Now may all world see that light
   which is(#1) your Israel boast bright every country.

The Friendly Beasts   227

1. Jesus, our brother, strong(#1), good,
   was humble born rough barn, friendly
   animals stood around him. Jesus, our
   brother strong(#1), good.

2. "I," said donkey, long brown hair,
   "I carry(#2) his mother, up-down-hill,[1]
   I carry(#2) his mother, Bethlehem; I,"
   said donkey, long brown hair.

3. "I," said cow, all white, red, "I gave
   him my manger[2] for bed, I gave him hay[3]
   lay(#3) his head; I," said cow,
   all white, red.

4. "I," said sheep with curly-horn,[4] "I gave
   him my wool for his warm clothes, he
   wear(#2) my coat Christmas morning; I," said
   sheep with curly-horn.

5. "I," said little bird, from roof high,
   "I sang him asleep that he should not cry,
   we sang him asleep, my mate[5] and I; I," said
   little bird, from roof high.

6. That way all animals, through some good
   fascinate(#1), in dark barn were glad tell
   gifts animals gave Jesus,
   gifts animals gave Jesus.

[1]Up-down-hill: R and L "cupped" hands, separated, palms facing down, move both hands up and down in a waving motion, from left to right, several times.
[2]Manger: R and L "5" hand positions, fingers pointing down and interlocking, palms facing each other.
[3]Hay: Right bent "5" hand position, palm facing up under the chin, brush upward with the heel of right hand against the chin several times.
[4]Curly-horn: R and L "O" hand positions, palms facing back at the temples, arc both up and back over the ear, changing both into "S" hand positions.
[5]Mate: R and L bent "5" hand positions, separated, palms facing body, bring both hands together locking fingers together.

228   He Is Born

Refrain:
   Jesus born, holy child, play horn,[1]
   windpipe-blow[2] merry. Jesus born, holy
   child, we all sing, Savior kind(#1).

1. Through years past, prophets finish
   forecast Jesus coming; through years
   past, now time finish come, last(#1).

Refrain

2. O how beautiful, O how pure(#2)
   this perfect child heaven; O how beautiful,
   O how pure(#2), gracious gift world.

Refrain

3. Jesus, Lord all world, coming as baby
   among us, Jesus, Lord all world, give
   us your heaven peace.

Refrain

[1]Horn: Sign the natural motion of blowing a horn.
[2]Windpipe-blow: There is no sign for the original word, "bagpipes." Suggest signing "wind,"
then "pipe."

Infant Holy, Infant Lowly   229

1. Baby holy, baby humble, for his bed cow
   stall;[1] cows low noise, little knowing, baby
   Jesus is(#1) Lord all. Fast moving angels
   singing, Christmas ring(#2), news bring;
   Jesus baby is(#1) Lord all.

2. Sheep lie-around(#3) sleeping, shepherds keep
   watch(#1), until morning new saw glory, heard
   story, information good news true. This way
   rejoice, free from sorrow, praises singing,
   meet tomorrow; Jesus baby was born for you.

[1]Stall: R and L "5" hand positions, fingers interlocking and pointing down, palms facing
each other.

O Little Town of Bethlehem

1. O little(#1) town Bethlehem, how still(#2)
   we see you asleep; above your deep real
   sleep,[1] silent(#1) stars-pass.[2] Yet[3] your
   dark street shine everlasting(#2) light;[4]
   hopes, fears ever since years,
   found you tonight.

2. For Christ born, Virgin-Mary,
   gathered(#2) all above, while people
   sleep, angels keep-watch(#1) wonder(#2) love
   O morning stars together, proclaim holy
   birth, praises sing God, King,
   peace all on-earth.

3. How silent(#2), how silent(#2),
   wonder(#2) baby give; true God give
   people hearts, bless his heaven. No person
   may hear Jesus coming, but in this world sin,
   where(#2) humble hearts will(#1) receive
   Jesus, still(#1) Jesus enters.

4. O holy baby from Bethlehem, come-down us
   we pray; take-away our sin, enter, become
   born in us today. We hear Christmas angels,
   great(#) glad news tell; O come us, live
   with us, our Lord Emmanuel.[5]

[1]Deep real sleep: In dreamless sleep, no thoughts, words, or pictures are being processed in the mind, so sign "real" and the sign for "sound asleep," which is signed "sleep," followed by R and L "A" hand positions, palms facing each other, move right down on top of the left.
[2]Stars pass: Signs beginning from the left and moving to the right, several times.
[3]Yet: Sign "but."
[4]Light: This is a directional sign and should be signed coming from God, fingertips touching back of left hand then reversing the sign going back us, indicating the street is shining.
[5]Emmanuel: Signed the same as Lord except with an "E" hand position.

When Christmas Morn is Dawning 232

1. Happen Christmas morning begin,
   I wish(#1) I could be near manger,[1]
   see God newborn Son. Near manger,
   see God newborn Son.

2. How kind you, our Savior, for us come
   earth. O may we not through sin, hate
   your humble(#1) birth. O may we not
   through sin, hate your humble(#1) birth.

3. We need you, O Lord Jesus, to-be(#1) our
   precious friend. Your love will guard, guide
   us, care us continue(#1) life. Your love will
   guard, guide us, care us continue(#1) life.

[1]Manger: R and L "5" hand positions, palms facing each other, fingers interlocking and fingertips pointing down.

This ASL translation © 1995 Augsburg Fortress

Cold December Flies Away 233

1. Cold month fade-away, rose red great(#3)
   bright. Spring perfect glory appear while
   all world wonder(#1) holy secret power tree
   which grow flower. On bless tree bloom[1]
   reddest[2] flower, on tree bloom rose[3] here love
   own[4] garden, full strong(#1) glory.

2. In depressed time of sin deep dark finish
   enter. All world lie(#3) like(#2) dead,
   eyes-closed sleeping. But, happen all seem
   lost night,[5] sunrise golden bright bring
   continue joy, bring continue joy our hope,
   highest hope, our hope bright begin,
   Son beloved heaven.

3. Now flower open, world wake. Inside
   pure flower found wonder(#2) fragrant.
   Spread over-all earth begin with birth;
   itself[6] beauty live. In flower fragrant
   live, flower spread with heaven bright,
   pleasant fragrant delight.

[1]Bloom: R and L "cupped" hand positions together before the body, palms facing each other, fingers point up, open and close several times starting from left to right.
[2]Reddest: Should be signed squeezing the eyebrows together and slightly bowing the head, making a strong movement downward with the right index finger, changing into a right "10" hand position and lift up high.
[3]Rose: In the same sign as "flower," except sign it with a "R" hand position.
[4]Own: Left "index" hand position, palm facing right, finger pointing up. Right "10" hand position, palm facing body, move right hand toward left index.
[5]Night: Should be signed as "all night."
[6]Itself: Left "index" hand position, palm facing right, finger pointing up. Right "10" hand position, palm facing body, move toward left but not touching.

234   O Come, All Ye Faithful

1. O come, all you faithful(#2), joy
   triumph(#2), O come you, O come you,
   Bethlehem. Come, see Jesus, born King,
   angels;

Refrain:
   O come, let us adore him, O come,
   let us adore him, O come, let us
   adore him, Christ, Lord.

2. True God, true God, Light from Light
   Eternal, look, Jesus avoid not Virgin-Mary;
   Son, Father, born not create;

Refrain

3. Sing, choirs angels, sing celebration;
   O sing, all you people heaven above!
   Glory God, all glory, highest;

Refrain

4. See how shepherds, call(#1) his cradle[1]
   leave(#1) shepherds sheep, come near, look;
   we same(#1) will(#1) go-to,
   turn our joy walk.

Refrain

5. Child, for us sinners, poor, manger[2] we
   will(#1) hug you with love, wonder(#2). Who
   would not love you, loving us true dearly?

Refrain

6. Yes, Lord, we welcome you, born this happy
   morning, Jesus, you all glory give.
   Word, Father, now person appearing:

Refrain.

[1]Cradle: Sign "manger."
[2]Manger: R and L "5" hand positions, palms facing each other, fingers interlocking and fingertips pointing down.

235   Rock-A-Bye, My Dear Little Boy

1. Rocking-chair, my precious little(#1)
   boy, precious little(#1) boy, wonder(#2)
   wonder(#1), my bless joy; sleep as I
   gentle(#1) love you, let my tender love
   hug you; give me, world gift God, here my
   arms lie(#3) true peace sleep.

2. Little(#1) Jesus, Baby Holy, Baby
   Bless, one with Father, but born become
   mine; as I rocking-chair you calm sleep,
   angel guard watch-care(#1); precious child,
   one day we will(#1) see what love finish
   mean for you me.

236   While Shepherds Watched Their Flocks

1. While shepherds watch(#1) sheep
   through night, all seated-around,[1] angel
   Lord appeared, glory shine around,[2]
   glory shine-around.

2. "Fear not!" said angel, for mighty(#2)
   fear finish take-over troubled mind. "Glad
   good news great(#3) joy, I bring all
   people, all people.

3. "You, city David,[3] today, born
   David generation Savior, himself Jesus
   Lord, this will(#1) be(#1) show, this
   will(#1) be(#1) show.

4. "Heaven baby you will(#1) find, people
   view display, all poor wrapped, thin clothes,
   lie(#3) manger, lie(#3) manger."

5. This way spoke angel, once, appeared
   shine group(#1) angels praising God on high,
   who this way spoke angel song, who this way
   spoke angel song:

6. "All glory be(#1) God on high, earth
   be(#1) peace; good will(#2) from-then-on
   heaven earth begin, never cease, begin,
   never cease."

[1]Seated-around: R and L bent "V" hand positions, palms facing down, hands separated, arc
both hands out, twisting the wrists, ending up with palms facing body, hands touching.
[2]Shine-around: Should be signed with both hands, from left to right.
[3]David: Right "D" hand position, palm facing body at the right temple, tap several times.

This ASL translation © 1995 The United Methodist Publishing House

Sing We Now of Christmas   237

1. Now we sing Christmas, Christmas,
   we sing here! Hear our grateful praise
   babe so precious.

Refrain:
   We sing Christmas, King born,
   Christmas! Now we sing Christmas, now
   we sing Christmas!

2. Angels call(#2) shepherds, "Leave(#2)
   your sheep rest, go to Bethlehem,
   find baby true bless."

Refrain

3. Bethlehem shepherd found baby; Joseph[1]
   Virgin-Mary gracious, seated[2] beside manger,[3]
   watch(#1) holy child.

Refrain

4. From eastern country kings came afar,
   carrying gifts Bethlehem, guide through star.

Refrain

5. Gold, perfume, kings brings, gifts
   great(#2) worth; never animal house
   past like(#2) great(#3) happy.

Refrain

[1]Joseph: Right "J" hand position, palm facing body at the left shoulder, describe a "J" on left shoulder several times.
[2]Seated: Should be signed with both bent "V." Move out and down slightly indicating that both were sitting by the manger.
[3]Manger: R and L "5" hand positions, palms facing each other, fingers interlocking and fingertips pointing down.

238   Angels We Have Heard on High

1. Angels we finish hear high, sweetly
   sing over land,[1] mountains
   answer sound joy music.

Refrain:
   Glory, high God Power(#1)!
   Glory, high God Power(#1)!

2. Shepherds, why this great(#3) joy?
   Why your joy music continue? What glad
   good news which inspire[2] your heaven song?

Refrain

3. Come, Bethlehem, see Christ, himself
   birth angels sing; come, adore bend-knee,
   Christ Lord, newborn King.

Refrain

4. See Jesus lie(#3) manger[3] whom groups
   angels praise; Virgin-Mary, Joseph,[4] give
   your aid, while our hearts, love we sing.

Refrain

[1]Land: Sign "dirt," then the sign for "spread."
[2]Inspire: R and L flat "O" hand positions, palms facing body at the heart, fingers pointing up, move both hands up opening into "5" hand positions.
[3]Manger: R and L "5" hand positions, palms facing each other, fingers interlocking and fingertips pointing down.
[5]Joseph: Right "J" hand position, palm facing body at the left shoulder, describe a "J" on left shoulder several times.

Silent Night, Holy Night   239

1. Silence(#2) night, holy night, all
   calm, all bright round[1] Virgin-Mary
   mother, baby! Holy baby, true soft,
   sweet, sleep, heavenly peace, sleep
   heavenly peace.

2. Silence(#2) night, holy night, shepherds
   quake[2] sight; glory stream[3] from heaven
   afar, heaven group(#1) sing Alleluia!
   Christ, Savior born,
   Christ, Savior born!

3. Silence(#2) night, holy night, Son
   God, love pure(#2) light; bright ray[4] from your
   holy face, with begin, redeem(#1)
   grace(#1), Jesus, Lord, your birth,
   Jesus, Lord your birth.

4. Silence(#2) night, holy night, wonder(#2)
   star show your light; with angels let us
   sing Alleluia our King; Christ Savior
   born, Christ Savior born!

[1]Round: Should be signed with a Right "open hand," palm facing up on the left side, move all the way to the right.
[2]Quake: R and L "5" hand positions, palms facing body and separated, fingertips pointing down, shake both hands several times.
[3]Stream: Should sign "shine" with both hands in reverse, coming from above.
[4]Ray: Same sign as "stream."

240   Hark! the Herald Angels Sing

1. Pay attention! announce angels sing,
   "Glory newborn king; peace earth, mercy(#2)
   kind, God, sinners make friends!" Joy
   all you nations, rise(#1), join(#3)
   triumph(#2) sky; with angel group(#1)
   proclaim, "Christ born Bethlehem!"

Refrain:
   Pay attention! announce angels sing,
   "Glory newborn King!"

2. Jesus, through high heaven adore;
   Jesus, everlasting Lord! Late night
   Jesus born, child Virgin-Mary.
   Became person, God can see; Welcome,
   body form God, please with us
   live, Jesus, our Emmanuel.[1]

Refrain

3. Welcome heaven born Prince Peace!
   Welcome Son Righteous(#2)! Light, life
   all he brings, rise(#1) with heal[2] his
   hand. Kind(#1) Jesus glory near, born that
   people may not die, born rise(#1) us,
   from grave(#1), born give us, second birth.

Refrain

[1]Emmanuel: May be signed with the Right "E," the same as Lord.
[1]Heal: Sign for "make," then the sign for "well"(#2).

That Boy-Child of Mary 241

Refrain:
   That boy, baby Virgin-Mary born animal
   house, manger[1] his bed in Bethlehem.

1. What will(#1) we call boy child in
   manger? What named give in Bethlehem?

Refrain

2. Boy baby name Jesus, God ever(#3)
   with us, God give for us in Bethlehem.

Refrain

3. How can boy baby save us, how can he
   help us, born here among us in Bethlehem?

Refrain

4. Gift Father, to person mother,
   birth boy baby our brother in Bethlehem.

Refrain

5. One with Father, he our
   Savior, heaven-sent help in Bethlehem.

Refrain

6. Glad we praise boy baby, love adore
   him, give ourselves Jesus in Bethlehem.

Refrain

[1]Manger: R and L "5" hand positions, palms facing each other, fingers interlocking and fingertips pointing down.

242   Love Came Down at Christmas

1. Love came-down Christmas, Love all
   beautiful, Love divine; Love was born
   Christmas; Star angels gave show.

2. Worship we God, Love body form, Love
   divine; worship we our Jesus, but
   where for blessed show?

3. Love will(#1) be(#1) our gift;
   love be(#1) yours, love be(#1) mine;
   love God all people, love for
   plea, gift, show.

From a Distant Home

1. We come seek Savior from far
   home, using same our guide, star
   true bright shining.

Refrain:
  Beautiful east star, that tells
  us God morning, heaven wonder(#2)
  light, O never cease your shining!
  Glory in highest, Son Heaven,
  upon earth, be(#1) peace, love all.

2. Shining gold, I bring newborn
   baby true holy, gift God power
   rule(#1) above, glory.

Refrain

3. Perfume, I bring baby God own
   choosing, show our prayers
   heaven ever(#3) rise(#3).

Refrain

4. Bitter perfume have I give
   baby Jesus, showing pain that Jesus
   will bear(#4) save us.

Refrain

‘Twas in the Moon of Wintertime

1. True middle winter, happen all birds
   gone south, that mighty(#2) great(#3) God
   sent angel group(#1) instead(#2); before(#1)
   angels light stars became dark, wander(#2)
   hunters heard song:

Refrain:
Jesus your King born, Jesus
born, highest God glory.

2. Within rough(#1) animal house, tender[1] baby
   was found; poor robe, rabbit skin wrap
   Jesus beauty; but as hunter brave came
   near, angel song sounded loud, high:

Refrain

3. Before(#1) moon winter not
   round, fair as surround glory, on
   small baby. Chief from far, before(#3)
   Jesus kneel, with gifts fox, animal coat.

Refrain

4. O children forest free, O seed great(#3)
   God holy child earth, heaven born
   today for you. Come kneel before(#3) radiant[2]
   boy, himself brings you beauty, peace, joy.

Refrain

[1]Tender: Suggest to sign "soft" at the heart or "warm."
[2]Radiant: Use the sign for "bright."

1. First Christmas, angel finish say,
   to certain poor shepherds field(#2)
   as sat-around;[1] field(#2) where(#2) shepherds
   sat-around, keep sheep, cold-winter
   night that true silent(#2).

Refrain:
   Christmas, Christmas, Christmas,
   Christmas, born King Israel.

2. Shepherds look-up(#1), saw star
   shine east, far; world star gave
   great(#2) light, star continued
   both day, night.

Refrain

3. Through light that same star three
   Wise Men came from country far; desire seek
   King intend follow star no matter star go.

Refrain

4. This star came near north-west, over
   Bethlehem take up place; there star both stop,
   stay, over place where(#2) Jesus lie(#3).

Refrain

5. Then enter Wise Men three, full love
   respect upon knee, offer there, his
   presence, gifts gold, incense perfume.

Refrain

[1]
Sat-around: R and L bent "V" hand positions, palms facing down and separated, arc both hands out, twisting wrists to end up with palms facing body, hands touching.

246   Joy to the World

1. Joy world, Lord arrive!
   Let world receive world King; let
   every person plan receive Jesus,
   heaven, nature sing,
   heaven, nature sing,
   heaven, heaven, nature sing.

2. Joy world, Savior reign!
   Let all songs use; while
   field(#2), flood, rock, hill
   land all over, repeat sounding
   joy, repeat sounding joy
   repeat, repeat, sounding joy.

3. No more let sin sorrows grow,
   nor sharp point troubles earth; he
   comes make his bless grow,
   far as wrong found, far
   as wrong found, far
   as, far as wrong found.

4. He rules(#1) world with truth,
   grace(#1), makes nations prove,
   glory his, righteous, wonder(#2)
   his love, wonder(#2) his love,
   wonder(#2), wonder(#2), his love.

This ASL translation © 1995 The United Methodist Publishing House

O Morning Star, How Fair and Bright

1. O Morning Star, how beautiful bright
   you shine truth light, O ruler(#1) kind
   humble! You Jesus grandfather, David[1] Son,
   my Lord ruler(#1), you finish won my heart
   serve you only! You are(#1) holy, fair,
   glory, all victory(#2), rich bless
   rule(#1) might(#1) over all things.

2. You heaven bright! Light divine! O
   deep within my heart now shine, make
   yourself altar![2] Fill me joy strength be(#1)
   your member(#1), ever(#3) join(#2) you love
   that cannot fail; toward your long(#2)
   control(#1) me; turn bless me; here sad
   eye heart long(#2) your glad!

3. What joy know, happen life finish, Lord
   we love is(#1) first last, end(#1) begin!
   He will(#1) some day, O glory grace(#1),
   carry us that happy place beyond all tears
   sin! Amen! Amen! Come, Lord Jesus! Crown
   glad, we desire for day your return.

[1]David: Right "D" hand position, palm facing body at the right temple, tap several times.
[2]Altar: R and L "A" hand positions, palms facing down and hands together, separate, then move both down slightly.

On This Day Earth Shall Ring

1. Today earth will(#1) sound with song
   children sing, Lord Christ our King, born
   on earth save us; God gave us Jesus.

Refrain:
   Alleluia, Alleluia, Alleluia, Glory
   highest, God.

2. Jesus condemn, ours happy,
   happen Jesus came-down earth, Bethlehem
   saw Jesus birth; cow, donkey near Jesus,
   from cold protect Jesus.

Refrain

3. God bright star, over Jesus head, Wise
   Men three led Jesus star; Wise Men kneel
   near his bed, gave gifts before him, praise
   him, adore him.

Refrain

4. Today angels sing; with angel song, earth
   will(#1) sound, praise Christ, heaven King,
   born earth save us; peace love he gave us.

Refrain

There's A Song in the Air

1. True song air! True star high!
   True mother deep prayer, baby low cry!
   star spread shine,[1] while beautiful
   sing, for manger[2] welcome King!

2. True excitement joy over wonder(#2)
   birth, for Virgin-Mary baby is(#1) Lord
   for world. Yes! star spread shine while
   beautiful sing, for manger, Bethlehem welcome King!

3. Bright that star found generation
   great(#2) worth; that song from far
   finish spread over world. Every home
   warm, beautiful sing in homes
   world that Jesus is(#1) King.

4. We rejoice light, we sound again
   song that spreads through night from
   heaven group(#1). Yes! we shout
   beautiful good news angels bring, we
   welcome Jesus as our Savior, King.

[1]Shine: Should be signed with both hands in reverse coming from above, indicating all the stars.
[2]Manger: R and L "5" hand positions, palms facing each other, fingers interlocking and fingertips pointing down.

250　Once in Royal David's City

1. Long ago Bethlehem found humble animal
house, where(#2) mother lie(#3) her baby manger[1]
for his bed; Virgin-Mary, love mother kind,
Jesus Christ, her little(#1) baby.

2. Jesus came-down earth from heaven
himself God, Lord all, barn his protect,
manger his bed. With poor,
mocked, humble lived on earth
our Savior holy.

3. Jesus like(#2) us grow-up; everyday,
like(#2) us Jesus grew; Jesus was
little weak, dependent, tears, smiles
like(#2) us Jesus knew; he feels for our
sadness, he shares our glad.

4. Our eyes last(#1) will(#1) see Jesus,
through his own redeem(#1) love; for that
child true precious, gentle, our
Lord heaven above; he lead his children,
place where(#2) Jesus gone.

[1]Manger: R and L "5" hand positions, palms facing each other, fingers interlocking and fingertips pointing down.

This ASL translation © 1995 The United Methodist Publishing House

251　Go, Tell It on the Mountain

Refrain:
　　Go, tell mountain, over(#2) hills, every place,
　　go, tell mountain, that Jesus Christ born.

1. While shepherds keep their watch(#1)
silence(#2) sheep through night,[1] look(#1)[2]
through-out heavens, there show, holy bright.

Refrain

2. Shepherds, fear, trembled,[3] when look(#1)!
   above earth, sound angel sing that announce
   Savior birth.

Refrain

3. Low manger,[4] humble Jesus was born,
   God sent us salvation that bless
   Christmas morning.

Refrain

[1]Night: Should be signed "over night" or "all night."
[2]Look: The first "look" should be signed from left to right, indicating throughout the heavens, then "throughout" should not be signed.
[3]Trembled: R and L "5" hand positions, palms facing body and separated, fingers point down, shake hands several times.
[4]Manger: R and L "5" hand positions, palms facing each other, fingers interlocking and fingertips pointing down.

When Jesus Came to Jordan   252

1. Happen Jesus came "J"-river, John[1] baptize[2]
   Jesus, didn't come for pardon,
   but as man with no sin. Jesus came share
   repent with people themselves mourn
   sins, speak vital sentence,
   with which good news begins

2. Jesus came share tempt, our great(#2)
   grief(#2), loss, for us our salvation die
   upon cross. True happen little bird come-
   down on Jesus, Son of Man, private years
   finish end(#1), time grace(#2) began.

3. Come, Holy Spirit, aid us keep vow we
   make; this day enter us, every bond
   break.[3] Come, give our lives direction(#2),
   gift we covet(#1) most; share resurrection
   that leads Pentecost.[4]

[1]John: Suggest, Right "J" hand position on the back of the left, palm face body, describe a J several times or use a sign name you already have for the disciple John.

[2]Baptize: First sign "water," then the sign for "baptize" in order to show difference between the church and baptize.

[3]Break: Should be signed with "bound," then separate hands as in "save."

[4]Pentecost: Use the sign for "Pontius Pilate" or any other sign name you already have for Pentecost.

254   We Three Kings

1. We three kings from East; bring gifts
   we travel far, field(#2), river, open
   wet land, mountain, following star.

Refrain:
   Star wonder(#2), star bright, star with
   like(#2) king beauty bright, west lead,
   still(#1) proceed, guide us your perfect light.

2. Born King, Bethlehem plain,[1] gold I bring,
   crown him again, King forever, cease never,
   over us all reign.[2]

Refrain

3. I have smell offer; smell own God
   near; prayer, praise voices sing,
   worship God high.

Refrain

4. Perfume is(#1) mine; gum bitter
   perfume means life much gloom; sorrow,
   crying, bleed, dying, bury stone tomb.

Refrain

5. Glory now see Jesus rise(#1); King,
   God, sacrifice: Alleluia, Alleluia,
   sounds through, earth, heavens.

Refrain

[1]Plain: R and L "open hand" positions, palms facing down, fingers pointing out, move hands out, arc right to the right and arc left to the left.
[2]Reign: "Regulate" will take care of the meaning of phrase "over us all reign."

We Would See Jesus 256

1. We would see Jesus; see his star
   shining above rough animal house while
   angels sing; there manger[1] lie(#3) hay;[2]
   let us give our gifts before(#3) King.

2. We would see Jesus, Virgin-Mary son most
   holy, light world everyday; shine show
   through every task most humble, Jesus
   God, life, truth, way.

3. We would see Jesus, on mountain, teach,
   with all people gathered(#2) pay attention;
   while birds, flowers heaven above
   announce, bless which simple
   trust finish found.

4. We would see Jesus, his work heal,
   evening before sun-set; divine man,
   Jesus real make known God made man,
   loving service met.

5. We would see Jesus, early-morning, still(#1)
   as past Jesus call(#1), "Follow me!" Let
   us rise(#1), all humble service look-down;
   Lord, we are yours, we give ourselves you.

[1]Manger: R and L "5" hand positions, palms facing each other, fingers interlocking and fingertips pointing down.
[2]Hay: Right bent "5" hand position under the chin, palm up, fingers point out, brush upward with heel of right hand against chin several times.

257   We Meet You, O Christ

1. We meet you, O Christ, many face;
   your image we see simple, wise. You live
   fine house, live small house; we see you,
   worker, cross your back.

2. Many, many, alive, gone far; involve
   our life, you live near. Imprison system,
   you long(#2) be(#1) free; we see you
   Lord Jesus, still(#1) bear(#4) your cross.

3. We hear you, O man, agony cry(#3);
   for freedom you march, riot you die. Your
   picture newspapers we read, we see. Cross
   must be(#1) found through person decree.

4. You choose become one with earth; dark
   grave prepares for your begin. Your death
   is(#1) your rise(#1), create your word;
   cross starts life, our hope made new.

1. O wonder(#2) sight! O vision(#2) fair,
   glory that church will(#1) share, which
   Jesus on mountain shows, where(#2) bright
   than sun, he shine![1]

2. From generation, generation story
   declare, how with three disciples there
   where(#2) Moses,[2] Elijah[3] meet, Lord have
   earnest friendly talk.

3. Law, prophets, there have place, two
   chosen witness, grace(#1); Father voice
   from cloud proclaims his only Son.

4. With shine[4] face, bright display, Jesus
   come-down clear that day what glory will(#1)
   be angels above themselves joy in God
   with perfect love.

5. Faithful(#2) hearts rise(#3) high,
   through this great(#3) secret vision;
   for which joy family we rise(#3) voice,
   prayer, hymn praise.

[1]Shine: Should be signed in reverse coming from above.
[2]Moses: R and L "G" hand positions at the temples, palms facing down, move out to the respective sides of the body, closing the "G" hands.
[3]Elijah: Make an "E" with the Right hand, then sign "prophet" or any other name sign you have for this particular prophet.
[4]Shine face: Should be signed with both hands coming from the face, not off the back of left hand.

260   Christ, upon the Mountain Peak

1. Jesus, on mountain peak, found alone
glory, bright; let us if we brave speak,
with angels praise Jesus: Alleluia!

2. Tremble,[1] Jesus feet, we saw Moses[2] Elijah[3]
speech(#2). All prophets law shout through
prophets joy welcome: Alleluia!

3. Swift, cloud glory came, God proclaim in
thunder, Jesus as Son through name! Nations
cry(#3) loud wonder(#2): Alleluia!

4. This is(#1) God beloved Son! Law,
prophets fade before(#3) Jesus; first, last,
only-one, let world now adore him: Alleluia!

[1]Tremble: R and L "5" hand positions, separated, palms facing the body and fingertips pointing down, shake hands several times.
[2]Moses: R and L "G" hand positions at the temples, palms facing down, move out to the respective sides of the body, closing the "G" hands.
[3]Elijah: Make an "E" with the Right hand, then sign "prophet."

This ASL translation © 1995 Hope Publishing Company

261   Lord of the Dance

1. I danced morning happen world begun, I
danced moon, stars, sun, I came-down from
heaven, I danced earth. Bethlehem I
finished my birth.

Refrain:
Dance, then, wherever you may be; I Lord
Dance, said he. I lead you all wherever
you may be, I lead you all dance, said he.

2. I danced for writers, Lawyers, but they
   not dance, they not follow me; I danced for
   fishermen, for James,[1] John;[2] fishermen came
   me, dance continue.

Refrain

3. I danced Sunday, happen I heal[3] lame,
   holy people said, true shame; they whip,
   they remove clothing, they crucified me;
   they left(#2) me cross die.

Refrain

4. I danced, Friday, sky change black;
   hard(#1) dance with devil ride back(#2);
   they bury my body, they thought I dead,
   but I dance, I still(#1) continue.

Refrain

5. They kill me, I resurrection heaven,
   I true life that will(#1) never, never die;
   I live you, if you live me; I Lord,
   Dance, said he.

Refrain

[1]James: Sign a right "J," then "disciple" or any other name sign you use for this particular disciple.
[2]John: Right "J" on back of left hand, palm facing body, describe a "J" several times or use any other name sign for this disciple.
[3]Heal: Sign for "make," then the sign for "well"(#2).

Heal Me, Hands of Jesus

1. Heal me, hands Jesus, search
   my pain; inspire[1] my hope, remove my
   fear, bring me peace again.

2. Clean me, blood Jesus, bitter
   take-away; let me forgive as person
   forgive, bring me peace today.

3. Know me, mind Jesus, show me
   all my sin; scatter memory guilt,
   bring me peace with-in.

4. Fill me, joy Jesus; anxiety
   will(#1) cease, heaven calm be(#1)
   mine, for Jesus brings me peace!

[2]Inspire: R and L flat "O" hand positions, palms facing body at the heart, fingers pointing up, move both hands up opening into "5" hand positions.

263 When Jesus the Healer Passed Through Galilee

1. Happen Jesus, healer, passed through
   "G"-country, Heal us, heal us today!
   deaf came hear, blind came see.
   Heal us, Lord Jesus!

2. Disabled[1] man was lower through roof.
   Heal us, heal us today! His sins were
   forgiven, his walking proof.
   Heal us, Lord Jesus!

3. Death king daughter cause king
   weep(#1). Heal us, heal us today! Jesus
   took-hand[2] girl, Jesus rise(#1) from dead.
   Heal us, Lord Jesus!

4. Happen blind man cried(#3)-out Lord,
   Heal us, heal us today! His faith made him
   well(#2), his sight made new.
   Heal us, Lord Jesus!

5. Sick white skin, were made well, demon
   cast-out. Heal us, heal us today! Bent[3]
   woman rise(#1) laugh, shout.
   Heal us, Lord Jesus!

6. Twelve were given power(#1) sent-out
   two-two.[4] Heal us, heal us today! make sick
   well(#2) spread good news.
   Heal us, Lord Jesus!

7. True still(#1) lot sick, suffer today.
   Heal us, heal us today! We gather(#2)
   together heal, pray; Heal us, Lord Jesus!

[1]Disabled: Left "open hand" position, palm face body. Right "D" hand position, palm face down, index finger points out, tap fingers of right D between left thumb and left index several times.
[2]Took-hand: Natural motion of taking someone's hand and lifting the person up.
[3]Bent: Right "X" position, palm face out, move forward.
[4]Sent-out two-two: R and L "V" or "2" hand positions, fingers up, palms facing out, move out to the respective sides of the body.

Silence, Frenzied, Unclean Spirit

1. "Silence(#2), very much excite, not
   clean spirit!" cried(#3) God heal Holy One.
   "Cease your careless talk(#1)! People can't
   control(#2); flee as night, before sun."
   Jesus words demon trembled,[1] from person
   injure(#2) demon gone(#3), while crowd that
   assemble stood wonder(#1), shocked(#1), hush.

2. Lord, demon still(#1) succeed, small
   dark thoughts mind: cruel(#1) rule(#1)
   voices, loud, force, confused thoughts that
   control(#1), doubts that mix heart anxiety,
   fears made ugly reason sight, guilt that
   makes our loving very much excite, dreams
   that darken heart with fear.

3. Silence(#2), Lord, not clean spirit in
   our mind, our heart; speak your word that
   happen we hear word, all our demon will(#1)
   depart. Clear our thought, calm our feel;
   still(#2) broken, struggle heart. Through
   power(#1), your heal make us faithful(#2),
   true, whole.

[1]Tremble: R and L "5" hand positions, fingers pointing down, palms facing body, shake hands several times.

1. O Christ, healer,[1] we finish come pray
   for health, plea for friends. How can we
   fail except made new, happen touched
   through love that continue?

2. From every sickness, people endure(#1)
   our bodies cry-out(#3) be(#1) free; yet[2] our
   hearts, we would confess that well(#2)
   our real need.

3. How strong, O Lord, our desires,
   how weak our knowledge ourselves? Free us
   healing truths, not aware-of pride
   resists, put[3] aside.

4. Conflicts[4] that destroy our health, we
   recognize world disease; our everyday life
   declare our evil. Is(#1) there no help,
   O Christ, for us?

5. Grant(#2) that we all, made one faith,
   your community(#1) may find well(#2) that,
   improve us, will(#1) touch all world.

[1]Heal: Sign for "make," then the sign for "well"(#2).
[2]Yet: In ASL this meaning is signed "but."
[3]Put-aside: R and L "open hand" positions, both palms facing right, fingers pointing out, brush both to the right, as the natural motion of pushing something aside.
[4]Conflict: R and L "index" or "1" hand positions, separated, palms out, fingertips pointing up at an angle, move both hands up until "index" fingers cross.

266   Heal Us, Emmanuel, Hear Our Prayer

1. Heal[1] us, Emmanuel,[2] hear our prayer; we
   wait feel your touch; deep wound souls
   you mend new, Savior, we same(#3).

2. Our faith is(#1) feeble, we confess,
   we weak trust your word;
   but will(#1) you pity us less(#1)?
   We would not wish(#1) that from you, Lord!

3. Remember person himself once
   apply(#2) trembling[3] for free burden;
   "Lord, I believe," with tears man cried(#3);
   "O help my disbelief(#1)!"

4. Woman also(#1) herself touched you
   in crowd, heal good taken,[4]
   was answered, "Daughter, go peace:
   your faith finish made you well(#2)."

5. Like(#2) woman, with hope fears
   we come touch you, if we may;
   Don't send us home without hope;
   send no one not-yet healed home.

[1]Heal: Sign for "make," then the sign for "well"(#2).
[2]Emmanuel: May be signed with the Right "E," the same as Lord.
[3]Trembling: R and L "5" hand positions, fingers pointing down, palms facing body, shake hands several times.
[4]Taken: Right "5" hand position at the heart, fingers pointing to the left, move right hand out closing into an "S" hand position.

O Love, How Deep

1. O love, how deep, how broad, how high,
   love fill heart with joy, that God, Son
   God, should take our living form for
   our understand!

2. For us baptized, for us Jesus bear(#4),
   his holy time without food, hungry pain,
   for us temptation clear he knew; for us
   devil conquered.

3. For us Jesus prayed; for us he taught;
   for us his daily works he made; through
   words show, actions that way, still(#1)
   seek now himself, but us.

4. For us evil power(#1) deceive, whip,
   mock purple robe dress, he bear(#4) shame
   cross, death, for us gave up his
   dying breath.

5. For us Jesus rise(#1) from dead again;
   for us he went-to heaven reign; for us
   Jesus sent his Spirit here, guide,
   strengthen, cheer.

6. All glory our Lord God for love true
   deep, true high, true broad: Trinity whom
   we adore, forever, forever more.

269   Lord, Who Throughout These Forty Days

1. Lord, who through past forty days,
   for us finished without food, pray?
   Teach us with you mourn our sins,
   stay close you.

2. As you with Devil finish contend(#2),
   finished win(#2) victory(#1), O give us
   strength in you fight conquer sin.

3. As you finish hunger bear(#4), thirst,
   same teach us gracious Lord, die self,
   especially live through your most holy word.

4. Through now days penitent, through your
   passion(#2), yes, ever(#3) life, death,
   Jesus, live with us.

5. Live with us, that true, this life
   suffer(#2) since past, Easter(#2) continue
   joy we may attain last(#1).

270   The Lord's Prayer

Our Father yourself heaven,
hallowed your name, your kingdom
come, your will(#2) done, earth
as in heaven. Give[1] us now
day our daily bread; forgive
us our sin, as we forgive
others who sin against us.

Lead us not into temptation,
but deliver(#1) us from evil, for
your kingdom, power,
glory forever. Amen.

¹Give: Should be signed as a directional verb.

The Lord's Prayer 271

1. Our Father, yourself true heaven,
   hallowed your name. Your kingdom come,
   your will(#2) done(#2), hallowed your name.

2. Done(#2) earth as in heaven, hallowed
   your name. Give¹ us now day our
   daily bread, hallowed your name.

3. Forgive all our sins, hallowed your
   name. As we forgive others sin against us,
   hallowed your name.

4. Lead us not into temptation, hallowed
   your name. But deliver(#1) us from evil,
   hallowed your name.

5. Your kingdom, power, glory,
   hallowed your name. Forever, ever,
   hallowed your name.

6. A-men, a-men, a-men, hallowed your name.
   A-men, a-men, a-men, hallowed your name.

¹Give: Should be signed as a directional verb.

Sing of Mary, Pure and Lowly

1. Sing, Virgin-Mary, pure, humble, girl
   mother, wise, kind. Sing God own Son most
   holy, who became Virgin-Mary little child.
   Beautiful child, beautiful mother, God,
   Lord himself came earth, Word became person,
   our very brother, became person like(#2) us,
   through Jesus birth.

2. Sing Jesus, son Virgin-Mary, home
   "N"-town. Toil cannot weary love endure(#2)
   till death. Always love he gave Virgin-Mary,
   although love separated Jesus
   from Virgin-Mary, out-world preach,
   heal, suffer, till cross Jesus died.

3. Joy mother, full glad, Virgin-Mary arms,
   your Lord born. Mourn mother, full
   sadness, all your heart with pain
   broken. Glory mother, now reward with
   crown, Jesus hand, generation, generation,
   remember your name will(#1) be(#1) blessed,
   every country.

Jesus' Hands Were Kind Hands

1. Jesus hands kind(#1) hands, doing
   good all, heal pain, sick, bless
   children small(#2), wash tired feet,
   saving people who fall; Jesus hands
   kind(#1) hands, doing good all.

2. Take[1] my hands, Lord Jesus, let
   hands work for you; make hands strong(#1),
   gentle(#2), kind(#1) all I do. Let me
   watch(#2) you, Jesus, till I gentle(#1)
   same, till my hands are(#1) kind(#1) hands,
   quick work for you.

[1]Take: Natural motion of taking my hand.

Woman in the Night   274

1. Woman during night, tired from giving
   birth, guard our precious light;
   peace on earth!

Refrain:
   Come, join(#2) song, women, children
   men; Jesus makes us free live again.

2. Woman in crowd, creep-up[1] behind
   touch[2] allow; seek, you will find!

Refrain

3. Woman by(#1) well(#3), question Jesus;
   find your friends, tell; drink your
   heart desire!

Refrain

4. Woman at feast, let righteous look;
   come, go peace; love Jesus with
   your hair!

Refrain

5. Woman in house, raise be(#1) meek,
   leave(#1) your second place; pay
   attention, think, speak!

Refrain

6. Women on road, welcomed made new,
   traveled far, wide; witness, Lord!

Refrain

¹Creep-up: R and L "index" hand positions, fingertips point down and palms facing body, move indexes up and down alternating as move forward, the natural motion of tiptoeing. ²Touch: Right "5" hand position with middle finger extended, touch back of left hand with right middle finger.

275   The Kingdom of God

1. Kingdom, God,
   like(#2) tiny(#2) seed(#3).
   When seed(#3) sow earth, seed(#3) small(#1).
   Seed(#3) like(#2) kingdom God secret.

2. For happen seed(#3) sow,
   seed(#3) grows becomes large plant(#1),
   largest all plants, grows like(#2) tree.
   Seed(#3) like(#2) kingdom God, secret.

3. Grows, true birds can rest
   in tree, inside tree dark,
   hid from any evil danger.
   Seed(#3) like(#2) kingdom God secret.

4. True we can compare kingdom seed(#3)
   which grow tree larger than all trees,
   from only small(#1) seed(#3).
   Seed(#3) like(#2) kingdom God secret.

The First One Ever   276

1. First one since, oh, ever(#2) know
   birth Jesus was Girl Virgin-Mary,
   Virgin-Mary Girl "G"-country, bless
   she, herself believes. Oh, bless
   she herself believes, Lord, oh,
   bless she herself believes. She
   Virgin-Mary Girl "G"-country, bless
   she herself who believes.

2. First one since, oh, ever(#2) know
   Messiah, Jesus, happen he said, "I am(#1)
   he," was "S"-country woman who drink from
   well(#3), bless she, herself
   perceive(#2). Oh, bless she
   herself perceive(#2) Lord, oh, bless
   she herself perceive(#2). Was
   "S"-country woman herself drink from
   well(#3), bless she,
   herself perceive(#2).

3. First ones since, oh, ever(#2) know
   rise(#1) Jesus, his glory were three
   women went-to tomb, bless women,
   themselves see. Oh, bless are women
   themselves see Lord, oh, bless
   women themselves see. Three women
   themselves went-to tomb, bless
   women themselves, see.

Tell Me the Stories of Jesus

1. Tell me story Jesus I love hear;
   things I would ask him tell me if
   Jesus here; scenes near way-side,
   stories sea, stories Jesus,
   tell stories me.

2. First let me hear how children
   surround Jesus, I will(#1) fancy his
   bless rest me; words full kindness,
   deeds full grace(#1), all love,
   light Jesus face.

3. Into city I follow children crowd,
   waving palm-trees, high hand; one his
   follower, yes, I would sing loudest
   praises, "Jesus is(#1) King!"

Hosanna, Loud Hosanna

1. Praise, loud praise God, little
   children sang; through court temple,
   beautiful song sounded. Jesus, himself
   finish bless children, hug close Jesus,
   children sang praises, simple, best.

2. From city children followed among
   rejoice crowd; victory(#2) palm-waving,
   singing clear loud. Lord earth heaven
   continue low honor, not look-down little
   children should wait Jesus call(#1).

3. "Praise God highest!" that old song
   we sing, for Jesus is(#1) our Redeemer(#1),
   Lord, heaven our King. O may we ever(#3)
   praise him with heart, life, voice, his
   happy presence eternally rejoice!

Filled with Excitement   279

1. Fill with excitement, all happy crowd,
   spread clothes, growth tree, on city
   street. There distance, crowd begin see,
   riding donkey, comes Son of God.

Refrain:
   From every place, many, many voices sing
   praises, Jesus himself comes name God. With
   great(#3) shout welcome, loud triumph(#2)
   song begins: Praise God, Praise God King,
   Praise God, Praise God King.

2. As that entrance Old Town, we sing
   praise Jesus, our King, living Savior,
   himself still(#1) call(#1) today, asking us
   follow him with love, faith.

Refrain

All Glory, Laud, and Honor

Refrain:
　　All glory praise honor you, Redeemer(#1),
　　King, whom voices children made sweet
　　praises sound.

1. You are(#1) King Israel, you King
　　David Son, himself Lord name come,
　　King Bless One.

Refrain

2. Group angels praising you high,
　　we with all world sing make answer.

Refrain

3. People, Hebrews with hymns before(#3)
　　you; our prayer praise songs before(#3)
　　you we present(#1).

Refrain

4. You, before(#1) your strong(#1) feel,
　　children sang their hymns praise you, now
　　high honor, our melody we sing.

Refrain

5. You finished accept their praises;
　　accept prayers we bring, who all good
　　delight, you good, gracious King.

'Tis Finished! The Messiah Dies

1. True finished! Jesus dies, forgive
   for sins, but not Jesus sins. Accomplish
   sacrifice, great(#3) redeem(#1)
   work done(#2)

2. Curtain torn; in Jesus alone
   living way heaven is(#1) seen; center
   wall breakdown, all world
   may enter in.

3. True finished! All my guilt, pain, I
   want no other sacrifice; for me, Jesus
   crucified; true finished! I true
   justice(#2).

4. Reign sin, death, finished, all
   may live free from sin; Devil finish lost
   Devil power; true take-up victory.

285   To Mock Your Reign, O Dearest Lord

1. Mock your reign, O precious Lord,
   they made crown thorns; place you with
   mock along that road from which no one
   come-back. They couldn't know, as we
   know now, how glory that crown;
   that thorns would flower your head, your
   sorrows heal ourself.

2. Mock applaud, O gracious Lord, they
   took-away purple robe; your passion(#2)
   changed, for all they thought, like(#2)
   soldier joke. They couldn't know,
   like(#2) we know now, although we deserve
   blame, you want hide our shame with
   your robe of mercy(#2).

3. Rod, O patient Lord, they forced
   into your hand, acted out their awful
   game, chosen end. They couldn't know,
   like(#2) we know now, although nations
   found, collapse, your kingdom will(#1)
   continue grow till love welcome all.

286   O Sacred Head, Now Wounded

1. O bless Lord, now wounded, with grief,
   shame burdened, now mocking surrounded with
   pains, your only crown: how weak you
   with suffer, with hurt, wrong, reject! How
   does that face fade, which, past,
   bright like morning!

2. My Lord, what you finish suffer, for
   sinners gain; mine sin, but yours dead
   pain. Look, here I fall, my Savior! This I
   deserve your place; look-on me with favor,
   promise me your grace.

3. What language shall I speak thank you,
   loving friend, because this your dying
   sorrow, your pity continue? O make me
   yours forever, should I become weak, Lord,
   let me never, never forget my love you.

O Love Divine, What Hast Thou Done   287

1. O Love divine, what you done(#2)!
   Living God finish die for me! Father with
   everlasting Son forgave all my sins upon
   cross. This everlasting God for me finish
   die! My Lord, my Love, crucified!

2. True crucified for me—you, bring us
   rebels back God. Believe, record true,
   you bought with Jesus blood.
   Pardon for sins come from Jesus. My Lord,
   my love, is(#1) crucified!

3. See Jesus, all people who pass near
   bleed Prince life, peace! Come, sinners,
   see your Savior die, say, "Was ever(#3)
   grief like(#2) Jesus?" Come, feel with
   me his blood apply(#2): My Lord,
   my love, is(#1) crucified!

Were You There

1. Were you there happen people crucified
   my Lord? Were, you there happen people
   crucified my Lord? Oh, oh, sometimes,
   crucifixion causes me tremble, tremble, tremble.
   Were you there happen people crucified my Lord?

2. Were you there happen soldiers nailed
   Jesus cross? Were, you there happen soldier
   nailed Jesus cross? Oh, oh, sometimes,
   crucifixion cause me tremble, tremble, tremble.
   Were you there happen soldiers nailed Jesus cross?

3. Were you there happen soldier wounded
   Jesus side? Were, you there happen soldier
   wounded Jesus side? Oh, oh, sometimes,
   crucifixion cause me tremble, tremble, tremble.
   Were you there happen soldier wounded him side?

4. Were you there happen sun refused shine?
   Were you there happen sun refused shine? Oh,
   oh, sometimes, crucifixion cause me tremble, tremble, tremble.
   Were you there happen sun refused shine?

5. Were you there happen people lie(#3)
   Jesus, tomb? Were, you there happen people
   lie(#3) Jesus, tomb? Oh, oh, sometimes,
   crucifixion cause me tremble, tremble, tremble.
   Were you there happen people lie(#3) Jesus, tomb?

Ah, Holy Jesus

1. O, holy Jesus, what you done(#2)
   happen we judge you with false hate?
   Through enemy mock, through
   your own reject, O most pain!

2. Who was guilty? Who brought this upon
   you? Sorry my false work, Jesus finish
   ruin you! Was I, Lord Jesus, I deny you;
   I crucified you.

3. See Good Shepherd, because sheep
   offered; slave finish sin, Son finish
   suffer. For our suffer, while we never
   pay attention, God took our place.

4. For me, kind Jesus, you become
   person, your living sorrow, your life
   offering; your death great(#2) pain, your
   bitter passion(#2) for my salvation.

5. Therefore(#3), kind Jesus, since I
   cannot pay you, I true adore you, will(#1)
   ever(#3) pray you, I think your pity, your
   love continue I not deserve.

Go to Dark Gethsemane

1. Go dark garden, you that feel devil
   power(#1); your Redeemer(#1) struggle see,
   watch with Jesus one bitter hour. Turn
   not from Jesus griefs, learn Jesus
   Christ pray.

2. See Jesus judgment room, beaten, bound,
   mocked, accuse(#1); O bitter, hate! O pains
   Jesus soul bear(#3)! Avoid not suffering,
   shame, loss; learn Jesus bear(#4) cross.

3. Calvary mourn mountain walk; there,
   adore Jesus feet, note that miracle time,
   God own sacrifice, complete(#1). "Life
   is(#1) finished!" hear Jesus cry(#3);
   learn Jesus Christ die.

4. Early hurry tomb where(#2) they lie(#3)
   Jesus body, all alone, gloom. Who
   took[1] Jesus away? Jesus risen! He
   meets our eyes; Savior, teach us
   true rise(#1)

[1]Took: Right "5" hand position at the heart, fingertips point left, move right hand forward, changing into an "S" hand position.

1. People crucified my Lord, Jesus
   silence(#1) never whisper[1] word;
   people crucified my Lord,

Refrain:
   Jesus silence(#1) never whisper word,
   not one word, not one word, not one word.

2. They crucified Jesus cross, Jesus
   silence(#1) never whisper word; they
   crucified Jesus cross,

Refrain

3. They wound Jesus side,[2] Jesus
   silence(#1) never whisper word;
   they wound Jesus side,

Refrain

4. Jesus blood drip-down, Jesus
   silence(#1) never whisper word; Jesus
   blood drip-down,

Refrain

5. Jesus bow-down head died, Jesus
   silence(#1) never whisper word; Jesus
   bow-down head died,

Refrain

[1]Whisper: Use the sign for "mumble." Right "4" hand position at the mouth, palm facing left, wiggle fingers only.
[2]Side: Right "open hand" position at the right side of the body, palm facing left, fingers point out, move hand down.

What Wondrous Love Is This

1. What wonder(#2) love this, O my
   soul, O my soul, what wonder(#2) love
   this, O my soul! What wonder(#2) love
   that caused Lord joy bear(#4) awful evil for
   my soul, for my soul, bear(#4) awful evil
   for my soul.

2. What wonder(#2) love this, O my
   soul, O my soul, what wonder(#1) love
   this, O my soul! What wonder(#1) love
   that caused Lord life sacrifice his life for
   my soul, for my soul, sacrifice his life
   for my soul.

3. God Jesus I will(#1) sing, I will(#1)
   sing, for God Jesus, I will(#1) sing, for God Jesus,
   himself great(#3) God, while many,
   many people join(#2) subject, I will(#1) sing,
   I will(#1) sing; while many, many people
   join(#2) subject I will(#1) sing.

4. Happen from death I free, I continue
   sing, I continue sing, happen from death I
   free, I continue sing; happen from death I
   free, I sing joy, through eternity I
   continue sing, I continue sing, through
   eternity I continue sing.

Alas! And Did My Savior Bleed 294

1. Regret! My Savior true bleed, my King
   true die? Would he give-up that holy
   leader for sinners same I?

2. Was for sin that I finish-done, he grief
   upon cross? Amaze pity! Grace not known!
   Love more than measure!

3. Therefore(#3) dark might(#2) hide sun,
   shut glory, happen God, mighty(#2) maker,
   died for his only world sin.

4. That way I might(#2) hide my blush-face
   while his precious cross appear(#3);
   dissolve my heart thankful,
   melt mine tears-eyes.

5. But tears-eyes never able satisfy
   responsibility love I owe. Here, Lord,
   I give myself, that all I can do.

In the Cross of Christ I Glory 295

1. Cross Jesus, I glory, high over
   destroy time; all light holy
   story surrounds leader high great(#3).

2. Happen grief life overcome-me, hopes
   false, fears annoy, never will(#1) cross
   leave me. Look, cross shines[1] with peace joy.

3. Happen sun happy shining light,[2]
   love upon my way, from cross bright
   shines, adds more glory, day.

4. Death, bless, pain, pleasure, through
   cross made holy; peace there
   that knows no measure, joys through
   all time wait.

5. In cross Jesus, I glory, high over,
   destroy time; all light holy
   story surrounds leader high great(#3).

[1]Shines: Should be signed with both "5" hands and in the direction of the intent of the word.
[2]Light: Should be signed as a directional veneer.

296   Sing, My Tongue, the Glorious Battle

1. Sing, my language, glory contest(#3),
   sing end(#1) challenge, now above cross,
   winner victory(#1), sound-loud triumph(#2)
   made quiet; tell how Christ, world
   Redeemer(#1), as person won day.

2. Tell how, happen last(#1) full
   appointment time was come, Christ, Word,
   born from woman, left(#2) for us, his home
   heaven; show us person life made
   perfect, shine as light amid gloom.

3. That way with thirty years
   accomplished(#1), Jesus left "N"-town
   intend, promise, willing(#3), made his work,
   met his death. Like(#2) little
   sheep, he humbly give-up his life through
   dying on cross.

4. Faithful(#2) cross, you show
   triumph(#2), now for us, high great(#3)
   tree, none full green, none full bloom,
   none fruit, your followers may become;
   example world redeem(#1), for heavy
   concern(#1) death you.

5. Unto God be(#1) praise, glory: Father,
   Son, Holy Spirit, honor now, everlasting(#2)
   continue(#1); praise, glory highest,
   while continue(#1) years.

Beneath the Cross of Jesus   297

1. Beneath cross Jesus, I willing(#3)
   take-up my place, darken mighty(#1) stone
   within weary land;[1] home within dry land,
   rest way, from hot noon sun, burdens day.

2. Upon cross Jesus, mine eye times can
   see, dying form person himself suffered
   cross for me; from my sorrow heart, with
   tears, two wonder(#2) I confess; wonder(#2)
   redeem(#1) love, my not worthy.

3. I take-up, O cross, your shadow,[2] for my
   living place; I ask no other sunshine than
   sunshine his face; content let world pass,
   know no profit know no loss, my sin
   self my only shame, my glory all cross.

[1]Land: Sign for "dirt" then the sign for "spread."
[2]Shadow: Can be signed as "form."

298, 299 When I Survey the Wondrous Cross

1. Happen I search wonder(#2) cross, which
   Jesus died, my valuable gain I consider(#2)
   but loss, continue contempt all my pride.

2. Forbid, Lord, that I should boast, save
   death Jesus, my God; all vain things that
   delight me most, I give-up things Jesus blood.

3. See, from his head, his hands, his feet,
   sorrow, love mixed continue every place.
   Past, ever same love, sorrow meet, trouble
   make true valuable crown?

4. If all kingdom world mine, that offering
   be(#1) very small; love true amazing, true
   divine, demands my soul, my life, my all.

300 O the Lamb

O Jesus, loving Jesus, Jesus
Calvary! Jesus that was
crucified, yet(#1) lives again
purpose, Jesus take-up place
for me!

Jesus, Keep Me Near the Cross

301

1. Jesus, keep me near cross; there
   precious water, free all, continue heal,
   begin from Calvary mountain.

Refrain:
   In cross, in cross, be(#1) my glory
   ever(#3), until my strong(#1) feel soul
   will(#1) find rest beyond river.

2. Near cross, tremble[1] soul, love,
   mercy(#1) found me; there bright morning
   star shine light around me.

Refrain

3. Near cross! O Jesus from God, bring
   scenes before(#3) me; help me walk every
   day with shadow cross over me.

Refrain

4. Near cross, I watch, wait, hoping,
   trusting ever(#3), till I arrive very
   happy land[2] beyond river.

Refrain

[1]Tremble: R and L "5" hand positions, fingertips down, palms facing body, shake hands
several times.
[2]Land: Sign for "dirt," then the sign for "spread."

Christ the Lord is Risen Today

1. Christ, Lord rise(#1) today,
   Alleluia! Earth, heaven, groups sing,
   Alleluia! Sing your joys, triumph(#2)
   high, Alleluia! Sing, you heavens,
   earth answer, Alleluia!

2. Love redeem(#1) work done(#2),
   Alleluia! Fought battle, struggle won(#1),
   Alleluia! Death vain forbids him rise(#1),
   Alleluia! Jesus finish opened heaven,
   Alleluia!

3. Lives again our glorious King,
   Alleluia! Where(#2), O death, now your
   pain? Alleluia! Once Jesus died, our soul
   save, Alleluia! Where(#2) your victory(#2),
   proud death? Alleluia!

4. Rise(#1) we now happen(#1) Jesus finish led,
   Alleluia! Follow our high honor King,
   Alleluia! Made like(#2) Jesus, like(#2)
   Jesus we rise(#1), Alleluia! Ours, cross,
   grave, heavens, Alleluia!

5. Welcome, Lord earth, heaven, Alleluia!
   Praise you, through both given,
   Alleluia! You we welcome, triumph(#2) now,
   Alleluia! Welcome your Resurrection,
   Alleluia!

6. King, glory, soul, joy, Alleluia!
   Everlasting(#2) life this, Alleluia!
   Want know you your power(#1) prove, Alleluia!
   This way sing, this way love, Alleluia!

The Day of Resurrection

1. Day resurrection! Earth, tell
resurrection far; annual feast glad,
celebration God. From death life
eternity(#1), from earth unto heaven,
our Jesus finish brought us over(#2),
with songs victory(#2).

2. Our hearts pure from evil, that we
may see Lord rays ever(#2) resurrection
light; listen his voice, may hear,
true calm, plain, his own "All welcome!"
hearing, may sing victor(#2) hymn.

3. Now let heavens be(#1) joy. Let
earth song begin. Let around[1] world keep
triumph(#2), all that is(#1) there. Let
all things seen, secret, sing glad
coordinate, because Jesus, Lord finish
rise(#1), our joy continues.

[1]Around: The natural motion indicating a round world with "cupped" hands; then sign "world."

This ASL translation © 1995 The United Methodist Publishing House

Easter People, Raise Your Voices

1. Easter people, rise(#2) your voices,
sounds heaven earth should ring. Jesus
finish bring us heaven choices; heaven
music, let music sound. Alleluia!
Alleluia! Easter people, let us sing.

2. Fear death can't stop us from our press(#3) here below. For our Lord empowered(#1) us triumph(#2) over(#2) every enemy. Alleluia! Alleluia! Now we onward victory(#2)

3. Every day is(#1) Easter, with resurrection song. Happen trouble move faster our God himself makes right wrong. Alleluia! Alleluia! See power(#1) heaven group.

305   Walk On, O People of God

Refrain:
Walk-on, O people God; walk-on, O people God! New law, God new union, all world new begin. Walk-on, O people God; walk-on, O people God.

1. Look-on Calvary-mountain-top, on-rock found cross; death that gives begin new living, new people, new light. Jesus finish brought us salvation with his death, rise(#1) again. Every thing comes new begin, all world new begin.

Refrain

2. Jesus accepts bear(#4) all our sin, bound, pain; as he destroys sin, Jesus brings us life plenty, life new joy. Jesus brings all people together all things, with God. World grows new flowers, all world new begin.

Refrain

3. Heaven, earth surround, our
   soul find pardon last(#1). Now heaven gates
   open for sinner, all us. Israel walks
   journey(#3); now we live, salvation our song;
   Jesus resurrection finish free us. There
   new worlds, search.

Refrain

The Strife Is O'er, the Battle Done   306

1. Alleluia! Alleluia! Alleluia!
   Struggle finished, battle done(#2);
   victory(#1) life won(#2); song
   triumph(#2) finish begun, Alleluia!

2. Power(#1) death finish-done worse(#1),
   but Jesus their great(#2) many scatter; let
   shouts holy joy sing-out, Alleluia!

3. Three-days-pass quick[1] sad; Jesus rise(#1)
   glory from dead; all glory our rise(#1)
   Jesus! Alleluia!

4. Lord, through beat(#3) which wound you,
   from fear death pain your servants free,
   that we may live, sing you, Alleluia!
   Alleluia! Alleluia! Alleluia!

Note: At the end of each verse, the last Alleluia should be opened into "5" hand positions.
[1]Three-days-pass-quick: Should be signed, "day, day, day, three."

Christ Is Risen

1. Christ rise(#1)! Shout praise God!
   Celebrate today. Jesus rise(#1)!
   Hush wonder(#2); all world amazed!
   Dry land surround, see, spread tree finish
   grow. Heal permits(#2) plenty grace(#1)
   come experience love not known.

2. Christ rise(#1)! Rise(#3) your
   spirits from real loss hope. Walk with glad
   morning. See what love can do, courage.
   Drink wine resurrection, not servant, but
   friend; Jesus is(#1) our strong good-friend.
   Joy, peace will(#1) continue.

3. Christ rise(#1)! Earth, heaven
   never again same. Break bread new life
   where(#2) world continue(#1) pain. Tell
   fierce demon group(#1): "Christ
   rise(#1)! You fade-away!" God First, Last(#3)
   with us. Sing Praise God every person.

This ASL translation © 1995 Hope Publishing Company

Thine Be the Glory

1. Yours be(#1) glory, rise(#1), conquer
   Son; continue victory(#1), you finish
   over-come death. Angels bright robes move
   stone-away, kept folded[1] clothes where(#2)
   Jesus body lie(#3).

Refrain:
   Yours glory, rise(#1) conquer Son;
   continue(#1) victory(#1) you
   over-come death.

2. Look! Jesus meet you, rise(#1) from grave; love he welcome you, dissolve fear, gloom. Let church with glad hymns, triumph(#2) sing, because our Lord now lives; death finish lose pain.

Refrain

3. We doubt you no more, glory Prince life. Life nothing without you; aid us our struggle. Make us more than conquerors, through your continue love; bring us safe through "J"-country your home above.

Refrain

[1]Folded: Natural motion of folding clothes.

On the Day of Resurrection 309

1. On day resurrection, "E"-town we return; while confused, amazed, frightened, Jesus comes meet us, not known.

2. Then this stranger[1] asks-question,[2] "What this trouble you?" Meets us, our pain, suffering; Jesus walks with us, not known.

3. In our trouble, words come from his; like(#1) burn-fire[3] our hearts, explains scripture meaning. Jesus speaks us, not known.

4. Then(#1) we near arrive our home.
   Then(#1) we invite stranger enter, Jesus
   follow our urge; Jesus stay with us,
   not known.

5. Day sorrow forgotten happen
   stranger becomes servant. Take bread,
   bless, break, Jesus himself made known.

6. Open-eyes[4] make new conviction(#2), return
   Jerusalem[5] past happen[6] pain; telling all
   that Jesus risen. Jesus through us
   made known.

[1]Stranger: Sign "new," then the " person" ending sign.
[2]Asks-question: Should be signed in reverse, indicating Jesus is asking the question.
[3]Burn-fire: Should be signed at the heart, or sign "inspire."
[4]Open-eyes: Should be signed at the eyes, more like "surprise."
[5]Jerusalem: Sign "old," then the sign "town."
[6]Happen: Should be signed several times from left to right, indicating more than one happening.

310   He Lives

1. I serve rise(#1) Savior, he world today;
   I know he living, no matter enemy may
   say. I see his hand mercy(#1), I hear his
   voice cheer, just(#2) time I need him,
   he always near.

Refrain:
   He lives, he lives, Christ Jesus lives today!
   He walks with me,[1] talks with me along life way.
   He lives, he lives, salvation give-me. You ask
   me[2] how I know he lives? He lives in[3]-my heart.

2. All world surround me I see his loving
   care(#1), although my heart becomes weary, I
   never lose hope. I know that he lead during
   all trouble, destroy; day his appear(#3)
   will(#1) come last(#1).

Refrain

3. Rejoice, rejoice, O Christian, rise(#3)
   voice, sing eternity(#1) hallelujahs Jesus
   Christ King! Hope all who seek him, help all
   who find; none other loving, true good, kind.

Refrain

[1]Me: Should be signed with R and L "cupped" hands, separated at the body, palms face
body, fingers pointing towards each other, move down the body.
[2]Ask me: Should be signed in reverse, since people are asking.
[3]In: Should be signed at the heart.

Now the Green Blade Riseth   311

1. Now green plant-grows(#1), from bury
   seed(#1), seed(#3) bury dark ground, many
   days finish plant(#2); Love lives again,
   like(#2) seed(#3) grows green.

2. Soldiers lie(#3) Jesus in grave, Love
   itself finish(#2) kill, think that he never
   awake again, bury ground like(#2) seed(#1)
   that sleeps not see: Love come again,
   same seed(#3) grows green.

3. Jesus rise(#1) Easter like(#2) growing
   seed(#3), Jesus, himself for[1] three days,
   grave finish bury; rise(#1) from dead,
   my rise(#1) Lord see; Love come
   again, same seed(#3) grows green.

4. Happen our hearts cold, grief,
   pain, Jesus touch can call(#1) us again life,
   part our hearts like(#2) dead, like(#2)
   empty past: Love come again, same
   seed(#3) grows green.

[1]For: Should be signed as "since."

312   Hail the Day That Sees Him Rise

1. Welcome day Jesus ascend, Alleluia!
   his throne above skies, Alleluia! Christ,
   short time with people, Alleluia!
   Return home heaven, Alleluia!

2. There glory victory(#1) happens,
   Alleluia! Open now heaven gates,
   Christ finish conquer death, sin, Alleluia!
   Accept King glory, Alleluia!

3. Look(#1)! heaven Lord receive,
   Alleluia! Yet[1] he loves earth he leaves(#2),
   Alleluia! Although[2] return his throne,
   Alleluia! He still(#1) call(#1) world
   his own, Alleluia!

4. Look(#1)! he lift-up-hands[3] above,
   Alleluia! See! he shows proof[4] his love,
   Alleluia! Pay attention! his gracious
   voice proclaim, Alleluia! Bless his
   church below, Alleluia!

[1]Yet: In ASL this meaning is signed "but."
[2]Although: In ASL this meaning is signed "but."
[3]Lift-up-hands: Should be signed as naturally lifting up hands.
[4]Shows proof: After signing "proof," point to the palms of the hands.

Christ Is Risen   313

1. Christ rise(#1), Christ live,
   dry your tears, don't afraid! Death
   dark could not keep Jesus, not tomb
   where(#2) Jesus buried. Don't look-for among
   dead for Jesus himself lives forever; tell
   world Christ rise(#1), announce he
   gone(#1)[1] before(#3).

2. If Lord never rise(#1), we nothing
   believe; but his promise, we can trust:
   "You will(#1) live, because I live." As we
   share death from Adam,[2] true also in Christ we
   live again; death finish lose power, fear,
   Christ, Lord finish come reign.

3. Death lost past control, let world
   rejoice, shout! Christ, firstborn live,
   gives us life leads us out. Let us thank
   our God, himself cause hope rise(#1) from
   dead. Christ rise(#1), Christ give
   life eternity(#1), life value.

[1]Gone: Should be signed up and out, indicating above.
[2]Adam: Right "A" hand position at the temple, palm out, tap right thumb at the temple several times.

314 In the Garden

1. I come garden(#1) alone while dew[1]
   still(#1) on roses,[2] voice I hear sounds
   my ear, Son God made known.

Refrain:

   He walks[3] with me,[4] He talks with me, He tells
   me[5] I true his own; joy we share while we
   wait, none other, past ever(#2) known.

2. He speaks, sound his voice sweet
   birds hush singing,
   music he gave me,[6] within
   my heart continue.

Refrain

3. I want stay garden(#1) with him, although,
   night surround me become dark, but he bid(#1)
   me go; although voice grief, his voice
   continue call(#1) me.

Refrain

[1]Dew: Sign for "water," then the sign for "wet" from the left to the right, indicating all over.
[2]Roses: Sign for "flower," except right "R" hand position.
[3]Walk: Should be signed very slowly.
[4]Me: R and L "cupped" hand positions, separated at the body, fingertips pointing toward each other and touching body, move down.
[5]Tells me: Should be signed directionally.
[6]Gave me: Should be signed directionally.

1. Come, you faithful(#2), raise(#1) shout
   victory(#1) glad; God finish bring Israel
   into joy from sadness, free from Egypt King
   terrible control, Jacob[1] sons, daughters, led
   people, walk dry not become wet,
   through water Red Sea.

2. True new life person today; Christ finish
   defeat power(#1), three day sleep in death,
   as sunrise; all time our sins, long dark,
   flee from his light, himself we
   sing worship praise continue.

3. Now best time, bright glory day, with
   King celebrate, happen joy give; happen glad
   Jerusalem,[2] that with true love welcome
   continual(#1) praise, Jesus resurrection.

4. Not might(#1) gates death, not tomb dark
   entry, not soldiers, not stone keep you
   like(#2) person; but today amid twelve you
   finish appear(#2), give your peace which
   more than people know.

5. "Alleluia!" now we cry(#3) our King
   eternity(#1), himself, victory(#1), defeat
   tomb dark entry; "Alleluia!" with Son,
   God, Father praising, "Alleluia!"
   still(#1) again Spirit inspire.[3]

[1]Jacob: Right "J" at the forehead, palm facing body, make a "J" several times on the forehead.
[2]Jerusalem: Sign "old" then the sign "town."
[3]Inspire: R and L flat "O" hand positions, palms facing body at the heart, fingers pointing up, move both hands up, opening into "5" hand positions.

He Rose

1. People crucified my Savior, put-him-on-cross,[1]
   people crucified my Savior, put-him-on-cross,
   people crucified my Savior, put-him-on-cross,
   Lord will(#1) carry my spirit home.

Refrain:
   Jesus rise(#1), Jesus rise(#1), Jesus rise(#1)
   from dead! Jesus rise(#1), Jesus rise(#1),
   Jesus rise(#1) from dead! Jesus rise(#1),
   Jesus rise(#1), Jesus rise(#1) from dead,
   Lord will carry my spirit home.

2. Then(#1) friend beg(#2) Jesus body lie(#3)
   tomb, then(#1) friend beg(#2) Jesus body
   lie(#3) tomb, then(#1) friend beg(#2) Jesus
   body lie(#3)-in tomb, Lord will(#1) carry my
   spirit home.

Refrain

3. Sister Mary[2] run(#2), look for Jesus,
   Sister Mary run(#2), look for Jesus,
   Sister Mary run(#2), look for Jesus,
   Lord will carry my spirit home.

Refrain

4. Angel came[3] from heaven roll(#1)-away stone,
   angel came from heaven roll(#1)-away stone,
   angel came from heaven roll(#1)-away stone,
   Lord will carry my spirit home.

Refrain

[1]Put-him-on-cross: Should be signed as one continuous sign, "put cross."
[2]Mary: Right "M" over head on left side of temple, palm facing body, move right "M" over head ending at right temple.
[3]Came: Should be signed as a directional verb from above.

O Sons and Daughters, Let Us Sing   317

1. O sons, daughters, let us sing! King
   heaven, glory King, defeat death, hell(#1),
   rise(#3), triumph(#2).

Refrain:
   Alleluia! Alleluia!

2. That Easter morning, sunrise, faithful(#2)
   women walk-along way, seek tomb where(#2)
   Jesus lie(#3).

Refrain

3. Angel dressed white, women see, himself
   sat, tell three women, "Your Lord not here,
   go "G"-country."

Refrain

4. That night disciples met fear; Jesus
   appear(#3) disciples, said, "My peace
   be(#1) with you."

Refrain

5. During this most holy day, our hearts,
   voices, Lord, we sing you, great(#3)
   joy, praise.

Refrain

6. Happen Thomas[1] first good news heard,
   about disciples see rise(#1) Lord, he
   doubted disciples word.

Refrain

7. "My wounded side, O Thomas, see; my
   hands, my feet, I show you; not doubt,
   but believe."

Refrain

8. Thomas not again deny; he saw feet,
   hands, side; "You are(#1) my Lord, God,"
   he cried(#3).

Refrain

9. True bless, are(#1) people, themselves
   not yet seen, yet faith finish continue,
   because people eternity(#1) life
   will(#1) receive.

Refrain

[1]Thomas: Right "T" hand position on the back of left wrist, palm facing down, touch wrist, then move out to the end of the fingertips of left hand, or use any other name sign for this particular disciple.

1. Christ alive! Let Christians
   sing. His cross found empty sky-line-there.
   Let street, homes with praises sound. His
   love, no matter, death will never stop.

2. Christ alive! Not limited future
   years "P"-town, he comes demand his
   right(#1), now, live every place, time.

3. Not put throne, far-away high, not
   touch, not moved through people pains,
   but daily, amid life, our Savior, God reigns.

4. Every insult(#3), split,[1] war, where(#2)
   color, scorn(#1), money divide(#1), he
   continue suffers, yet[2] loves more, lives,
   although ever(#3) crucified.

5. Christ alive, come bring good news,
   this, every generation, till earth, all people
   rejoice with joy, with justice(#2), love, praise.

[1]Split: Use the sign for "divide"(#2).
[2]Yet: In ASL this meaning is "but."

319   Christ Jesus Lay in Death's Strong Bands

1. Christ Jesus lie(#3) death strong-power(#1),
   because our sins forgiven; but now God right(#2)
   hand he stands, brings us life from heaven;
   same way let us joy sing God true loud
   thankful songs, Alleluia! Alleluia!

2. True strange, terrible struggle happen life,
   death contend(#1); victory(#1) remain with life;
   reign death end(#3). Take-away power, no
   more death reigns, empty grave alone remain;
   death pain lost forever! Alleluia!

3. This way let us keep celebration, where(#2)
   Lord invites us; Christ himself joy all,
   Sun that warms, lights us. Through his
   grace(#1) he gives-me always sunshine heart;
   night for sin end(#3)! Alleluia!

4. Then(#1) let us celebrate this Easter day on
   true Faith heaven; Word grace finish clean-away
   old, evil influence(#4). Christ alone, our
   souls will(#1) care(#1); he our real
   food, drink, indeed; faith lives upon no
   other! Alleluia!

This ASL translation © 1995 The United Methodist Publishing House

1. Deep-in grave he lie(#3), Jesus my
   Savior, waiting new day, Jesus my Lord.

Refrain:
   Rise(#1) from grave he rise(#1), with
   mighty(#2) triumph(#2) overcome his foes;
   he rise(#1) victor(#1) from dark place, he
   lives forever with his angels reign. He
   rise(#1)! He rise(#1)! Alleluia! Christ rise(#1)!

2. Without success soldiers watch(#1) his
   grave, Jesus my Savior; without success
   soldiers close grave, Jesus my Lord.

Refrain

3. Death cannot keep Jesus grave, Jesus
   my Savior, he destroy death power(#1),
   Jesus my Lord.

Refrain

Hail Thee, Festival Day   324

Refrain (Easter):
Welcome, celebration day! bless day
hallowed(#1) ever(#3); day happen our Lord
rise(#1), destroy kingdom death.

Refrain (Ascension):
Welcome, celebration day! wonder(#2) day
hallowed(#1) ever(#3); day happen our
rise(#1) Lord ascend heaven reign.

Refrain (Pentecost):
Welcome, celebration day! bless day
hallowed(#1) forever; day happen Holy
Spirit shine world full grace(#1).

Easter Stanzas:
1. All beauty earth, from winter without
    life occur! Every good gift year now with
    Ruler(#1) returns:

Refrain

2. Rise(#1) from grave now, O Lord, maker
    life, world. Walk way death, new life
    you give us all:

Refrain

Ascension Stanzas:
1. He himself past crucified on cross,
    Ruler, Lord all people. All things create
    on earth, sing glory God:

Refrain

2. Daily beauty grows adorn with glory
    bloom; heaven gates open, gives wonder(#2)
    light:

Refrain

Pentecost Stanzas:
1. Bright like(#1) fire, people themselves
    wait your appear(#2), you yourself Lord
    finish foretell, quick, descend:

Refrain

2. From Father you come with many not
   explain gifts, give all people much bless from God:

Refrain

All Season Stanzas
3. God almighty, Lord, Ruler(#1) world,
   heaven, guard us from harm; clean us
   from evil within:

Refrain

4. Jesus, healthy world, inform our minds,
   great(#3) Redeemer(#1), Son Father authority,
   only Son from God:

Refrain

5. Spirit life power(#1), now move in us,
   place our begin, knowledge that informs us
   all, life that all may live:

Refrain

6. Praise giver good! O lover create
   concur, give heal our lives, order(#1)
   our ways your peace:

Refrain

Hail, Thou Once Despised Jesus

1. Welcome, you past hate Jesus! Welcome,
   King from "G"-country! You suffer, forgive
   us; you free salvation bring. Welcome, you
   universal Savior, himself finish accept our
   sin, shame! Through your merit we find
   kindness; life give through your name.

2. Easter Jesus, God appoint, all our sins
   you accept; through almighty lover made holy,
   you finish make full suffer. Every sin may
   forgive through good your blood; open
   gate heaven, we made friends with God.

3. Jesus welcome! throne[1] glory, there
   forever live; all heaven group(#1) angels
   adore you, seated near your Father. There for sinners you plea;
   there you take-up our
   place; you for Christians plea, till
   glory appear(#2).

4. Worship, honor, power(#1), bless Christ
   worthy receive; loud praises, continue
   right(#3) for us give praises. Help, you
   bring angels spirits, bring your pleasant,
   honor song, help sing Jesus merit, help
   sing Jesus praise!

[1]Throne: R and L "C" hand positions, palms facing down and separated, move both hands
back in an arc toward the body, indicating the arms of a large chair.

This ASL translation © 1995 The United Methodist Publishing House

1. Head that once crowned with thorns
   now crowned glory; king crown beautiful
   mighty(#2) victor(#2) head.

2. Highest place that heaven offers,
   belong him through right(#1); King, kings,
   Lord, lords,[1] heaven eternity(#1) light.

3. Joy all themselves live above, joy all
   below, whom he give his love, give
   his name know.

4. For them, cross with all shame, with
   all grace(#1), give; their name
   everlasting name, their joy, joy heaven.

5. They suffer with Lord below; they
   reign with him above; their profit,
   their joy know, not understand his love.

6. Cross he bear(#4) life, health,
   no matter shame, death him, his people hope,
   his people abundance, their everlasting way.

[1]King, kings: Lord, lords: May be signed with the right hand then reversed and signed with the left hand.

Christ Jesus Lay in Death's Strong Bands

1. Crown Jesus with many crowns, Jesus
   upon his throne.[1] Pay attention, heaven
   hymns strong(#1) more glory than other music.
   Awake my soul, sing about Jesus himself
   died for me, welcome him as your king
   through all eternity(#1).

2. Crown him Lord life, himself
   triumph(#2) over-come grave, rise(#1)
   victory(#1) struggle for those he came save.
   His glory now we sing, himself died ascend,
   himself died, eternity(#1) life bring, lives
   that death may finish.

3. Crown him Lord peace, his power(#1)
   influence all world, that wars may cease, all
   prayer praise. His reign shall
   continue, surround wound feet beautiful
   flowers heaven offer fragrant ever(#3) pleasant.

4. Crown him Lord love; see his hands,
   side, wounds, yet visible beauty glory.
   Welcome, Redeemer(#1), welcome, because you died for me;
   your praise, glory shall
   continue through eternity.

[1]Throne: R and L "C" hand positions, palms facing down and separated, arc both hands toward the body, indicating the arms of a large chair.

Surely the Presence of the Lord 328

Surely presence Lord this place;
I can feel his power(#1), his grace(#1)
I can feel touch angel wings,
I see glory each face(#1);
surely presence Lord this place

Great Spirit, Now I Pray 330

Great(#3) Spirit, now I pray you,
I pray now you, great(#3) Spirit,
hear me; my soul weary, now I pray
that your spirit will dwell in me.

Holy Spirit, Come, Confirm Us 331

1. Holy Spirit, come, make us certain, truth
   that Christ makes known; we have faith,
   understand through your help gift alone.

2. Holy Spirit, come, comfort us, come
   as advocate plea; love Spirit from
   Father, give Christ help we need.

3. Holy Spirit, come, make new us, come
   yourself make us live; holy because your
   love presence, holy because gift you give.

4. Holy Spirit, come, possess us, you love,
   Trinity, Holy Spirit, Father, Holy Spirit, Son.

332   Spirit of Faith, Come Down

1. Spirit faith, come-down, show things
   God, make us know God, witness through blood.
   Your blood use clean, give us faith for
   understand, himself died for every sinner,
   finish sure die for me.

2. No one can true say that Jesus Lord,
   except, you true understand, accept God
   Word. Then, only then, we feel benefit
   Jesus blood, cry(#3) with much joy,
   "You are(#1) my Lord, my God!"

3. O that world might know Jesus, himself
   change all wrong! Spirit faith, descend(#2)
   show good his name; grace(#1) which all may
   find, save power(#1) gives, proof all people,
   touch every heart.

4. Inspire[1] living faith, no matter person
   receive, witness themselves, they have,
   conscious believe, faith that conquers all,
   can mountains move, save any person Jesus
   call(#1), made perfect with love.

[1]Inspire: R and L flat "O" hand positions, palm facing body at the heart, fingers pointing up, move both hands up opening into "5" hand positions.

This ASL translation © 1995 The United Methodist Publishing House

333   I'm Goin' Sing When the Spirit Says Sing

I will sing happen Spirit says sing,
I will sing happen Spirit says sing,
I will sing happen Spirit says sing,
obey Spirit Lord.

I will pray happen Spirit says pray,
I will pray happen Spirit says pray,
I will pray happen Spirit says pray,
obey Spirit Lord.

I will cry happen Spirit says cry,
I will cry happen Spirit says cry,
I will cry happen Spirit says cry,
obey Spirit Lord.

I will shout happen Spirit says shout,
I will shout happen Spirit says shout,
I will shout happen Spirit says shout,
obey Spirit Lord.

Note: Will should be "the will"(#1) and cry should be "the cry"(#1).

Sweet, Sweet Spirit 334

There pleasant, pleasant Spirit this place,
I know Spirit Lord; true many pleasant
express each face, I know people
feel presence Lord.

Pleasant Holy Spirit, pleasant heaven little
bird, stay here with us, fill us with your
love; for now bless, we raise(#2) our hearts
praise; no doubt we know that we finish
make new, happen we shall leave this place.

Of All the Spirit's Gifts to Me

1. Many gifts[1] Spirit give me, I pray that I
   will(#1) never cease accept value most: love, joy, peace.

2. Spirit show me love basic every gift
   sent[2] from above, every flower, every
   fruit, that God true love.

3. Spirit shows, if I have love, no evil
   can destroy; no matter great(#2)
   my pain, then(#1) this true joy.

4. No matter what future true secret,
   life itself ours on loan, everyday
   Spirit tell-me[3] share, go-forward peace!

5. We go peace, but know that, trouble
   world like(#2) now, our clear purpose
   share love, joy, peace.

[1]Gift: "Gifts, "give," should be signed directionally throughout.
[2]Sent: Sign directionally.
[3]Tell-me: Sign directionally.

This ASL translation © 1995 Hope Publishing Co.

Only Trust Him

1. Come, every person through burden sin,
   here mercy(#1) with Lord; he will(#1) sure
   give you rest, because trust his Word.

   Refrain:
   Only trust him, only trust him, only
   trust him now. He will(#1) save you, he
   will(#1) save you, he will(#1) save you now.

2. Because Jesus spread his precious blood,
   blest bless give; come-down now into red
   overflow that clean pure as snow.

Refrain

3. Yes, Jesus truth, way that leads you
   into rest; believe him without postpone,
   you full bless.

Refrain

4. Come join this holy group(#1), onward
   glory, dwell heaven land where joys
   forever continue.

Refrain

Where He Leads Me   338

1. I can hear my Savior call(#1),
   I can hear my Savior call(#1),
   I can hear my Savior call(#1),
   "Take-up your cross, follow, follow me."

Refrain:
   Place he leads me I will follow,
   place he leads me I will follow,
   place he leads me I will follow;
   I go with him, with him all way.

2. I go with him through garden,
   I go with him through garden,
   I go with him through garden,
   I go with him, with him all way.

Refrain

3. I go with him through judgment,
   I go with him through judgment,
   I go with him through judgment,
   I go with him, with him all way.

Refrain

4. He will(#1) give me grace(#1), glory,
   he will(#1) give me grace(#1), glory,
   he will(#1) give me grace(#1), glory,
   go with me, with me all way.

Refrain

339   Come, Sinners, to the Gospel Feast

1. Come, sinners, gospel(#2) celebrate;
   let every person Jesus visitor. None
   need absence(#1), because God
   finish bid all people.

2. Sent through my Lord, you I call(#1);
   invitation for all. Come, all world! come,
   sinner, you! All things Christ
   true ready now.

3. Come, all you soul with burden sin,
   you anxious people look-for rest; you poor,
   cripple, weak, blind, with Christ find
   friendly welcome.

4. My information as from God receive;
   you[1] may come Christ live. O let his
   love control your hearts, not let Jesus
   die for nothing.

5. Now time, no more delay!
   Lord accept day. You come,
   now, his call(#1), live for him,
   himself died for all.

[1]You: "You" and "your" in this stanza are plural.

Come, Ye Sinners, Poor and Needy   340

1. Come, you sinners, poor, needy, weak
   wound, sick, pain; Jesus ready now
   save you, full pity, love, power(#1).

Refrain:
   I will(#1) rise(#1), go Jesus; he
   will(#1) embrace with his arms; in
   arms my precious Savior, O there
   ten thousand delights.

2. Come, you thirsty, come, welcome, God
   free gift glory; true belief, true repent,
   every grace(#1) that bring you near.

Refrain

3. Come you weary, much trouble, lost,
   ruin through become worse; if you wait
   till you become better, you never come.

Refrain

4. Let not conscience(#3) make you wait,
   not just dream well(#1); all
   right(#1) he require understand
   you need him.

Refrain

341   I Sought the Lord

1. I look-for Lord, later I knew he
   inspired[1] my soul seek him, Jesus seek me.
   Not I that find, O Savior true; no,
   you found me.

2. You finish touch me, I accept; I
   walk, not sink(#1) storm water. Not
   I myself hold you, as you, precious
   Lord, yourself hold me.

3. I find, I walk, I love, but oh,
   whole love my answer, Lord, you.
   Because you with my soul; always
   you loved me.

[1]Inspire: R and L flat "O" hand position, palms facing body at the heart, fingers pointing up,
move both hands up opening into "5" hand positions.

Come Back Quickly to the Lord

1. Return quick Lord, only return Lord.
   No matter how serious your sins, how
   burden sins seem, true no sin he cannot
   bear(#4), no sinner he not accept, because
   our loving Lord great(#2) more than
   all sky.

2. Return quick Lord, only return Lord.
   Our Lord waits everyday with his doors
   open. He anxious wait for you everyday,
   every night. Lord wait through all-night
   for child himself finish gone[1] wander(#2).

3. Return quick Lord, only return Lord.
   No matter you think you finish sin, not
   right(#1) become his child, God will
   celebrate with big feast, happen sorrow
   bring you home. True, return his arms,
   return quick Lord.

[1]Gone: Should be signed directionally, out instead of down.

This ASL translation © 1995 The United Methodist Publishing House

Lord, You Have Come to the Lakeshore

1. Lord, you finish come water-lake not
   look-for wealth not wise people;
   you only asked me follow humbly.

   Refrain:
   O Lord, your eyes, finish search[1] me,
   while smiling say my name;
   now my boat left(#2) ground behind me;
   near you, I will seek other places.

2. You know things I possess(#2); my boat carries no gold, no guns; you will find only my fishing nets, my work.

Refrain

3. You need my hands, full care(#1) through my work, give people rest, continue love that never finish.

Refrain

4. You, yourself finish fish other oceans, ever(#3) long(#2) for persons that wait, my loving friend, this way you call me,

Refrain

[1]Search: Should be signed as "look me over," indicating God has searched you.

345   'Tis the Old Ship of Zion

Refrain:
True old church heaven, true old church heaven, true old church heaven, enter church, enter church.

1. Church finish win(#1) many thousand, church finish win(#1) many thousand, church finish win(#1) many thousand, enter church, enter church.

Refrain

2. Not danger in water, not danger in water, not danger in water, enter church, enter church.

Refrain

3. Church was good for my precious mother, church was good for my precious mother, church was good for my precious mother. enter church, enter church.

Refrain

4. Church was good for my precious father, church was good for my precious father, church was good for my precious father, enter church, enter church.

Refrain

5. Church will(#1) bring us all heaven, church will(#1) bring us all heaven, church will(#1) bring us all heaven, enter church, enter church.

Refrain

347 Spirit Song

1. O let Son God surround you with his
   Spirit his love. Let Son fill your heart,
   satisfy your soul. O let Son have things
   that keep you, Jesus Spirit like(#2) little
   bird will(#1) come into your life
   make you well(#2).

Refrain:
   Jesus, O Jesus, come, fill your people.
   Jesus, O Jesus, come, fill your people.

2. O come, sing this song with glad
   like(#2) your hearts fill with joy.
   Rise(#3) your hands, full(#1) surrender his
   name. O give him all your tears, sadness;
   give him all your years pain, you will(#1)
   begin new light, Jesus name.

Refrain

This ASL translation © 1995 Mercy Publishing c/o Maranatha! Music

348 Softly and Tenderly Jesus Is Calling

1. Quiet(#2), love Jesus call(#1), call(#1)
   for you, for me; see, gate Jesus wait,
   watch(#1), watch(#1) for you, for me.

Refrain:
   Come home, come home; you yourself
   weary, come home, earnest, love Jesus
   call(#1), call(#1), O sinner, come home!

2. Why should we wait happen Jesus plea,
   plea for you, for me? Why should we stay
     not pay attention his mercy(#1), mercy(#1)
   for you, for me?

Refrain

3. Time now short, moments almost finish.
   almost finish for you, for me; dark more
   more, death will happen, happen
   for you, for me.

Refrain

4. O for wonder(#2) love he finish promise,
   promise for you, for me! No matter we
   finish sin, he give mercy(#1), pardon,
   pardon for you, for me.

Refrain

Turn Your Eyes Upon Jesus   349

Look(#1) Jesus, Look toward
his wonder(#2) face,
things earth will(#1)
become strange fade,
light his glory, grace(#1).

350   Come, All of You

1. Come, all you, come, men, women,
   come, drink water provide(#2) for you; all
   you yourself thirsty, come drink water
   life, provide(#1) through Jesus your Lord.

2. Come, all you, come, persons
   burden, come, I will(#1) give you rest;
   don't wait long; all you that weary,
   come Christ, Jesus Lord all, Savior,
   King all people.

3. Come, all you, come, trouble mind,
   come, I will(#1) give you peace, peace
   mind; all you that hungry, come me,
   receive bread, water life, provide(#2)
   through Jesus your Lord.

4. Come, all you, come, hungry, poor,
   come receive your milk, wine, no money;
   come for free, bring no money; come me,
   receive bread, water life, provide(#2)
   through Jesus your Lord.

351   Pass Me Not, O Gentle Savior

1. Pass[1] me not, O gentle Savior, hear my
   humble cry(#3); while others You
   call(#1), don't pass me.

Refrain:
   Savior, Savior, hear my humble cry(#3);
   while others you call(#1), don't pass me.

2. Let me your place mercy(#1) find
   pleasant relief, kneel there really sorry;
   help my disbelief.

Refrain

3. Trust only your merit, would I seek
   your presence; heal my wound, depressed
   spirit, save me with your grace(#1).

Refrain

4. You begin all my comfort, more than
   life me, whom have I earth except you?
   Whom heaven but you?

Refrain

[1]Pass: Should be signed with a left "index" in front of the body, palm face out, finger up. With a right "index," palm face left, finger up, move from the right to the left, passing the left index.

It's Me, It's Me, O Lord   352

Refrain:
   True me, true me, true me, O Lord,
   I need prayer. True me,
   true me, O Lord, I need prayer.

1. Not my brother, not my sister, but
   me, O Lord, I need prayer.
   Not my brother, not my sister, but
   me, O Lord, I need prayer.
Refrain

2. Not preacher, not church leader, but
   me, O Lord, I need prayer.
   Not preacher, not church leader, but
   me, O Lord, I need prayer.

Refrain
> Not my father, not my mother, but
> me, O Lord, I need prayer.
> Not my father, not my mother, but
> me, O Lord, I need prayer.

Refrain

354   I Surrender All

1. All Jesus I surrender; all I free
   give-him; I will(#1) ever(#3) love, trust
   him, his presence daily live.

Refrain:
> I surrender all, I surrender all, all
> you, my bless Savior, I surrender all.

2. All Jesus, I surrender; humbly his feet
   I bow, world pleasures all give-up;
   accept me, Jesus, accept me now.

Refrain

3. All Jesus, I surrender; make me, Savior,
   all yours; let me feel Holy Spirit,
   truly know that you mine.

Refrain

4. All Jesus I surrender; Lord, myself I
   give-you; fill me with your love,
   power(#1); let your bless come-me.

Refrain

5. All Jesus I surrender; now I feel holy
light, true joy full(#1) salvation!
Glory, glory Jesus name.

Refrain

Depth of Mercy   355

1. Wonderful mercy(#1)! Happen true
   mercy(#1) still(#1) keep for me? Can my
   God his anger control(#2), me,
   worse(#1) sinner save?

2. Eversince I finished oppose his grace(#1),
   long-ago make angry before(#3) Jesus, would
   not pay attention his call(#1), troubled
   Jesus with thousand sins.

3. Jesus, I past denied; I again
   crucify, often contempt his holy name,
   caused Jesus shame.

4. There for me, Savior stands, shows-me
   his wounds, spread-show-me-hands.[1] God is(#1)
   love, I know, I feel; Jesus weeps,
   loves me still(#1).

5. Now influence me repent; let me now
   my sins sorry, now my sin rebel regret,
   weep(#1), believe, sin no more.

[1]Spread-show-me-hands: "Spread" should be signed in reverse, with palms up, looking at hands. "Show" should be signed directionally.

When We Are Living

1. Happen we living, in Christ
   Jesus, happen we dying, in Lord.
   Both in our living, our dying,

Refrain:
   We belong God, we belong God.
   We belong God, we belong God.

2. Through all our living, we our
   service must give. Good works
   service for offering. Happen we
   give, happen we receive,

Refrain

3. Amid time sorrow, time pain, happen
   sense beauty, love embrace, whether
   we suffer, sing rejoice,

Refrain

4. Across this wide world, we will(#1)
   always find people themselves
   cry(#1) with no peace mind, but happen
   we help people, happen we feed people,

Refrain

1. Only as I am(#1), without one plea,
   but because your blood give-me,[1]
   that you bid me come you,
   O Son of God, I go,[2] I go.

2. Only as I am(#1), wait not
   free my soul one sin,
   yourself blood can clean each
   sin, O Son of God, I go, I go.

3. Only as I am(#1), although confused
   with many conflict,[3] many doubt(#1),
   fighting, fears within, without,
   O Son God, I go, I go.

4. Only as I am(#1), poor, sad, blind;
   sight, riches, heal for mind,
   yes, all I need with you find,
   O Son God, I come, I come.

5. Only as I am(#1), you will(#1) accept,
   will(#1) welcome, pardon, cleanse, help;
   because your promise I believe,
   O Son God, I go, I go.

6. Only as I am(#1), your love not known
   finish remove every barrier;
   now, true yours, yes, yours alone,
   O Son God, I go, I go.

[1]Give-me: Right "and" hand, palm down, bring fingertips down touching back of left open hand, open right hand into "5" hand positions as it is moved out.
[2]Go: Should be signed as the directional form of "come."
[3]Conflict: R and L "index" hand positions, palms facing out, fingers pointing at an angle toward each other, move both hands up until the indexes cross.

     Dear Lord and Father of Mankind

1. Precious Lord, Father all people, forgive
   our foolish ways; make new our
   right mind, more pure lives your
   service find, with true respect, praise.

2. With humble faith, like(#1) people
   themselves heard, near sea, gracious
   call(#1) Lord, let us, like(#1) people past,
   without complaint, rise(#1) follow you.

3. O Sunday rest near "G"-country, O
   calm(#2) hills above, place Jesus knelt
   share with you silence(#1) eternity(#1),
   interpreted through love.

4. Give-us your peace, till all our
   struggles cease; remove from our souls
   pains, worry, let our order(#3) lives know
   beauty your peace.

5. Breathe through excite our desire(#1)
   your calm(#1), your heal; let emotion(#1)
   calm(#1), let body rest; speak through
   earthquake, wind, fire, O still(#2)
   voice calm.

Alas! and Did My Savior Bleed

1. Pity! my Savior bleed, my King die.
   Would he sacrifice that bless life for
   sinners same I?

Refrain:
   There cross, there cross, place I first
   understood, burden my heart fade; there
   through faith I received my understand,
   now I happy all-day.

2. True because sin I finish-done, he
   suffered on cross? Wonderful(#1) pity!
   Grace not understood! Perfect love
   none compare!

Refrain

3. True, dark hide sun, block light,
   happen God, powerful maker, died for his
   own people sins.

Refrain

4. That way may I hide my blush
   face(#1), while his precious cross
   appear(#2); touch my heart with
   thankful, melt mine eyes tears.

Refrain

5. But tears can never return
   responsibility(#1) love I obligation(#3).
   Here, Lord, myself I-give-you,
   True, all I can do.

Refrain

Rock of Ages, Cleft for Me

1. Support all time, open for me, let me
   hide myself you; let water, blood, from
   your wounds which flowed,[1] sin become good
   health, save from anger, make me pure.

2. Not work my hands can satisfy your law
   demands; could my zeal no delay know, could
   my tears forever continue, all for sin could
   not change; you must save, you alone.

3. I bring nothing my hand, I simple(#2)
   depend cross; naked I go you, for clothes;
   weak, depend you for grace(#1); dirty,
   I go begin; Savior clean me, I die.

4. While I live short life, happen mine
   eyes shall close, die, happen I soar[2] worlds
   not known, see you your judgment throne,[3]
   support all time, open for me, let me hide
   myself you.

[1]Flowed: Right "5" hand position at the right side of the body, palm facing left, fingers point out, move hand down, wiggling fingers at the same time.
[2]Soar: Should be signed as "gone"(#1) without the left hand; instead of moving down, move up and down.
[3]Throne: R and L "C" hand positions, palms facing down and separated, move both hands back in an arc toward the body, indicating the arms of a large chair.

Nothing But the Blood

1. What can remove my sin? Nothing(#1)
   except blood Jesus. What can make me
   well(#2) again? Nothing except
   blood Jesus.

Refrain

   O precious blood that makes me clean as
   snow; no other begin I know; nothing except
   blood Jesus.

2. For my pardon this I see: nothing except
   blood Jesus. For my clean this my plea:
   nothing except blood Jesus.

Refrain

3. Nothing(#1) for sin can change: nothing
   except blood Jesus. Nothing good that I
   done(#2): nothing except blood Jesus.

Refrain

4. This all my hope, peace: nothing except
   blood Jesus. This all my righteous(#2):
   nothing except blood Jesus.

Refrain

1. Can happen I should gain(#2) interest
Savior blood! Jesus died for me? We
ourselves responsible his pain. Who Jesus
death follow? Wonderful love! How can
happen that you, my God, should die for me?
Wonderful love, How can happen that you, my
God, should die for me?

2. All true secret: that Jesus dies! Who
can examine his strange plan? Impossible(#2)
first high angel tries tell real love
divine. All true mercy(#2)! Let earth
worship; let angel minds inquire(#1) no more.
All true mercy(#2)! Let earth worship; let
angels minds inquire(#1) no more.

3. He left his Father throne[1] above (true
free, true very, very great(#3) his grace(#1)!),
empty himself all but love, bled for Adam[2]
weak people. All true mercy(#1), involve
deep free, for O my God, found me. All true
mercy(#1), involve deep free, for O my God,
found me.

4. Long-ago my spirit keep quiet(#1),
strong(#1) bound sin during night; your eye
spread quick ray; I awoke; dark show light;
my chains disconnect, my heart free, I
rise(#1), went out, followed you. My chains
disconnect, my heart free. I rise(#1),
went out, followed you.

5. Now I not dread announce guilty wrong;
   Jesus mine; alive in him, my living Leader,
   provide(#1) righteous(#2) divine, brave I
   approach eternity(#1) throne, demand crown,
   through Christ my own. Brave I approach
   eternity(#1) throne, demand crown,
   through Christ my own.

¹Throne: R and L "C" hand positions, palms facing down and separated,
move both hands back in an arc toward the body, indicating the arms of a large chair.
²Adam: Right "A" hand position, palm facing out at the temple, touch thumb to temple
several times.

Because He Lives 364

1. God sent his Son, they call(#1) him
   Jesus; he came love, heal, forgive; he
   lived, died buy my pardon, empty
   grace there, prove my Savior lives.

Refrain:
   Because he lives, I can face tomorrow;
   because he lives, all fear fade; because
   I know he control future, life worth
   living only because he lives.

2. True precious hold, newborn baby, feel
   pride, joy he gives; but great(#2)
   still(#1), calm make sure, that baby can
   face(#2) doubt days because he lives.

Refrain

3. Then one day, I cross(#3) river; I
   fight life final war with pain; then
   as death becomes victory(#1), I see,
   lights glory, I know he reigns.

Refrain

365   Grace Greater Than Our Sin

1. Marvelous grace(#1) our love Lord,
   grace(#1) that exceeds our sin,
   our guilt. Beyond Calvary-mountain,[1]
   place Jesus blood was overflow.

   Refrain:
       Grace(#1), grace(#1), God grace(#1),
       grace(#1) that will(#1) pardon, clean;
       grace(#1), grace(#1), God grace(#1),
       grace(#1) that more great(#3)
       than all our sin.

2. Sin, loss hope, like(#2) cold ocean,
   bother soul with complete(#1) loss;
   grace(#1) that more great(#3), yes,
   grace(#1) not told, place protect
   mighty(#2) cross.

Refrain

3. Dark stain that we cannot(#1)
   hide. What can help wash-away? Look,
   there continue(#1) blood, you
   become more clean than snow today.

Refrain

4. Marvelous, very, very great(#2), perfect
   grace(#1), free give² all themselves
   believe. Yourself long(#2) see his face(#1),
   will(#1) you now accept his grace(#1)?

Refrain

¹Calvary-Mountain: Should be signed as "rock," "mountain," then "cross."
²Give: Should be signed directionally coming from God.

He Touched Me 367

1. Bound with heavy burden, beneath a lot¹
   guilt, shame, then hand Jesus touch-me,²
   now I not same.

Refrain:
   He touch-me, O he touch-me, O joy that
   fills my soul! Something happen, now I
   know, he touch-me made me well(#2).

2. Because I met this bless Savior,
   because, he clean, made me well(#2), I
   will(#1) never cease praise him; I shout
   praises while eternity(#1) onward.

Refrain

¹A lot: Sign "much."
²Touch-me: Should be signed at the heart, not off the back of the left hand or middle fingers
touching.

My Hope Is Built

1. My hope built nothing except
   Jesus blood righteous. I enough
   courage not trust person,
   but full(#1) depend Jesus name.

Refrain:
   On Christ strong(#1) support I depend,
   all other support fade-away sand;
   all other support fade-away sand.

2. Happen dark hide his beautiful face,
   I rely(#2) his continue grace(#1).
   Every strong(#1), terrible wind,
   my support continue with protect.

Refrain

3. Jesus promise, his agree, his life
   support me during trouble. Happen all
   surround me fails, Jesus all my
   hope support.

Refrain

4. Happen he shall come with
   trumpet[1] sound, O may I him true
   found! Prepared his
   righteous alone, perfect stand
   before(#3) throne![2]

Refrain

[1]Trumpet: Same sign as "trombone," except the right hand does not move, and the left fingers move up and down as tapping.
[2]Throne: R and L "C" hand positions, palms facing down and separated, move both hands back in an arc toward the body, indicating the arms of a large chair.

Blessed Assurance

1. Bless confidence, Jesus mine!
   O true vision, glory divine! Give[1]
   salvation, belong God, born his Spirit,
   washed his blood.

Refrain:

   This my story, this my song,
   praise my Savior all-day-long;
   this my story this my song,
   praise my Savior all-day-long.

2. Perfect obedience, perfect delight,
   visions[2] great(#2) joy before(#3) my eyes;
   angels descend(#2) bring[3] from above,
   touch mercy(#1), touch love.

Refrain

3. Perfect obedience, all now calm; I,
   with my Savior, true happy, bless,
   watch(#1) wait, look-above,[4] fill
   with his good, surround his love.

Refrain

[1]Give: Should be signed directionally with both hands coming from God. As a variation the hands may be rotated as they come from God.
[2]Vision: R and L "S" hand positions, palms facing down at the forehead, left is in front of the right, move hands to their respective sides of the body, opening into bent "5" hand positions.
[3]Bring: Should be signed directionally, coming from above.
[4]Look: Should be signed from left to the right.

Victory in Jesus

1. I heard old, old story, about Savior
   came from glory, how he gave-up his life on
   Calvary save person like(#2) me; I heard
   about his cry(#3), his precious blood
   make change, then I repent my sins,
   win(#1)-victory(#1).

Refrain:

   O victory(#1) Jesus, my Savior forever! He
   seek me, save me with his redeem(#1) blood;
   he love me before(#1) I knew him, all
   my love for him; he bring[1] me victory(#1),
   with clean power(#1).

2. I heard about his heal,[2] his clean power(#1)
   show, how he caused lame walk again caused
   blind see; then I cry(#3), precious Jesus,
   come, heal my discourage(#2) spirit, some
   how Jesus came, bring me victory.

Refrain

3. I heard about mansion[3] he finish build
   for me, heaven, I heard about streets gold
   beyond shining sea; about angels sing old
   redeem(#1) story, some pleasant day
   I sing heaven song victory.

Refrain

[1]Bring: Should be signed directionally.
[2]Heal: Sign for "make," then the sign for " well"(#2).
[3]Mansion: Should be signed as a classifier, sign "house" with a large sign.

This ASL translation © 1995 Mrs. Eugene M. Bartlett. Used by permission of Albert E. Brumley, Inc.

I Stand Amazed in the Presence

1. I true amazed presence Jesus,
   wonder(#1) how he could love me, sinner,
   found guilty wrong, not clean.

Refrain:

   How marvelous! How wonder(#2)! My song shall
   ever(#3) be(#1): How marvelous! How wonder(#2)!
   my Savior love for me!

2. Garden he pray for me: "Not my
   will(#2) but yours." He himself no tears his
   griefs, but sweat-drops(#2) blood for mine.

Refrain

3. In pity angels saw him, came from world
   light comfort him during sorrows he
   bear(#1) for my soul that night.

Refrain

4. He accept my sins, my sorrows, he
   made sins, sorrows his own; he endure(#1)
   burden Calvary(#1), suffer, died alone.

Refrain

5. Happen with saved glory, his face(#1) I
   shall see, will(#1) become my joy through
   generations sing about his love for me.

Refrain

372   How Can We Sinners Know

1. How can we sinners know our sins earth
   finish forgiven? How can my gracious
   Savior show my name write heaven?

2. What we finish feel, seen, with confidence
   we tell, share with all world proof free error.

3. We ourself believe that Christ died
   for us, we all received his not known
   peace, feel his blood clean.

4. We through his Spirit, prove, know
   things about God, things that free his
   love, he finish give-us.

5. True obedient, humble our heart with our
   Savior was, that Spirit give-us[1] same prove
   us with his cross.

6. Our world turn, our mind change all
   power(#1), both witness join(#1),
   Spirit God with ours.

[1]Give: Should be signed directionally coming from God.

This ASL translation © 1995 The United Methodist Publishing House

373   Nothing Between

1. Nothing between my soul, my Savior,
   not this world false dream;
   I finish renounce all sin pleasure;
   Jesus mine, nothing between.

Refrain:
> Nothing between my soul, my Savior,
> true that his bless face can see;
> nothing prevent his kind(#1);
> keep way open! let nothing between.

2. Nothing between, like(#2) world
   pleasure; habits life, although no
   harm(#1) see, must not separate my
   heart from him; he all important,
   true nothing between.

Refrain

3. Nothing between, like(#1) pride,
   place; self, friends shall not
   interfere; no matter I may suffer much
   trouble, I finish decide,
   true nothing between.

Refrain

4. Nothing between, no matter many
   difficult trouble, no matter all world
   convene against me, watch(#1) with
   pray, much self denial, I will(#1)
   triumph(#2) last(#1), true
   nothing between.

Refrain

Standing on the Promises

1. Depend promise Christ, my King,
   through eternal generations, let his
   praises ring(#2); glory highest, I will(#1)
   shout, sing depend promise God.

Refrain:
   Depend, depend, depend promise God my
   Savior; depend, depend, I depend
   promise God.

2. Depend promise that cannot fail,
   happen confusion, doubt, fear attack,
   through living Word God, I shall
   last(#3), depend promise God.

Refrain

3. Depend promise Christ, Lord, bound
   him eternity through strong(#1) love,
   overcome daily with Spirit power(#1),
   depend promise God.

Refrain

4. Depend promise I cannot fail, listen
   every moment Spirit call(#1) rest my
   Savior as my all, depend promise God.

Refrain

There Is a Balm in Gilead

Refrain
> There oil "G"-country, make wound
> well(#2), there oil "G"-country
> heal sin-sick soul.

1. Some times I feel discourage(#1), think
   my work worthless(#2). But then Holy
   Spirit revives my soul again.

Refrain

2. Don't ever(#3) feel discourage(#1),
   because Jesus your friend, if you look-for
   knowledge, he never refuse give.

Refrain

3. If you can't preach like(#2) Peter,[1] if
   you can't pray like Paul,[2] only tell[3] love
   Jesus, say he died for all.

Refrain

[1]Peter: Right "P" hand position, palm facing down over the left hand, tap middle finger of the "P" on the back of the left several times.
[2]Paul: Right "P" hand position, palm facing the body, at the right temple, tap the middle finger of the "P" at the temple several times.
[3]Tell: Should be signed as "announce."

It Is Well with My Soul

1. Happen peace, like(#2) river, come my
   way, happen sorrows like(#2) ocean increase;
   no matter my decide, you finish teach me say,
   all well(#1), all well(#1) with my soul.

Refrain:
   All well(#1), with my soul, all
   well(#1), all well(#1) with my soul.

2. No matter Satan should hurt, no matter
   trials should come, let this bless
   confidence control(#1), that Christ finish
   look[1] my weak belief, finish shed[2] his
   blood for my soul.

Refrain

3. My sin, oh, joy this glory thought! My
   sin, not part but whole, crucified on cross
   I bear(#4) sin no more, praise Lord,
   praise Lord, O my soul.

Refrain

4. Lord, haste day happen my faith shall
   see, clouds roll[3] like(#2) scroll;[4] trumpet[5]
   shall sound, Lord shall descend, anyway,
   all well(#1) with my soul.

Refrain

[1]Look: Should be signed directionally toward yourself.
[2]Shed: Right flat "O" hand position, palm facing down, bring finger tips down touch back of
left hand, moving out, opening right "O" into "5" hand position.
[3]Roll: R and L "open hand" positions, palms facing body, fingers pointing toward each other,
roll hands alternating over each other as both hands move out.

⁴Scroll: Should be signed as a "classifier" with R and L "C" hand positions, palms facing each other and separated, bend both wrists back and forth as you separate hands to their respective sides, indicating the unrolling of a scroll.

⁵Trumpet: Same sign as "trombone," except right hand does not move, and the left fingers are tapped up and down.

Amazing Grace 378

1. Wonder(#2) grace(#1)! True pleasant sound,
   that saved person like(#2) me, I once
   lost, but now I found, blind,
   but now I see.

2. True grace(#1) that taught my heart fear,
   grace(#1) my fears relieved;[1] true precious
   that grace(#1) appear, hour I first believed.

3. Through many danger(#2), toil, trap, I
   finish come; true grace(#1) finish bring me
   safe so-far, grace(#1) will(#1) lead me home.[2]

4. Lord finish promise good me, his word
   my hope free fear; he will(#1) my shield(#1),
   my part, as long(#1) as life endure(#2).

5. Yes, happen this body, heart shall fail,
   living shall cease, I shall possess(#2),
   within hid face(#1), life joy, peace.

6. Happen we finish touch place ten
   thousand years, bright, shine,[3] as sun, we
   finish no less days sing God praise than
   happen we first begun.

[1]Relieved: Should use the sign for "satisfaction."
[2]Home: Should sign "heaven."
[3]Shine: Should be signed directionally.

Blow Ye the Trumpet, Blow

1. You blow-trumpet[1]-blow! Glad holy sound God,
   let all people know, earth distant limit:

Refrain:
   Year rejoice now! Year rejoice
   now. Return you save sinners, home.

2. Jesus, our great(#3) high priest, finish
   full(#1) suffer, death; you weary spirits, rest;
   you mournful souls, true glad.

Refrain

3. Praise, Jesus, God, all suffer, death
   Jesus; redeem(#1) his blood through
   world proclaim.

Refrain

4. You slaves yourself sin, hell(#1), your
   liberation received, safe Jesus dwell,
   bless in Jesus live.

Refrain

[1]Blow-trumpet: Should be signed as a classifier, the same sign as "trombone," except right hand does not move and the left fingers are tapped up and down, the natural motion of blowing a trumpet.

There's Within My Heart a Melody

1. True within my heart melody, Jesus
   whispers pleasant, low: Fear not, I
   with you, peace, still(#2), all life
   trouble become weaker.

Refrain:
> Jesus, Jesus, Jesus, pleasant name I know,
> fill my every long(#2), keeps me singing
> as I go.

2. All my life destroy through sin,
   struggles, conflict[1] filled my heart with
   pain; Jesus touch broken heart, inspire[2]
   sleep music again.

Refrain

3. No matter sometimes he leads through
   waters deep, trouble before(#3) our way,
   although sometimes path seems rough, high,
   see his steps(#1) all way.

Refrain

4. Celebrate value his grace(#1), rest
   beneath his shelter, always look his
   smiling face(#1), that reason I shout, sing.

Refrain

5. Now Jesus return welcome me far
   beyond star sky; I shall travel world
   not known; I shall reign with Jesus high.

Refrain

[1]Conflict: R and L "index" hand positions, palms facing out, fingers pointing up at an angle, move both hands up to the point the index fingers cross.
[2]Inspire: R and L flat "O" hand positions, palms facing body at the heart, fingers pointing up, move both hands up opening into "5" hand positions.

Savior, Like a Shepherd Lead Us

1. Savior, like(#2) shepherd lead us, much
   we need your tender[1] care(#1); your pleasant
   field(#2) feed us, for our use your church
   prepare. Bless Jesus, bless Jesus! You
   finish bring us, we yours. Bless
   Jesus, bless Jesus! You finish bring us,
   we yours.

2. We yours, you true help us, you
   care(#1) our way; keep your followers,
   from sin defend us, seek us happen we go
   wander(#2). Bless Jesus, bless Jesus! Hear,
   O hear us happen we pray. Bless Jesus, bless
   Jesus! Hear, O hear us happen we pray.

3. You finish promise accept us, poor, true
   we sinful; you have mercy(#1) relieve[2] us,
   grace(#1) clean power(#1) free. Bless Jesus,
   bless Jesus! We will(#1) early turn you.
   Bless Jesus, bless Jesus! We will(#1)
   early turn you.

4. Early let us seek your favor, early let
   us do your will(#2); bless Lord, only Savior,
   with your love our hearts fill. Bless Jesus,
   bless Jesus! You finish love us, love us
   still(#1). Bless Jesus, bless Jesus! You
   finish love us, love us still(#1).

[1]Tender: Can be signed as "soft," but probably a better meaning would be signed as "warm."
[2]Relieve: Should be signed as "satisfaction."

This ASL translation © 1995 The United Methodist Publishing House

Have Thine Own Way, Lord

382

1. Have your own way, Lord! Have your
   own way! You true maker, I true clay.
   Form me, make me, follow your will(#2),
   while I wait, yield, still(#2).

2. Have your own way, Lord! Have your
   own way! Search me use me, Savior
   today! Wash me now, Lord, wash me
   now, as your presence humbly I bow.

3. Have your own way, Lord! Have your
   own way! Wound, weary, help me I pray!
   Power(#1), all power(#1), surely yours!
   Touch[1]-me, Heal[2]-me, Savior divine!

4. Have your own way, Lord! Have your
   own way! Keep remind me you real
   control(#1). Fill with your spirit till
   all shall see Christ only, always
   living me!

[1]Touch: Should be signed directionally at the heart.
[2]Heal: Sign "make" then the sign for "well"(#2).

383   This Is a Day of New Beginnings

1. Today[1] day new begin, time
   remember forward, time believe what[2] love
   bring, stop pain that gone.

2. Because, through life, death Jesus,
   God mighty(#2) Spirit, now as past, can
   make for us big(#1) difference, as faith,
   hope, begin again.

3. Then let us, with Spirit courage,
   leave(#1) past, leave(#2) behind our
   disappointment, guilt, grieve, seek new
   paths, sure will find.

4. Christ alive, goes before(#3)
   us show, share, what love can do.
   Today day new begin; our God
   make all things new.

5. Faith we will(#1) gather(#2)
   around-table,[3] taste, share, what love can
   do. Today day new begin; our God
   make all things new.

[1]Today: Should be signed with both "Y" hand positions, palms facing up, bend down wrists sharply, then repeat two times.
[2]What: Should be signed as "where"(#2).
[3]Around-table: Should be signed as a classifier, R and L bent "2" hand positions, palms down, hands together, twisting both wrists respectively out and bring hands back together again.

Love Divine, All Loves Excelling

1. Love divine, all love better than, joy
   heaven, earth come-down; place us your
   humble house; all your faithful(#2)
   mercy(#1), crown! Jesus, you all
   compassion, your love pure not limit;
   come us with your salvation; enter
   every trembling[1] heart.

2. Breathe, O breathe your loving Spirit
   into every troubled heart! Let us all,
   you receive; let us find that second rest.
   Take-away our desire sin; begin, end(#1)
   true, end(#3) faith as begin, found our
   hearts liberation.

3. Come, Almighty deliver(#1), let us all
   your life receive; quick return never, never
   more your temple leave. You we would always
   bless, serve you as your group(#1) above, pray,
   praise you without cease, glory your
   perfect love.

4. Finish, then, your new world; pure,
   clean let us become. Let us see your
   great(#3) salvation perfect made new you;
   change from glory into glory, till heaven
   we take-up our place, till we cast-out our
   crowns before(#3) you, lost wonder(#1),
   love, praise.

[1]Trembling: R and L "5" hand positions, palms facing body, fingers pointing down, shake hands several times.

385 Let Us Plead for Faith Alone

1. Let us plea for faith alone, faith
which through our work shown; God himself
true show just(#1), only faith
grace(#1) bless.

2. Active faith that lives within,
conquers hell(#1), death, sin, hallow(#1)
whom faith first made whole, form
Savior soul.

3. Let us for this faith contend(#3),
sure salvation end(#1); heaven finish
begin, everlasting life win(#1).

4. Only let us persevere(#3) till we see
our Lord appear(#2), never from support
remove, saved through faith, which works
through love.

386 Come, O Thou Traveler Unknown

1. Come, O you Traveler(#3) not known, whom
still(#1) I keep, but cannot see! My group(#1)
before(#3) gone(#1), but true left alone
with you. With you all-night I mean(#2) to
stay, wrestle till sunrise; with you all-night
I mean(#2) stay, wrestle till sunrise.

2. I need not tell[1] you about me, not happy,
sin, declare; yourself finish call(#1) my
name, look[2] your hands, read there. But who,
I ask you, who are(#1) you? Tell me your
name, tell me now. But, who, I ask you,
who are(#1) you? Tell me your name,
tell me now.

3. Yield me now, because I true weak, but confidence self loss hope! Speak my heart, bless speak, true conquer through my immediate prayer. Speak, now you never move later, tell me if your name love. Speak, now you never move later, tell me if your name love.

4. This Love! This Love! You died for me, I hear your whisper my heart. Morning begins, dark fades, pure, universal Love you true. Me, all, your mercy(#1) move; your life, your name Love. Me, all, your mercy(#1) move; your life, your name Love.

[1]Tell: Should be signed directionally.
[2]Look: Should be signed directionally toward the hands.

O Come and Dwell in Me   388

1. O come, dwell me, Spirit power(#1) within, bring glory liberation from sorrow, fear, sin.

2. Haste joy day which shall my sins consume(#2), happen old things shall fade, all things become new.

3. I want witness Lord, that all I do right, according-to your mind, word, true pleasing your sight.

4. I ask no high position; allow myself something desire, short time, later then change your eternal joy.

Freely, Freely

1. God forgive my sin Jesus name, I
   finish born again Jesus name, Jesus name
   I come you, share his love as he tell[1] me.

Refrain:
   He said, "Freely, freely you finish received,
   freely, freely give. Go my name, because
   you believe, others will(#1) know I live."

2. All power(#1) give Jesus name,
   earth, heaven Jesus name, Jesus name I
   come you, share his power as he tell me.

Refrain

[1]Tell: Should be signed directionally.

This ASL translation © 1995 Communique Music, Inc.

390

Forgive Our Sins as We Forgive

1. "Forgive our sins as we forgive," you
   taught us, Lord, pray; but you alone can
   give-us[1] grace able live words we say.

2. How can your pardon touch,[2] bless people
   not forgive heart, think about wrongs,
   not let old bitter fade?

3. Bright light your cross shows, truth we
   not understand; small(#1) debt not important
   owe us, how great(#2) our debt you.

4. Lord, clean center our hearts, bid
feel-hurt cease; certain all join love,
our lives will(#1) spread your peace.

[1]Give-us: Should be signed directionally.
[2]Touch: Should be signed directionally at the heart.

O Happy Day, That Fixed My Choice   391

1. O happy day, that decide my choose(#1)
you, my Savior my God! Surely warm feel
heart rejoice, tell joys all world.

Refrain:
Happy day, happy day, happen Jesus
washed-away my sins! He taught me watch(#1),
pray, live rejoice everyday. Happy day,
happy day, happen Jesus washed-away my sins!

2. O happy tie(#1), that keep my vow him,
himself merit all my love! Let cheerful
songs fill his house, while that holy place
I move.

Refrain

3. True done(#2): great(#3) perform done(#2)!
I true Lord, he mine; he call(#1) me, I
follow, act(#2) confess voice divine.

Refrain

4. Now rest, my long divided heart, found this happy center, rest. Here, I found noble part; here heaven pleasures fill my heart.

Refrain

5. High heaven, that heard earnest vow, that vow made new shall daily hear, till life recent hour I bow, bless death tie(#1) true precious.

Refrain

393   Spirit of the Living God

Spirit living God,
come-down new me.
Spirit living God,
come-down new me.
Melt me, form me,
fill me, use me.
Spirit living God,
come-down new on-me.

394   Something Beautiful

Something beautiful, something good;
all my confusion he understood;
all I had offer him
broken, struggle,
but he made something beautiful
my life.

Take Time to Be Holy

1. Take[1] time holy, speak often with your
   Lord; dwell him always, learn from his word.
   Become friends God children, help people
   themselves weak, forget nothing
   his bless seek.

2. Take time holy, world hurry-on; use
   much time secret with Jesus alone. Through
   look Jesus, like(#2) him you shall become,
   your friends your conduct(#1) like(#2) him
   you shall see.

3. Take time holy, let him become your
   guide, run not before(#3) him, no matter
   happens. Joy, sorrow, still(#1) follow Lord,
   look Jesus, still(#1) trust his word.

4. Take time holy, true calm your soul, each
   thought, each motive(#2) beneath his
   control(#1). This way, led through his spirit,
   begin love, you shall ready for service above.

[1]Take: This is an idiom and should be signed as "require."

O Jesus, I Have Promised

1. O Jesus, I finish promise, serve you till
   end(#1); you always near me,[1] my Master,[2] my
   friend. I shall not fear battle, if you
   near me not wander(#2) from path,
   if you will(#1) my guide.

2. O Let me feel you near me! World
   ever(#3) near; I see-sights that dazzle,
   tempting sounds I hear; my foes
   ever(#3) near me, surround me, within;
   but Jesus, come near, shield my soul
   from sin.

3. O let me hear you talking speech
   clear still(#2), above disturb strong(#1)
   feel, complaint self will(#2). O speak me
   make sure me, haste control(#1); O speak,
   make me listen, you care(#1) my soul.

4. O Jesus, you finish promise all people
   follow you that place you glory I shall
   your servant there. Jesus, I finish
   promise serve you end(#1); O give me grace(#1)
   follow, my Master, my Friend.

[1]Me: Should be signed as the whole person, with both "C" hand positions palms facing body, fingertips touching, move both hands down the body.
[2]Master: Use the sign for "manager."

1. I need you every hour, most gracious
   Lord; no tender voice like(#2) your can
   peace provide(#2).

Refrain:
   I need you, O I need you; every hour I
   need you; O bless me now, my Savior,
   I come you.

2. I need you every hour; stay near me;
   temptations lose power(#1) happen you near.

Refrain

3. I need you every hour, joy, pain;
   Jesus come quick dwell, or(#1) life empty.

Refrain

4. I need you every hour, teach me your
   will(#2); your real promise me fulfill.

Refrain

5. I need you every hour, most Holy One;
   O make me yours true, you bless Son.

Refrain

1. Jesus call(#1) us over disturb our life,
   fierce, no rest confuse; everyday his pleasant
   voice sounds, say, "Christian follow me!"

2. As past, disciples heard call(#1) near
   "G"-sea; turn from home, toil, family,
   leave(#2) all because Jesus.

3. Jesus calls(#1) us from worship empty
   world gold place, from each idol that
   would keep us, say, "Christian,
   love me more!"

4. Our joys, our sorrows, days toil,
   hours free trouble, still(#1) he call(#1),
   worry, pleasure, "Christian, love me more
   than these!"[1]

5. Jesus call(#1) us, through your
   mercy(#1), Savior, may we hear your
   call(#1) give[2] our hearts your obedience,
   serve love you best all.

[1]These: Should be signed as a gesture, with the right open hand, palm up, sweeping motion from left to right.
[2]Give: Should be signed directionally.

This ASL translation © 1995 The United Methodist Publishing House

399   Take My Life, And Let It Be

1. Take[1] my life, let life made holy, Lord,
   you. Take my moments, my days; let days
   fill continue praise. Take my hands, let
   hands sign, inspire[2] your love. Take my
   feet, let feet swift, beautiful for you.

2. Take my voice, let me sing always, only
   for my King. Take my lips, let them speak
   words from you. Take my money, my gold;
   none would I save(#2) for myself. Take my
   knowledge, use every power(#1) as you
   shall choose.

3. Take my will(#2), make yours;
   shall no longer mine. Take my heart as
   your own; heart shall your precious throne.[3]
   Take my love, my Lord, I give, your feet
   money store care(#1). Take myself, I
   will(#1) ever(#3) only all for you.

[1]Take: This use is an idiom and should be signed as "accept."
[2]Inspire: R and L flat "O" hand positions, palms facing body at the heart, fingers pointing up, move both hands up opening into "5" hand positions.
[3]Throne: R and L "C" hand positions, palms facing down and separated, move both hands back in an arc movement toward the body, indicating the arms of a large chair.

Come, Thou Fount of Every Blessing   400

1. Come, your begin every bless, touch[1]
   my heart sing your grace(#1); continue
   mercy(#1), never cease, call(#1) for songs
   loud praise. Teach[2] me some music poem, sing
   through excite language above. Praise
   height! I found, height your redeem(#1) love.

2. Here I rise(#3) my name; here through
   your help I come; I hope through your good
   pleasure, safe arrive home; Jesus seek me
   happen stranger, wander(#2) from church God;
   he rescue me from danger(#2), interfere
   his precious blood.

3. O grace(#1) true great(#3) person, daily
   I compel(#1)! Let your good like(#2) chain
   bind my wander(#2) heart you. Incline
   wander(#2), Lord, I feel, incline
   leave(#1) God I love; here my heart, O take[3]
   heart, shield heart for your place above.

[1]Touch: Should be signed at the heart.
[2]Teach: Should be signed directionally.
[3]Take: Should be signed as "accept."

402   Lord, I Want to Be a Christian

1. Lord, I want become Christian my heart,[1]
   my heart; Lord, I want become Christian, my
   heart. My heart, my heart, Lord, I want
   become Christian my heart.

2. Lord, I want become more loving my
   heart, my heart; Lord, I want become more loving
   my heart. My heart, my heart, Lord, I want
   become more loving my heart.

3. Lord, I want become more holy my heart,
   my heart; Lord, I want become more holy
   my heart. My heart, my heart, Lord, I
   want become more holy my heart.

4. Lord, I want become like(#2) Jesus my
   heart, my heart; Lord, I want become like(#2)
   Jesus my heart. My heart, my heart, Lord, I
   want become more like(#2) Jesus my heart.

[1]My heart: Should be signed at the heart.

Refrain:
　　Every time I feel Spirit inspire[1] my
　　heart, I will pray. Yes, every time I
　　feel Spirit inspire my heart, I will pray.

1. Upon mountain, my Lord spoke, Lord spoke
　　fire, smoke. I look-all-around,[2] true shine,[3]
　　I ask[4] my Lord, if all was mine.

Refrain

2. "J"-river-runs[5] true cold, chilly body,
　　not soul. Only one group(#1) travel(#3)
　　this path, goes-back-forth[6] heaven.

Refrain

[1]Inspire: R and L flat "O" hand positions, palms facing body at the heart, fingers pointing up, move both hands up opening into "5" hand positions.
[2]Look-around: Should be signed with the "look" sign from left, then sweep around to the right.
[3]Shine: Should be signed directionally.
[4]Ask: Should be signed directionally, toward God, as "ask a question."
[5]"J"-river-runs: Should be signed as all one sign.
[6]Goes-back-forth: Should be signed all as one sign.

405   Seek Ye First

1. Seek you first, kingdom God
   his righteous, all these[1]
   things shall become added unto
   you. Alleluia, alleluia!

2. Ask(#1) shall give[2]-unto you;
   seek you shall find; knock
   door shall open unto you.
   Alleluia, alleluia!

[1]These: Should be signed as a gesture, with the right open hand, palm facing up from the left and with a sweeping motion to the right.
[2]Give: Should be signed directionally.

406   Canticle of Prayer

Antiphon
We do not how pray like we should,
but Spirit plea for us with sounds
not understood for words.

1. Ask(#1), will(#1) give you;
   seek, you will(#1) find; knock,
   will open you:

Antiphon

2. For all themselves ask(#1)
   receive, all themselves seek find;
   all themselves knock, will open:

Antiphon

Close to Thee

1. You my everlasting part, more than
   friend, life me, ever-since my journey(#3)
   Jerusalem,[1] Savior, let me walk with you.
   Close you, close you, close you, close you
   ever-since my journey(#3) Jerusalem,
   Savior, let me walk with you.

2. Not for ease, world pleasure, not for
   fame my prayer shall; glad will(#1) I
   toil, suffer, only let me walk with you.
   Close you, close you, close you, close you,
   glad will(#1) I toil, suffer, only let
   me walk with you.

3. Lead me through valley dark, carry me
   over(#2) life not regular confuse; then gate
   life eternity may I enter, Lord, with you.
   Close you, close you, close you, close you,
   then gate life eternity may I enter,
   Lord, with you.

[1]Jerusalem: May be signed "Old Town" or "J"-town or "J"-old-town.

The Gift of Love

1. No matter I may speak with brave excite,
   have gift all inspire,[1] have not love, my
   words are empty, as using many word with
   little thought, feel no hope gain(#2).

2. No matter I may give all I possess(#2),
   struggle true, my love declare, but
   not give through love within, profit
   quick change strange small(#1).

3. Come, Spirit, come, our hearts
   control(#1), our spirits long(#2) true
   made well(#2). Let love guide every deed;
   through this we worship, true free.

[1]Inspire: R and L flat "O" hand positions, palms facing body at the heart, fingers pointing up, move both hands up opening into "5" hand positions.

410 I Want a Principle Within

1. I want belief within watch(#1), fear
   God sensibility[1] sin, pain feel sin near.
   I want first approach feel pride, wrong
   desire, catch wander(#2) my will(#2),
   end(#3) arouse excite.

2. From you that I no more may wander(#2),
   no more your good grieve, give[2]-me devotion
   great(#2) wonder(#1) I pray, tender(#1)[3]
   conscience(#1) give. Quick as love for God,
   my conscience(#1) make; awake my soul happen
   sin near, keep soul awake.

3. Almighty God truth, love, me your power(#1)
   give; remove large hardness from my soul. O
   may least omission(#1) pain my inspire[4] soul,
   compel(#1) me that life again, which
   makes wound well(#2).

[1]Sensibility: R and L "5" hand positions, palms facing the body, middle fingers touching at the heart, twist both wrist down and out.
[2]Give: Should be signed directionally.
[3]Tender: May be signed either "warm" or "soft."
[4]Inspire: R and L flat "O" hand positions, palms facing body at the heart, fingers pointing up, move both hands up opening into "5" hand positions.

Dear Lord, Lead Me Day by Day   411

1. Precious Lord, lead me, everyday; make
   me faithful(#2), wise, strong(#1); happy most
   all know that my precious Lord loves me true.

Refrain:
> Praise God, begin love, praise from
> morning till sunset; praise home, praise
> church; praise God every place earth.

2. Precious Lord, lead me everyday; make me
   follow, obey faithful(#2) your words life,
   that your love ever(#3) remain.

Refrain

3. Now with confidence, I sing joy praises
   our God, with honest heart, I give
   tender[1] care(#1), sympathy(#1).

Refrain

[1]Tender: May be signed "warm" or "soft."

413   A Charge to Keep I Have

1. Order(#1) keep I have, God
   glory, never dying soul
   save, prepare for sky.

2. Serve present(#3) time, my
   call(#1) fill; O may call(#1), all my
   power(#1) begin do my ruler(#1) will(#2)!

3. Provide(#1) me with watch(#1) care(#1),
   as in your sight live, oh, your servant,
   Lord, prepare perfect reason give!

4. Help me watch(#1) pray, on
   yourself rely(#2), confident, if I my
   trust deceive, I shall forever die.

414   Thou Hidden Love of God

1. Your hidden love God, himself height,
   center part not understood, no person
   knows, I see from far your beautiful light,
   within long(#2) for your rest; my
   heart pain, neither can heart
   rest, till heart finds you.

2. True mercy all that you finish bring
   my mind seek peace you; yet while I seek,
   I don't find you, no peace my wander(#2)
   end(#3), all my step(#1) you watch(#1) care(#1)?

3. Is(#1) there thing beneath sun that
   struggles with you my heart share? Surprise,
   separate from that place reign alone, Lord
   every change position; then shall my heart
   from earth free, happen heart finish
   find rest you.

4. O Love, your great(#3) aid give, save me
   from low thought care(#1); melt this self
   will(#2) from my heart, from all hidden
   confusion there; make me your obedient child,
   that I may continue cry(#3) "God, Father."

5. Each moment attract from earth take
   my heart that humble waits your call(#1);
   God speak my soul, say, "I your love,
   your God, your all!" Let me feel your
   power(#1), hear your voice, taste your
   love, all my choice.

Take Up Thy Cross   415

1. "Take-up your cross," Savior said, "if
   you would become my disciple, deny yourself,
   leave(#1) world, humbly follow me."

2. Take-up your cross, let not cross burden
   fill your weak spirit with warn; his
   strength shall bear(#4) your spirit, support
   your heart, strength your prepare(#1).

3. Take-up your cross, not pay-attention
   shame, not let your foolish pride rebel;
   your Lord for you cross endure(#1), save
   your soul from death, hell(#1).

4. Take-up your cross follow Christ, not
   think till death give-up; for only people
   themselves bear(#4) cross may hope
   wear(#2) glory crown.

416   Come Out the Wilderness

Refrain:
   I depend Lord, I depend Lord,
   I depend Lord, himself died Calvary.[1]

1. Tell me, how you feel happen you came
   out, area no people live, come out area no
   people live? Tell me, how you feel happen
   you come out, area no people live,
   depend Lord?

Refrain

2. You finish love everyone happen you
   come out, area no people live, come out area
   no people live? You finish love everyone
   happen you come out, area no people live,
   depend Lord?

Refrain

3. Your soul finish feel happy happen you
come out, area no people live, come out area
no people live? Your soul finish feel
happy happen you come out, area no people
live, depend Lord?

Refrain

[1]Calvary: May be signed "rock," then "mountain," then "cross."

This ASL translation © 1995 The United Methodist Publishing House

O for a Heart to Praise My God   417

1. O for heart praise my God, heart free
from sin, heart that always feel your blood
true free shed[1] for me.[2]

2. Heart accept, yield, patient, my
great(#3) Redeemer(#1) throne, place Christ
heard speak, place Jesus reigns alone.

3. Humble-lowly, regret heart, believe,
true, clean, which neither life, death can
part from Christ himself dwell within.

4. Heart every thought make new, full love
divine, perfect, right, pure, good,
copy, Lord yours.

5. Your life gracious Lord, give; come
quick from above; write your new name
on-my-heart,[3] your new, best name Love.

[1]Shed: Right flat "O" hand position, palm facing down over left wrist, bring fingertips down touching back of left hand, move out, opening right into "5" hand position.
[2]Me: Should be signed the whole person with both hands, fingertips moving down the body.
[3]On-my-heart: Should be signed at the heart.

This ASL translation © 1995 The United Methodist Publishing House

418   We Are Climbing Jacob's Ladder

1. We climb(#1) Jacob[1] ladder; we
   climb(#1) Jacob ladder, we climb(#1)
   Jacob ladder; soldiers cross.

2. Every climb(#1) higher, higher; every
   climb(#1) higher, higher, every climb(#1)
   higher, higher; soldiers cross.

3. Sinner, do-you[2] love my Jesus? Sinner,
   do-you love my Jesus? Sinner, do-you
   love my Jesus? Soldiers cross.

4. If you love him, why not serve him?
   If you love him, why not serve him?
   If you love him, why not serve him?
   Soldiers cross.

5. We climb(#1) higher, higher; we
   climb(#1) higher, higher, we climb(#1)
   higher, higher; soldiers cross.

[1]Jacob: May be signed with inscribing a "J" on the forehead, since Jacob is the father of the twelve tribes. Or may be signed with a right "J," then the sign for Israelites, or any other name sign you give to Jacob.
[2]Do you: Should be signed as "ask a question," all one sign.

This ASL translation © 1995 The United Methodist Publishing House

419   I Am Thine, O Lord

1. I yours, O Lord, I finish hear your
   voice, told your love me;[1] but I long(#2)
   rise(#1) arms faith true close
   attract you.

Refrain:
> Attract me near, near, bless Lord, cross
> place you finish died. Attract me near,
> near, near, bless Lord, your precious,
> bleed[2] side.

2. Consecration me now your service, Lord,
   through power(#1) grace(#1) divine; let my
   soul look up with continue(#1) hope, my
   will(#2) true lost you.

Refrain

3. O pure delight one hour that before(#3)
   your throne[3] I pass-by, happen I kneel
   prayer, with you, my God, I talk as
   friend with friend.

Refrain

4. There true strength love that I cannot
   know till I cross(#3) narrow sea; there
   heights joy that I may not reach
   till I rest peace with you.

Refrain

[1]Me: Should be signed the whole person.
[2]Bleed side: Sign "red," then right "5," palm facing left at the right side, move down, wiggling fingers.
[3]Throne: R and L "C" hand positions, palms facing down and separated, move both hands back toward the body in an arc, indicating the arms of a large chair.

420   Breathe on Me, Breath of God

1. Breathe me,[1] Breath God, fill me with life new,
   that I may love same you love, do same you would do.

2. Breathe me, Breath God, till my heart pure,
   till with you I will(#2) one will(#2) do, endure(#1).

3. Breathe me, Breath God, till I whole
   yours, till all pleasure out-world part
   me shine with your light divine.

4. Breathe me, Breath God, true shall I never die,
   but live with you perfect life your eternity.

[1]Me: Should be signed as the whole person.

421   Make Me a Captive, Lord

1. Make me prisoner, Lord, then I become
   free. Force me give up my sword, I become
   conqueror. I defeat life warn happen
   through myself I bear(#4); make me prisoner
   within, strong(#1) shall become my hand.

2. My heart weak, poor until find Jesus;
   heart no begin action sure, heart varies with wind.
   Heart cannot free move till you finish
   made heart work; take-away freedom with your
   wonderful love, eternity shall reign.

3. My power(#1) faith(#1), low till I
   finish learn serve; lack excite shine,
   lack breath courage. Cannot control
   world until itself[1] control; flag can only
   open happen you shall breathe from heaven.

4. My will(#2) not mine till you finish
   make yours; if would reach king throne,[2]
   must itself resign crown. Only stands free,
   amid conflict[3] struggle, happen on your body
   finish depend, found you life.

[1]Itself: Left "index" position, palm facing right, finger pointing up. Right "10" hand position, palm facing left, move right toward left, but not touching.
[2]Throne: R and L "C" hand positions, palms facing down and separated, move both hands back in an arc toward the body, indicating the arms of a large chair.
[3]Conflict: R and L "index" hand positions, palms facing out, fingers pointing up at an angle, move both up to a point the indexes cross.

Jesus, Thine All-Victorious Love   422

1. Jesus, you all victory(#1) love shed[1] my
   heart much; then shall my feet no more
   wander(#2), begin found God.

2. O that in-me[2] holy light might now begin
   shine; destroy worthless(#1) basis(#2)
   desire, make mountain move!

3. O that now from heaven might come, all
   my sins destroy! Come, Holy Spirit, for
   you I call(#1), Spirit excite, come!

4. Make pure excite, come through my heart,
   light-up[3] my soul; scatter your life
   through every part, make holy whole.

[1]Shed: Right flag "O" hand position above the head, palm facing body, bring the hand to the heart, opening into "5" after touching the heart.
[2]Me: Should be signed the whole person.
[3]Light-up: Should sign "bright."

424   Must Jesus Bear the Cross Alone

1. Must Jesus bear(#4) cross alone, all
   world free? No, there cross for every
   person, there cross for me.[1]

2. How happy angels above, themselves
   past went sorrow here. But now they
   experience not mix love, joy without tear.

3. Make holy cross, I bear(#4) til
   death shall free me; then go heaven my
   crown wear, for there crown for me.

[1]Me: Should be signed the whole person.

This ASL translation © 1995 The United Methodist Publishing House

425   O Crucified Redeemer

1. O crucified Redeemer(#1), whose life we
   finish destroyed, you we rise(#3) our guilty
   hands, humbly accept our guilt. Today we
   see your love spread open our gaze; crowd
   street, country road, Calvary display.

2. We hear your cry(#3) pain, we see your
   life crucified like battle area true red
   blood, our neighbor blood, O Lord; that other
   battle, fight for daily life, place might(#1)
   right, self king, we see your crown head.

3. Sounds create force out through pain,
   care(#1), pain many, many hearts that break
   silent loss hope; O crucified Redeemer(#1),
   these your cry(#3) pain; O may pain break
   our selfish hearts, love come-in reign.

This ASL translation © 1995 Community of Resurrection

Behold a Broken World

1. See broken world, we pray, place
   want, war increase, give[1]-us, Lord, this
   our day, old dream peace.

2. Dream sword become plows, spears[2] become
   shovel, guns from war destroy, world with
   peace made again.

3. Place every battle flag fold, every
   trumpet[3] quiet(#1), place wars shall
   cease all world, awake dream fill.

4. No force guns shall rule(#1) neither
   justice(#1) cease control(#1); neither shall
   highest vision(#2) fail dreamers day.

5. O Jesus, himself died save, lost world
   redeem(#1), rise(#1) triumph(#2) from
   grave, see our awake dream.

6. Bring, Lord, your better world begin,
   your kingdom, Love rule(#1), place peace
   with God, peace earth, peace eternity reign.

[1]Give: Should be signed directionally.
[2]Spear: Natural motion of throwing a spear.
[3]Trumpet: Same sign as "trombone," with the exception that the right hand does not move and the left fingers are tapped up and down.

1. Where(#2) cross(#3) crowd ways life,
   place sound cry(#3) people, class,
   above noise selfish struggle, we
   hear your voice, O Son man.

2. Visit place, very bad, need, dark
   door-way dark with fears, from paths
   place hide attract greedy, we catch
   vision[1] your tears.

3. Since tender[2] child dependent, from
   woman grief, man burden toil, from
   hungry soul, from sorrow pressure,[3] your
   heart true never known move back(#1).

4. Cup water give for you still(#1) keep
   new your grace(#1); yet(#1) you long(#2) these
   crowd see pleasant compassion your face(#1).

5. O Jesus from mountain make haste heal[4]
   these hearts pain; among these restless crowd
   dwell; O walk city streets again.

6. Till all world shall learn your love,
   follow place your feet finish walk,
   till, glory from your heaven above, shall
   come city our God.

---

[1]Vision: R and L "S" hand positions, palms facing down at the forehead, left in front of the right, move hands to their respective sides of the body, opening into bent "5" hand positions.
[2]Tender: May be signed "warm" or "soft" at the heart.
[3]Pressure: Left "S" hand position, palm facing right, Right "open" hand position, palm facing down, over the left, move right hand down, pushing the left hand down.
[4]Heal: Sign "make" then the sign for "well"(#2).

1. For heal[1] people, Lord, we pray with
   one accord; for just(#1) equal share
   things that earth give; life love action
   help us rise(#1), pledge our word,
   help us rise(#1), pledge our word.

2. Lead us forward into free; from loss
   hope your world free, that redeem(#1) from
   war, hate, all may come, go peace. Show
   us through care(#1), good fear will(#1)
   fade, hope increase, fear will(#1) fade,
   hope increase.

3. All that destroy abundant living, let
   from earth forbid(#1); pride position, class,
   school, belief that obscure your plan. Our
   common[2] quest for justice(#1) may we
   hallowed(#2) life short time, may we
   hallowed(#2) life short time.

4. You, Creator God, finish write your
   great(#3) name people heart; for our grow
   your like(#2) bring life Christ mind(#2),
   that through our response(#1), service earth
   itself determine happen may find, earth
   itself determine happen[3] may find.

[1]Heal: Sign "make," then the sign for "well"(#2).
[2]Common: R and L "Y" hand positions, palms facing down, move both simultaneously, counterclockwise, several times.
[3]Happen: Should be signed several times beginning from the left and continuing to the right.

430   O Master, Let Me Walk with Thee

1. O Jesus, let me walk with you, humble
   paths service free; tell me your secret;
   help me bear(#4) pain from toil,
   worry from care.

2. Help me slow heart inspire[1] through some
   clear, winning word love; teach me disobedience
   feet stay(#1), guide them home way.

3. Teach me your patience; still(#1) with
   you close, precious company, work that keeps
   faith pleasant strong, trust that
   triumph(#2) over(#2) wrong.

4. Hope that sends shining-ray far-down
   future broad way, peace that only you
   can give, with you, O Jesus, let me live.

[1]Inspire: R and L flat "O" hand positions, palms facing body at the heart, fingers pointing up, move both hands up opening into "5" hand positions.

431   Let There Be Peace on Earth

Let there peace earth, let
begin with me; let there peace
earth, peace that meant become.
With God our creator, we all
children. Let us walk with each-other
perfect cooperation. Let peace begin
with me; let this moment now.

With every place I walk, let this my earnest vow; accept each moment, live each moment peace eternity. Let there peace earth, let peace begin with me.

Jesu, Jesu, 432

Refrain:
    Jesus, Jesus, fill us with your love, show
    us how serve neighbor we have from you.

1. Kneel feet his friends, silent(#2) wash
   their feet, Jesus himself acts as slave them.

Refrain

2. Neighbors rich, poor, neighbors black,
   white, neighbors near, far-away.

Refrain

3. These people we should serve, these people
   we should love; all these neighbors, us you.

Refrain

4. Loving call(#1) us kneel, serving like(#1) we slaves,
   this way we should live with you.

Refrain

5. Kneel feet our friends, silence(#2) wash
   wash their feet, this way we should live with you.

Refrain

All Who Love and Serve Your City

1. All people love, serve your city, all
   themselves bear(#4) daily pressure,[1] all
   themselves cry(#3) peace, justice(#1), all
   themselves speak bad language,
   all themselves bless:

2. Your day loss, sorrow, your day weak
   struggle, honor, peace, love avoid,
   seek Lord, himself your life.

3. Your day wealth, plenty, wasted work,
   wasted play, remember word Jesus,
   "You work while still(#1) day."

4. For all days true days judgment,
   Lord wait still(#1), come near all
   themselves scorn him, offering peace
   from Calvary-hill(#1).

5. Rise(#1) Lord, shall city become city
   loss hope? Come today, our Judge, our
   Glory, Jesus name, "Lord there!"

[1]Pressure: Left "S" hand position, palm facing right, Right "open" hand position, palm down over the left, move right hand down, pushing the left hand down.

Cuando El Pobre

(When the Poor Ones)

1. Happen poor people, themselves have
nothing, share with stranger,[1] happen
thirsty give water all us, happen cripple
weak body strength others, then we know
that God still(#1) walks that road with
us, then we know that God still(#1) walks
that road with us.

2. Happen last(#1), all people themselves
suffer find their comfort, happen they hope
no matter hope seems without hope, happen
we love although hate sometimes seems all
surround us, then we know that God still(#1)
walks that road with us, then we know that God
still(#1) walks that road with us.

3. Happen our joy fills up our cup
overflow, happen our lips can speak no
words other than true, happen we know that
love for simple things better, then we
know that God still(#1) walks that road
with us, then we know that God still(#1)
walks that road with us.

4. Happen our homes will with good, abundance,
happen we learn make peace instead war,
happen each stranger that we meet call(#1)
neighbor, then we know that God still(#1)
walks that road with us, then we know that
God still(#1) walks that road with us.

[1]Stranger: May be signed as "new," then the sign for "person"; or "strange," then the sign for "person."

O God of Every Nation

1. O God all people, every class, land,[1]
   redeem(#1) your whole world with your
   almighty hand; place hate, fear divide
   us, bitter danger cast-out, love,
   mercy(#1) guide us, heal[2] our struggle world.

2. From search for wealth, power, scorn(#1)
   truth, right(#1), from trust bombs[3] that
   destroy through all-night, from pride class,
   position, blind your way, deliver every
   person, eternity God, we pray.

3. Lord, strength all themselves labor
   that all may find free from fear sounds
   swords, from dread war increase; happen hope,
   courage wander(#2), Lord, let your voice
   heard; with faith that none can change,
   your servants support.

4. Keep bright us vision(#2)[4] days happen
   war shall cease, happen hate, division
   give-up love, peace, till begin morning
   glory happen truth, justice(#1) reign,
   Christ shall rule(#1) victory(#1) over(#1)
   all world area.

[1]Land: The sign for "dirt," then the sign for "spread."
[2]Heal: Sign for "make," then the sign for "well"(#2).
[3]Bomb: R and L "S" hand positions, held together, left in front of the right, palms facing down. Move both hands up and out, opening into "5" hand positions.
[4]Vision: May be signed with R and L "S" hand positions, held together, left in front of the right at the forehead, palms facing down. Move both hands up and out, opening into "C" hand positions.

The Voice of God Is Calling

1. Voice God call(#1), summon(#1)
   our day; Isaiah[1] heard Israel, we now
   hear God say: "Whom shall I send help my
   people, need? Whom shall I send
   free bond shame, greedy(#3)?

2. "I hear my people cry(#3) poverty(#1),
   mine(#2) factory; no field(#2), business
   silent(#1), no city street still(#2). I
   see my people become bad dark, lose hope.
   Whom shall I send break chain which
   they bear(#4)?"

3. We pay-attention, O Lord, your
   summon(#1), answer: We here! Send us upon
   your trip, let us your servants become.
   Our strength dirt, what remain, our years
   like(#1) fade hour; but you can use our
   weakness increase your power(#1).

4. From comfort, plenty save us; from pride
   place declare free sin; clean us low desire;
   rise(#3) us high decide; accept us, make us
   holy; teach us your will(#2) way. Speak,
   see! we answer; command, we obey!

[1]Isaiah: Right "I" hand position, then sign "prophet," or any other name sign you have for the prophet Isaiah.

This Is My Song

1. This my song, O God all people,
   song peace for land far, mine. This
   my home, country place my heart; here my
   hopes, my dreams, my holy place; but other
   hearts, other lands beating[1] with
   hope, dreams, as true, high as mine.

2. My country sky bluer[2] than ocean,
   sunlight shines,[3] flowers, trees; but other
   lands[4] finish sunlight too, flowers, sky
   every place as blue as mine. O hear
   my song, you God all people, song peace
   for their lands, for mine.

3. This is my prayer, O Lord all world
   kingdoms: Your kingdom come; on earth your
   will(#2) do. Let Christ rise(#3) till all
   shall serve him, hearts united learn live as
   one. O hear my prayer, you God all people;
   myself, I give you; let your will(#2) do.

[1]Beating: Should be signed with a right "A" hand position at the heart, palm facing body, move hand out and back several times indicating heart beating.
[2]Bluer: Should be signed beginning from the left above the head and move to the right, while looking up.
[3]Shines: Should be signed directionally.
[4]Lands: May be signed "dirt," then the sign for "spread."

Forth in Thy Name, O Lord

1. Forward your name, O Lord, I go(#2),
   my daily labor pursue; you, only you,
   resolve know all I think, speak, do.

2. Task your wisdom finish give, O let me
   cheerful full; all my work your presence
   find, prove your good, perfect will(#2).

3. You may I found my right hand, whose
   eyes my secret wealth see, labor onward
   your command, offer all my work you.

4. For you, delight use no-matter-what your
   generous(#1) grace finish give; move onward
   with even joy, close walk with you, heaven.

This ASL translation © 1995 The United Methodist Publishing House

We Utter Our Cry

1. We express[1] our cry(#3): that peace may
   gain victory(#1), that earth will remain,
   faith must not fail. We pray with our life
   for world our care(#1), for people reduce
   through doubt, loss hope.

2. We cry(#3) from fright our daily scene
   for strength say "No" for all that bad: plans
   bear(#4) confusion, fade life, all strength
   waste(#1) things used make death.

3. We rise(#3) our hearts for children not
   yet born; give wisdom, O God, that we may
   help, provide new, take-care-of(#3), this
   good Earth, save future, wonder(#1) birth.

4. Creator life, come share we pray, your
   Spirit earth, show Way leaders
   sit-around-tables[2] discussing peace, that
   people may from unfair influence, deceit
   become free.

5. Come with us, Lord; love protect,
   march, help us inspire[3] with strong(#1) feel
   your church, match[4] all our talk, high
   decide with life, not rest, action involved.

6. No matter evil, pressure[5] we face, Lord
   inspire, heal[6] give understanding, grace
   think, make peace with each heart-beat,
   breath, choose Christ before king,
   life before death.

[1]Express: R and L "S" hand positions at the heart, palms facing the body. Move both hands up and out opening into "5" hand positions.
[2]Sit-around-tables: R and L bent "V" hand positions, fingers point out, palms facing down in front of the body, twisting both wrists respectively out in arc motions, ending up with fingers pointing toward body.
[3]Inspire: R and L flat "O" hand positions, palms facing body at the heart, fingers pointing up, move both hands up opening into "5" hand positions.
[4]Match: R and L bent "4" hand positions, palms facing body, move both hands toward each other, interlocking fingers.
[5]Pressure: Left "S" hand position. Right "open" hand position, palm down, over the left, move right down, pushing left hand down.
[6]Heal: Sign "make," then sign "well"(#2).

Let There Be Light

1. Let there light, let there
   understanding, let all people gather(#1),
   let people face(#2) each other.

2. Open our speaking, open our
   minds ponder, open door agree, open
   into grace(#1).

3. Perish(#2) sword, perish(#2) angry
   judgment, perish(#2) bombs,[1] hunger,
   perish(#2) fight for gain.

4. Hallowed(#1) our love, hallowed(#1)
   deaths martyrs, hallowed(#1) their holy
   freedom, hallowed(#1) your name.

5. Your kingdom come, your Spirit
   change language, your people speak
   together, your spirit never fade.

6. Let there light, open our hearts
   wonder(#1), perish great(#2) fear,
   hallowed(#1) world God made.

[1]Bombs: R and L "S" hand positions held together, palms facing down, Left is in front of the Right, move both hands up and out, opening into "5" hand positions, indicating exploding.

441   What Does the Lord Require

1. What Lord require for praise, offering?
   What sacrifice, desire, honor you bring? Do
   just(#1), love mercy(#1), walk humbly
   with your God.

2. Rulers(#1) earth, listen! Should you
   not know justice(#1)? Will(#1) God hear
   your plea, while lawbreaking, cruel(#1)
   grows? Do just(#1), love mercy(#1),
   walk humbly with your God.

3. All people earn wealth through business,
   for whom workers toils, think not win God
   aid, if greedy(#1) your business make dirty.
   Do just(#1), love mercy(#1), walk humbly
   with your God.

4. How shall our life fill God law true
   hard, high? Let Christ provide our will(#2)
   with grace(#1) make strong(#1). Then
   just(#1), mercy(#1), we walk
   humbly with God.

This ASL translation © 1995 Albert F. Bayly

442   Weary of All Trumpeting

1. Weary all loud music, weary all kill,
   weary all songs that sing promise, not
   fulfill, we would sing, O Christ, one song;
   we would join(#3) sing that great(#3)
   music, pure, strong place with
   heaven ring(#2).

2. Captain Christ, O humble Lord, servant
   King, your dying bid us put-down[1] foolish
   sword, bid us cease deny. Proclaim with
   your Spirit's breath through each height,
   hallowed(#1); yourself give death, call
   us all follow.

3. Triumph(#1) your cross summon all living;
   summon us live through loss, gain all through
   give, suffer all, that we may see triumph(#1)
   surrender; leave(#2) all, that we may become
   partners[2] your glory.

[1]Put-down: Should be signed as a classifier, the natural motion of putting the sword back into the sheath on the left side.
[2]Partners: R and L bent "4" hand positions, palms facing the body, move both hands toward each other, interlocking the fingers.

O God Who Shaped Creation 443

1. O God yourself shape world, earth very
   confuse begin, your word power(#1)
   spoken, look, dark fade! You made us
   your image, you brought us into begin, you
   bless our baby walk, share your glory earth.

2. O God, with pain, grief, mother see her
   child start wrong path, tempt, but make
   dirty; true your heart broken happen hate,
   desire increase, happen world you made,
   care-for(#1) scorn ways lead peace.

3. Although your heart broken happen people
   scorn your ways, you never cease your search
   through evil dark confusion; happen we cease
   our run, your joys, O God, plenty like(#2)
   joy search woman happen money found.

4. O God, happen little(#2) value lose
   bright, pleasures lose delight, happen weary
   through our wander(#2), we seek your care(#1),
   like(#1) mother, with compassion you share
   your warm love; you prepare banquet make
   us well through your grace.

5. Mercy(#1), compassion, your good made
   known; with tender(#1) you touch us, broken
   hearts healed.[1] You require us as your children,
   you remove our pride shame; with freedom
   began mercy(#1) we bless your holy name!

[1]Healed: Sign "make," then the sign for "well"(#2).

444   O Young and Fearless Prophet

1. O young, brave Prophet, old "G"-country,
   your life still(#1) summons serve people;
   make our thoughts, actions less inclined
   please crowd, stand humble courage for
   truth with hearts not fright.

2. We marvel purpose that keep you, move
   onward while ever(#3) hill-top[1] before(#3)
   you appear(#3) cross; your face same always
   look onward, place love, duty show, while we
   betray true quick, leave you cross alone.

3. O help us stand avoid against conflict[2]
   cruel way, place hate, desire, false
   control(#2), Christ holy influence; forbid
   false love, country that binds us his
   call(#1), himself rise(#3) above people, unity all.

4. Inspire[3] us, protest against our greedy(#1) wealth, while others starve-hunger, plea for work, health; place homes with small(#2) children cry(#3) out for want bread, themselves live their lives pain burden beneath gloom fear.

5. O young, brave Prophet, we need your presence here, amid our pride, glory see your face appear(#2); once again hear your challenge above noisy day, again lead us onward along God holy way.

[1]Hill-top: Should be signed as a classifier, the natural motion of making a hill, on the left, then repeat on the right.
[2]Conflict: R and L "index" hand position, palms out, fingers pointing up at an angle, move both up to a point the indexes cross.
[3]Inspire: R and L flat "O" hand positions, palms facing body at the heart, fingers pointing up, move both hands up opening into "5" hand positions.

Happy the Home When God Is There   445

1. Happy home happen God there, love fills every heart; happen people wish, people prayer, people heavenly rest.

2. Happy home place Jesus name pleasant every ear; place children early speak his fame, parents keep him precious.

3. Happy home place prayer heard, praise accustom rise(#3); place parents love holy Word, all wisdom value.

4. Lord, let us our homes agree this bless peace gain; unite our hearts love you, love all will(#1) reign.

447   Our Parent, by Whose Name

1. Our Parent,[1] through whose name all Power(#1), known, themselves your love proclaim, each family your own: direct(#2) all parents, guard well(#1), with continue love as protector which your people live.

2. O Jesus, yourself, child within earth home, with heart still(#1) pure, true become adult: our children bless every place, that they may all see your face(#1), know you, may grow grace(#1).

3. Bless Spirit, yourself can bind our hearts unity, teach us find love from self become free; all our hearts love increase that every home, through this free, may dwell place peace.

[1]Parent: May be signed "mother," then "father."

448   Go Down, Moses

1. Happen Israel live Egypt[1] land, let my people free; burden true hard(#1) they could not stand, let my people free.

Refrain:
> Go again, Moses,[2] far Egypt land;[3] tell old
> "P"-king let my people free!

2. Therefore(#3) said Lord," bold Moses
   said, let my people free; "if not, I strike(#1)
   your firstborn child dead," let my people free.

Refrain

3. No more shall they bondage toil, let
   my people free; let them leave with Egypt
   riches, let my people free.

Refrain

4. We need not always cry(#1), mourn,
   let my people free; weary slave chains
   neglect, let my people free.

Refrain

5. Come, Moses, you will not become lost,
   let my people free; rise-up(#3) your rod,
   come across, let my people free.

Refrain

6. As Israel stood near water, let my
   people free; God command sea divide, let
   my people free.

Refrain

7. Happen they finish touch other land,
   let my people free; they sang triumph(#1)
   songs, let my people free.

Refrain

8. O Moses, cloud will lead way, let my
   people free; fire through night, dark
   through day, let my people free.

Refrain

9. Your enemy shall not before(#3) you
   stand, you will have fair(#1) Canaan[4] land.[5]

Refrain

10. This world great(#2) sorrow,
    O let us go-ahead Canaan.

Refrain

11. O let us from chain become free,
    let us all with Christ become free, let
    my people free.

Refrain

[1]Egypt: May be signed with a right "X" hand position, palm facing out, held at the forehead.
[2]Moses: May be signed with R and L "G" hand positions, palms down, at the respective temples, move both hands to the respective sides, closing the index and thumbs together.
[3]Land: May be signed with "dirt," then the sign for "spread."
[4]Canaan: Right "C" hand position and sign country with a "C" on the back of the left forearm.
[5]Land: Sign for "dirt" with both hands, then the sign for "spread."

450   Creator of the Earth and Skies

1. Creator earth, sky, whom all truth,
   power(#1) belong, give us your truth make
   us wise, give us your power(#1),
   make us strong(#1).

2. We not yet know you: sky our statue for
   foolish rise(#3); all our self-made
   not happy make us trust ourselves more.

3. We not yet love you: far, wide destroy
   our hate spreads; evils made through people
   pride avoid not repent leaders.

4. We long(#2) end(#3) this world struggle:
   How shall we follow your way? Speak us all
   your words life, until our dark change day.

Be Thou My Vision   451

1. Become my vision,[1] O Lord my heart; nothing
   important all else me, only that you true. You
   my best thought, through day, through all-night
   awake, sleep, your presence my light.

2. Become my wisdom, you my true word; I
   ever(#3) with you, you with me, Lord; you
   only you, first my heart, great(#3) God
   heaven, you my value.

3. Great(#3) God heaven, my victory-won(#1),
   may I touch heaven joys, O bright heaven
   Sun. Heart my own heart, no matter happens,
   still(#1) my vision, O Ruler(#1) all.

[1]Vision: R and L "S" hand positions, palms facing down, at the forehead, left in front of the
right, move hands to their respective sides of the body opening into bent "S" hand positions.

452   My Faith Looks Up to Thee

1. My faith looks-up you, you Jesus,
   Christ, Savior divine! Now hear me while
   I pray, take-away all my guilt, O let me
   from this day be(#1) whole yours!

2. May your rich grace give strength(#1)
   my faith(#1) heart, my zeal inspire;[1] as you
   finish died for me, O may my love you, pure,
   warm, not change, living excite!

3. While life dark confusion I walk, grief
   around me spread, you my guide; bid dark
   change to day, day sorrow tears-away, never
   let me ever(#1) wander(#2) from your side.

4. Happen end(#1) life pass(#1) dream,
   happen death not friendly silent(#1)
   endure(#2) shall over me appear; bless
   Savior, then, love, fear, doubt(#1) remove;
   O bear(#4) me safe above, saved soul!

[1]Inspire: R and L flat "O" hand positions, palms facing body at the heart, fingers pointing
up, move both hands up opening into "5" hand positions.

453   More Love to Thee, O Christ

1. More love you, O Christ, more love you!
   Hear prayer I say bend-kneel. This my
   honest plea: More love, O Christ, you;
   more love you, more love you!

2. Past earthly joy I long(#2), seek peace,
   rest; now you alone I seek, give what best.
   This all my prayer: More love O Christ,
   you; more love you, more love you!

3. Let sorrow do work, come grief, pain;
   pleasant your people themselves announce,
   pleasant their control(#2), happen they
   can sing with me: More love, O Christ,
   you; more love you, more love you!

4. Then shall my recent breath whisper your
   praise; this last(#1) cry(#3) my heart shall
   rise(#3); this continue my prayer: More love,
   O Christ, you; more love you, more love you!

Open My Eyes, That I May See   454

1. Open-my-eyes,[1] that I may see brief(#1)
   view truth you plan for me; place my hands
   wonderful key that shall open make me free.

Refrain:
   Silent(#2) now I wait for you, ready,
   my God, your will(#2) see. Open-my-eyes,
   (st. 2—Open-my-ears,[2])
   (st. 3—Open-my-heart,[3])
   (make bright me, Spirit divine!

2. Open-my-ears, that I may hear voices
   truth you speak clear; while sounds
   fall-my-ear, everything false will disappear.

Refrain

3. Open-my-mouth, let me bear(#4) glad warm truth every place; open-my-heart, let me prepare love with your children every place share.

Refrain

[1]Open-my-eyes: Should be signed at the eyes, as in "awake."
[2]Open-my-ears: Should be signed at the ears, all one sign.
[3]Open-my-heart: Should be signed at the heart, all one sign.

455   Not So in Haste, My Heart

1. Not true haste, my heart! Have faith God, wait; although Jesus wait long, he never comes late.

2. He never comes late; Jesus knows best; anger not yourself vain; until Jesus comes, rest.

3. Until he comes, rest, not feel evil will(#2) hours-pass,[1] feet that wait for God fast arrive goal.

4. Fast arrive goal that not gain with speed; then keep you still(#2), my heart, for I shall wait his lead.

[1]Hours-pass: Should be signed as one sign, several repeats of "hour."

458   Dear Lord, for All in Pain

1. Precious Lord, for all themselves pain we pray you; O come, strike(#1) again your enemy.

2. Give your servants skill calm
   bless, give tired sick, give quiet.

3. Lord, people themselves know pain
   may not cease, come near, that anyway
   they may experience peace.

'Tis So Sweet to Trust in Jesus   462

1. True pleasant trust Jesus, accept him
   his word, just(#1) rest his promise, know,
   "Therefore(#3), said Lord."

Refrain:
   Jesus, Jesus, how I trust him! How I
   proved him again, again! Jesus, Jesus,
   precious Jesus! O for grace trust him more!

2. O how pleasant trust Jesus, just(#1)
   trust his clean blood; simple(#1) faith
   plunge-me[1] beneath(#1) heal, clean overflow.

Refrain

3. Yes, true pleasant trust Jesus, just(#1)
   from sin, self cease; just(#1) from Jesus
   simple accept life, rest, joy, peace.

Refrain

4. I true glad I learn trust you,
   precious Jesus, Savior, friend; I know
   you with me, continue with me end(#1)

Refrain

[1]Plunge-me: May be signed with a Right "10" hand position, palm facing left, twist wrist to
the left, then move down forcefully.

Lord, Speak to Me

1. Lord, speak me, that I may speak living
   sounds your voice; as you finish search,
   true, let me seek your wrong children
   lost, alone.

2. O strength me, that while I stand
   strong(#1) rock, strong(#1) you, I may offer
   love hand people struggle with lot trouble.

3. O teach me, Lord, that I may teach
   precious things you give; speak your words,
   that words may touch hid depths many heart.

4. O fill me with your love, Lord, until
   my very heart overflow kind thought warm
   feel word, your love tell, your praise show.

5. O use me, Lord, use me, just(#1) as
   you will(#2) happen, place, until your
   bless face I see your rest, your joy your
   glory share.

I Will Trust in the Lord

1. I will(#1) trust Lord, I will(#1) trust
   Lord, I will(#1) trust Lord, till I die; I
   will(#1) trust Lord, I will(#1) trust Lord,
   I will(#1) trust Lord, till I die.

2. Sister, will(#1) you trust Lord, sister,
   will(#1) you trust Lord, sister, will(#1) you
   trust Lord, till you die; sister, will(#1)
   you trust Lord, sister, will(#1) you trust
   Lord, sister, will(#1) you trust Lord,
   till you die.

3. Brother, will(#1) you trust Lord, brother,
   will(#1) you trust Lord, brother, will(#1)
   you trust Lord, till you die; brother, will(#1)
   you trust Lord, brother, will(#1) you trust
   Lord, brother, will(#1) you trust Lord,
   till you die.

4. Preacher will(#1) you trust Lord,
   preacher, will(#1) you trust Lord, preacher,
   will(#1) you trust Lord, till you die;
   preacher, will(#1) you trust Lord, preacher,
   will(#1) you trust Lord, preacher, will(#1)
   you trust Lord, till you die.

465   Holy Spirit, Truth Divine

1. Holy Spirit, Truth divine, make clear
   this soul mine; Word God, inward light[1]
   inspire[2] my spirit, clear my sight.

2. Holy Spirit, Love divine, glow[3] within
   heart mine; arouse every high desire;
   destroy self your pure delight.[4]

3. Holy Spirit, Power(#1) divine, fill,
   give this will(#2) mine courage; grant(#1)
   that I may strong(#1) live, brave bear(#4),
   great(#3) try(#1).

4. Holy Spirit, Right(#1) divine, King
   within my conscience(#1) reign; become my Lord,
   I shall strong(#1) bound, forever free.

[1]Light: Should be signed directionally.
[2]Inspire: R and L flat "O" hand positions, palms facing body at the heart, fingers pointing up, move both hands up opening into "5" hand positions.
[3]Glow: Should be signed directionally.
[4]Delight: May be signed the same as "excite," except instead of alternating hands at the heart, move both hands up at the same time.

This ASL translation © 1995 The United Methodist Publishing House

467   Trust and Obey

1. Happen we walk with Lord, light his word,
   what[1] glory he scatter-on our way! While we
   do his good will(#2), remain with us
   still(#1), with all themselves
   will(#1) trust, obey.

Refrain:
> Trust, obey, for no other way true
> happy Jesus, but trust, obey.

2. Not burden we bear(#3), not sorrow we
   share, but our toil he will(#1) true make
   equal; not grief, not loss, not frown, not
   cross, but become bless, if we trust, obey.

Refrain

3. But we never can prove delights[2] his love
   until we lay-on-altar;[3] for kindness he
   shows, for joy he gives, for people
   themselves will(#1) trust, obey.

Refrain

4. Then, fellowship pleasant, we will(#1)
   sit-around[4] his feet, we will walk by-his-
   side[5] in-way; what he says we will(#1) do,
   place he sends we will(#1) go; never
   fear, only trust, obey.

Refrain

[1]What: Should be signed as "where"(#2).
[2]Delights: May be signed as "excite," except instead of alternating the hands at the heart, move both hands up.
[3]Lay-on-altar: R and L "A" hand positions, palms facing down, thumbs together, move both hands to their respective sides, then twist wrists so that palms are facing each other, and move down.
[4]Sit-around: R and L bent "V" hand positions, fingers pointing out, palms facing down in front of the body, twist both wrists respectively out in an arc motion, ending with fingers pointing toward body.
[5]By-his-side: Should be signed as a classifier, R and L "index" hand positions, palms facing out and together, fingers pointing up, move both hands out together.

Dear Jesus, in Whose Life I See

1. Precious Jesus, whose life I see all
   that I would, but fail become, let your
   clear light[1] shine forever, shame, guide
   this life mine.

2. No matter what[2] I dream what I do during
   my weak days always different, help me,
   burden through things not yet done, O
   you who deeds, dreams were one.

[1]Light-shine: Should be signed directionally with both hands.
[2]What: Should be signed as "where"(#2).

1. Jesus is(#1)[1] all world me, my life, my
joy, my all; he is my strength
every-day, without him I would fail.
Happen I sad, him I go, no other can cheer
me true; happen I sad, me makes me glad,
he my friend.

2. Jesus is(#1) all world me, my friend,
trouble pain; I go him for bless, he
gives bless again, again. He sends sunshine
rain, he sends harvest gold growth;
sunshine, rain, harvest growth,
he my friend.

3. Jesus is(#1) all world me, true him
I will(#1) become; O how could I this friend
deny, when he true me? Following
him I know I right, he watch-over(#1) me
day all-night; following him through day
all-night, he my friend.

4. Jesus is(#1) all world me, I want no
better friend; I trust him now, I trust him
happen life days-pass[2] swift end(#1).
Beautiful life with same friend, beautiful
life that continue; eternity life, eternity
joy, Jesus my friend.

[1]May be signed without the verb to be "is."
[2]Days-pass: Should sign "days" several times.

470   My God, I Love Thee

1. My God, I love you, not because I hope
   for heaven there, not because, if I love
   not, I must forever die.

2. You, O my Jesus, because you show me
   love on-Cross, for me you bear(#4),
   nails,[1] sword, many various shame.

3. Then why, O bless Jesus Christ, should
   I not love you well(#1)? Not because
   win heaven, not escape hell(#1).

4. Not with hope gain anything, not seek
   rewards, but as yourself finish love me,
   O everlasting Lord.

5. True would I love you, precious Lord,
   your praise will(#1) sing; because you
   my love God, my eternity King.

[1]Nails: Should be signed as a classifier, a wide Right "G," strike across the upheld Left "index" position, several times.

This ASL translation © 1995 The United Methodist Publishing House

471   Move Me

Inspire[1] me, inspire me; inspire me
do your will(#2). Inspire me, inspire
me, inspire me do your will(#2).

[1]Inspire: R and L flat "O" hand positions, palms facing body at the heart, fingers pointing up, move both hands up opening into "5" hand positions.

This ASL translation © 1995 Richard Alan Henderson

Near to the Heart of God

1. True many place quiet rest, near heart
   God; place where(#2) sin cannot injure,
   near heart God.

Refrain:

   O Jesus, bless Redeemer(#1) send(#2)[1] from
   heart God; keep us who wait before(#3) You
   near heart God.

2. True many place comfort pleasant, near
   heart God; place where(#2) we our Savior
   meet, near heart God.

Refrain

3. True many, place full free, near heart
   God; place where(#2) all joy, peace,
   near heart God.

Refrain

[1]Send: Should be signed directionally coming from God.

Lead Me, Lord

Lead me, Lord, lead me your
righteousness(#2); make your way
plain(#1) before(#3) me. For way
you, Lord, you, Lord only,
that makes me live safe.

474   Precious Lord, Take My Hand

1. Precious Lord, take-my-hand,[1] lead
   me-on, let me stand, I tired, I weak,
   I poor; through storm, through all-night,
   lead me, light:[2]

Refrain:

    Take-my-hand, precious Lord, lead me home.

2. Happen my way become gloomy, precious
   Lord stay near, happen my life almost
   gone, hear my cry(#3), hear my call,
   hold-my hand[3] prevent my fall:

Refrain

3. Happen dark appear(#2), night near,
   day finish, gone(#1), river I stand
   guide my feet, hold-my-hand:

Refrain

[1]Take-my-hand: Should be signed naturally, taking the hand.
[2]Light: Should be signed directionally.
[3]Hold-my-hand: Should be signed naturally, taking the hand.

475   O Come Down, O Love Divine

1. Come-down, O Love divine, you seek my
   soul, visit my soul with your own
   faithfulness glowing; O Comforter, come
   near, appear(#3) my heart, inspire heart,
   your holy enthusiasm give.

2. O let excite free inspire, until earth
   desires change dirty, dirt, till warm
   use up; let your glory light shine always my
   sight, provide me full while my path lighted.

3. True desire strong(#1), with which soul
   will(#1) long(#2), shall far better than
   power(#1) people tell; because none guess
   grace(#1), till love create place where(#2)
   Holy Spirit lives.

Lonely the Boat   476

1. Lonely(#1) boat, sailing sea, rock-boat[1]
   cold stormy night; rough sea seem true wide,
   with waves true high. Lonely(#1) boat
   sailed real sea, straight wind; O Lord,
   great(#2) peril-danger do all harm(#1).

2. Strong(#1) winds began, all wind rage,
   rock-boat small lonely(#1) boat; large
   waves high, rock-boat, lost afloat.[2] Sailor
   stood alone, wonder(#1) what-do;[3] O Lord,
   sailor was without help, wonder what-do.

3. Trembling[4] with fear, real loss hope,
   look-all-around[5] for help, sailor saw light
   above. "Help can found; my God here,
   my small boat, stand near me; O I
   trust Savior, now my life continue.

4. "Plea for your mercy(#1), O Lord, no
   matter sinner like(#2) me, command, O Lord,
   calm sea, as "G"-country! Please save my
   life from all danger, give peaceful life;
   O please give mercy(#1), O Lord,
   times calm, struggle.

5. "Storms our lives, cruel(#2) cold, sure
   will(#1) start again, give warn lives,
   give warn us life stormy sea. Power(#1)
   great(#3), God hand there, strong(#1)
   control(#1). O Lord, calm, peace comes
   from you. Peace comes my heart alone."

[1]Rock-boat: Sign as a classifier, making a boat with both cupped hands and rock back and forth by twisting both wrists.
[2]Afloat: Sign as a classifier, both cupped hands seem to float along.
[3]What-do: Should be signed as R and L "D" hand positions, palms facing body, fingers pointing up, move both hands in a counterclockwise circle, closing and opening the index fingers at the same time.
[4]Trembling: R and L "5" hand positions, palms facing body, fingers pointing down, shake both hands.
[5]Look-all-around: "Look" should be signed from the left, moving all around to the right.

478   Jaya Ho
(Victory Hymn)

1. We come before(#3) you, O Great(#3)
   Holy, O Great(#3) Holy. We bow(#2) our
   heads you, great(#3) Holy, O Great(#3)
   Holy. Kneel, your feet we bow(#2)
   quiet(#2), respect, then sing your praise
   ever(#2) repeat.

2. Lord, let us see you, give-us vision.
   Give-us[1] vision![2] Sin deny(#1), love Lord,
   forgive us. Love Lord, forgive us. Accept
   us, take care us your strong protect; safe
   your refuge, we will(#1) sing your praise.

[1]Give-us: Should be signed in reverse, coming back to the body.
[2]Vision: Right and left "S" hand positions, palms facing down, held at the forehead, with left in front of right. Move both hands to their respective sides of the body, opening into bent "5" hand positions.

Jesus, Lover of My Soul 479

1. Jesus, lover of my soul, let me go you,
   while near water move, while strong wind
   still(#1) high. Hide me, O my Savior, hide,
   till life storm finish; safe protection
   guide; O receive my soul last.

2. Other protection I have none, depend my
   without help soul on you; leave
   me not alone, still(#1) support, comfort me.
   All my trust you continue hold, all my help
   from you I bring; cover my weak
   head with shadow your arm.

3. You, O Christ, all I want, more than
   all you I find; rise-up(#1) fall, cheer-up
   faint, heal sick, lead blind. Just(#1)
   holy your name, I true wicked; I true
   false full sin, you full truth, grace(#1).

4. Plenty grace(#1) with you found,
   grace(#1) cover all my sin; let heal continue
   plenty, make, keep me pure within. Your
   life begin, free let me accept you;
   pop-up my heart; rise(#1) all eternity

480   O Love That Wilt Not Let Me Go

1. O Love that will(#1) not let me
   leave(#1), I rest my weary soul you; I give
   you life I owe, that your love like ocean
   deep may worthy, full become.

2. O Light that follow all my way, I yield
   my flickering-light you; my heart made new
   like borrow ray, that your sunshine, bright
   like(#2) day may brighter, fairer(#1) become.

3. O Joy that seek me through pain, I
   cannot close my heart you; I follow rainbow
   through rain, feel promise worthy,
   during morning no tears.

4. O Cross that lift-up[2] my head, I courage
   not ask leave you; I lay low life glory
   dead, from ground there grows new life that
   will(#1) continue.

[1]Flickering: Right "O" hand position, open and close the "O" several times.
[2]Lift-up: Should be signed as a classifier, Right "S" hand position, palm down, bend wrist up, as lifting up head, etc.

This ASL translation © 1995 The United Methodist Publishing House

482   Lord, Have Mercy

1. Lord, have mercy(#1).
   Christ, have mercy(#1)
   Lord, have mercy, mercy(#1).

2. Lord, have mercy(#1).
   Christ, have mercy(#1)
   Lord, have mercy(#1).

This ASL translation © 1995 The United Methodist Publishing House

Kyrie Eleison 483

Lord, have mercy(#1).
Lord, have mercy(#1).
Lord, have mercy(#1).

Kyrie Eleison 484

Lord, Lord, have mercy(#1)

Let Us Pray to the Lord 485

Let pray Lord.
Lord, have mercy(#1).
Let pray Lord.
Christ, have mercy(#1).
Let pray Lord.
Lord, have mercy(#1).

Alleluia 486

Alleluia, Alleluia, Alleluia.

487   This Is Our Prayer

This true our prayer.
This true our prayer,
O God.

488   Jesus, Remember Me

Jesus, remember me happen you
come into your kingdom.
Jesus, remember me happen you
come into your kingdom.

491   Remember me

Remember me, remember me,
O Lord, remember me.

492   Prayer Is the Soul's Sincere Desire

1. Prayer true heart sincere(#1) desire,
   not said, express,[1] inspire[2] hid excite that
   trembles heart.

2. Prayer true burden soft sound,
   fall-tears, quick look-up,[3] happen none
   but God near.

3. Prayer true simple(#1) language that
   baby can say; prayer high great(#3)
   music that touch position honor high.

4. Prayer true regret sinner voice,
   return from sinners way, while angels their
   songs, rejoice, cry(#3), "Look, they pray!"

5. Prayer true Christian vital(#1) voice,
   Christians born certain place; their
   secret word enter gates death; they enter
   heaven with prayer.

6. O Jesus, through whom we come God, Life,
   Truth, Way: path prayer yourself finish
   walk; Lord, teach us how pray!

¹Express: R and L "S" hand positions at the heart, palms facing the body, move both hands up and out opening hands into "5" hand positions.
²Inspire: R and L flat "O" hand positions, palms facing body at the heart, fingers pointing up, move both hands up opening into "5" hand positions.
³Look-up: Should be signed directionally.

This ASL translation © 1995 The United Methodist Publishing House

Kum Ba Yah   494
(Come By Here)

1. Come through here, my Lord, come through
   here. Come through here, my Lord, come
   through here. Come through here, my Lord,
   come through here, O, Lord, come through here!

2. Some pray, Lord, come through here.
   Someone pray, Lord, come through here.
   Someone pray, Lord, come through here.
   O, Lord, come through here!

3. Someone cry(#1), Lord, come through
   here. Someone cry(#1), Lord, come through
   here. Someone cry(#1), Lord, come through
   here. O, Lord, come through here!

4. Someone needs you, Lord, come through
   here. Someone needs you, Lord, come through
   here. Someone needs you Lord, come through
   here. O, Lord, come through here!

5. Someone sing, Lord, come through here.
   Someone sing, Lord, come through here.
   Someone sing, Lord, come through here.
   O, Lord, come through here.

6. Let us praise, Lord, come through here.
   Let us praise, Lord, come through here.
   Let us praise, Lord, come through here.
   O, Lord, come through here!

496   Sweet Hour of Prayer

1. Pleasant hour prayer! pleasant hour
   prayer! that call(#1) me from world worry,
   bid me, Father throne[1] make all my wants,
   wish(#1) known. Seasons great(#2) pain,
   grief, my heart finish find relief,[2] often
   escape tempt contact(#2) through your return,
   pleasant hour prayer!

2. Pleasant hour prayer! pleasant hour
   prayer! joys I feel, joy I share those
   whose anxious spirits ache with strong(#1)
   desire for your return. With same I haste
   place God my Savior shows God face(#1), glad
   take-up my place, wait for you,
   pleasant hour prayer!

3. Pleasant hour prayer! pleasant hour
   prayer! your move shall my request bear(#4)
   him whose truth, faithful(#2) promise wait
   soul bless. Since he bid me seek his
   face(#1), believe his word trust his grace,
   I cast-on[3] him my every worry wait for Jesus,
   pleasant hour prayer.

[1]Throne: R and L "C" hand positions, palms facing down and separated, move both hands
back in an arc toward the body, representing the arms of a large chair.
[2]Relief: May be signed as "satisfy."
[3]Cast-on: May be signed as "cast-out."

Send Me, Lord 497

Leader: Send[1] me, Lord.
1. *All:* Send me, Jesus, send me, Jesus,
   send me, Jesus, send me, Lord.

Leader: Lead me, Lord.
2. *All:* Lead me, Lord, lead me, Lord,
   lead me, Lord, lead me, Lord.

Leader: Fill me, Lord.
3. *All:* Fill me, Lord, fill me, Lord,
   fill me, Lord, fill me, Lord.

[1]Send: Should all be signed as "send"(#1).

My Prayer Rises to Heaven

Refrain:

> My prayer rise(#3) heaven, secret God
> power(#1), as smoke ascend happen precious
> incense[1] burns. Have mercy(#1) us, Lord,
> give us your grace(#1). My voice glory Lord
> God finest, as night birds sings begin day.
> This my offering God, Lord all.

1. As dry earth looks heaven for life rain,
   save flower, tree, same I rise(#3) my hands
   high prayer; defend me from all people
   themselves try hurt me.

Refrain

2. O Lord God, how I wish(#1) that I can
   live with you for remain my life; living
   your house, I would feel satisfy that my
   prayers would always your sight.

Refrain

3. O Lord God, you true love, justice(#1),
   truth; all your judgments just(#1). O Lord
   God, you truth beyond compare. Lord, you
   will(#1) I trust.

Refrain

[1]Incense: May be signed as "smell" or "sweet smell."

This ASL translation © 1995 Vietnamese Ministries

Serenity

Sunday rest, "G"-country! O calm hills[1] above,
where Jesus kneel share with you silence(#2)
eternity interpret through love. Let
your still(#2) dews[2] quiet(#2), till
all our hard work cease; take-away from our
souls, struggle, stress,[3] let our order(#1)
lives confess beauty your peace.

[1]Hill: Should be signed as a classifier, the natural motion of making a hill from the left to the right.
[2]Dew: Sign "water" then the sign for "wet," starting from the left to the right.
[3]Stress: May be signed as "pressure," Left "S" hand position, palm facing right, Right "open" hand position, palm down over the left, move right hand down, pushing the left hand down.

This ASL translation © 1995 The United Methodist Publishing House

Spirit of God, Descend upon My Heart   500

1. Spirit God, come-on[1]-my heart; cause my
   heart turn-away from earth; through all
   heart-beat;[2] help my weak, mighty(#2) as you,
   make me love you as I ought-to love.

2. I ask no dream, no prophet miracles,
   happen apart hid person body, no angel
   visit, no open sky; but take-away
   dark my soul.

3. You ask me love you, God, King? All,
   all your own, soul, heart, strength, mind.
   I see your cross; there teach my heart stay.
   O let me seek you, O let me find.

4. Teach[3] me feel that you true always near;
   teach me struggle soul bear(#4). Inspect
   rise(#2) doubt, rebel sound breath, teach me
   patience, not answer prayer.

5. Teach me love you as your angels love,
   one holy strong(#1) feel fill all my body;
   love from heaven come-down little bird, my
   heart same altar(#1), your love glow-light.

[1]Come-on: Should all be one sign directionally to the heart.
[2]Heart-beat: Should be signed at the heart all one sign with a right "A" hand position.
[3]Teach-me: Should be signed directionally coming toward body, all one sign.

501   O Thou Who Camest from Above

1. You yourself came from above, pure
   heaven light give, arouse shine-bright
   holy, love, upon humble altar my heart.

2. There let shine for your glory, shine
   with continue light, trembling[1] begin
   return, humble prayer, earnest praise.

3. Jesus, make certain my heart desire,
   work, speak, think for you; still(#1) let
   me guard holy light, still(#1) inspire[2]
   your gift me.

4. Ready for all your perfect will(#2) my
   acts faith, love repeat, till death your
   continue mercy(#1) determine, make my
   sacrifice complete(#1).

[1]Trembling: R and L "5" hand positions, palms facing body, fingers pointing down, shake both hands.
[2]Inspire: R and L flat "O" hand positions, palms facing body at the heart, fingers pointing up, move both hands up opening into "5" hand positions.

Thy Holy Wings, O Savior

1. Your holy angels, O Savior, spread
   gentle(#1) over me, let me rest free fear
   through good, bad, you. Become my strength,
   part, my support, hid place, let my every
   moment live within your grace(#1).

2. O wash me water Noah[1] clean power(#1);
   give me will(#2) spirit, heart both clean,
   good. Accept into your care(#1) your
   children, great(#2), small(#2), while we
   pleasant sleep, protect us one, all.

[1]Noah: May be signed as a Right "N" at the right cheek or any other name sign for Noah.

This ASL translation © 1995 Gracia Grindal and Lahrae Knatterud

Let It Breathe on Me

Let Holy Spirit breathe me; let Holy
Spirit breathe me; let breath Lord
now breathe me. Let Holy Spirit
breathe me; let Holy Spirit breathe
me; let breath Lord now breathe me.

This ASL translation © 1995 Martin & Morris Music, Inc.

The Old Rugged Cross

1. On hill far, found old rough cross,
   example suffer, shame; I love that old
   cross, place precious, best, for world lost
   sinners was kill.

Refrain:
   True I love old rough cross, till last(#1) I
   gave-up memory victory(#1); I will hang(#1)
   old rough cross, exchange cross some day
   for crown.

2. O that old rough cross, true despise(#1)
   through-out world, finish wonder(#2) attract
   for me; for precious Jesus, God left(#1)
   his glory above bear(#4) cross dark Calvary

Refrain

3. That old rough cross, stain with blood,
   true divine, a wonder(#2) beauty I see,
   because that old cross Jesus suffer, died,
   pardon make holy me.

Refrain

4. That old rough cross, I will(#1) ever(#3)
   stay true, cross shame, blame glad bear(#4);
   then he call(#1) me some day, my home
   far-away, place his glory forever I share.

Refrain

1. Happen our trust shake, beliefs we
   think safe, happen spirit sick seeks
   but cannot find heal, God active
   burden faith not yet full develop(#1).

2. Sun, world, one-another, void mean(#2),
   freeze spirit like(#2) stone; always our
   research lead us height not known. Faith
   must die or come full surround faith begin,
   God alone.

3. Discipline(#1) pray, happen prayer hard
   believe, hard work care(#1), happen not
   enough grieve; faith, grow learn accept
   understand we receive.

4. God true love, that way redeem(#1) us,
   Christ we crucify; that God eternity
   answer world eternity reason. May we this
   faith, grow content live, die!

506   Wellspring of Wisdom

1. Begin wisdom, hear our cry(#3). Way
   before(#3) hard, dry. We seek begin
   satisfy our thirst for make holy waters,
   wisdom for your faith fill sons, daughters.

2. Begin, New Day, fade, fear war, night.
   As carriers your loving light, we meet
   close(#2) your light, rise(#3) lights hope
   much higher.

3. Garden Grace, your gifts plenty, holy
   show all around, whole earth holy ground.
   We learn, from all life express,[1] reason grow
   sow seed(#3) bless.

4. Call(#1) Compassion, help us bring our
   ardent, need for care(#1), empty everything
   your embrace, as we endeavor proclaim your
   holy name forever.

[1]Express: R and L "S" hand positions at the heart, palms facing the body, move both hands
up and out opening both hands into "5" hand positions.

507   Through It All

Through all, through all, I finish
learned trust Jesus. I finish
learned trust God, through all,
through all, I finish learned
depend God word.

Faith, While Trees Are Still in Blossom

1. Faith, while trees still(#1) bloom,[1]
   plan pick-out fruit; faith can feel
   thrill(#2) harvest happen buds[2] begin grow.

2. Long(#1) before(#1) morning light, faith
   expect sun. Faith eager for sunrise,
   for work that must done(#2).

3. Long(#1) before(#1) rains-coming,[3] Noah[4]
   went-to build boat. Abraham, lonely
   wander(#2) saw light beyond dark.

4. Faith, support, calm water not divide
   sea, Hebrew people found path, made
   Hebrews free.

5. Faith believe that God faithful(#2);
   God will(#1) become what God will(#1)
   become. Faith accepts call(#1), respond,
   "I willing(#3), Lord, send me."

[1]Bloom: May also be signed as "flower."
[2]Bud: Should be signed as a classifier, R and L "cupped" hands together, representing a bud.
[3]Coming: Should be signed as "rain."
[4]Noah: May be signed with a right "N" at the right cheek or use any other name sign for Noah.

509   Jesus, Savior, Pilot Mel

1. Jesus, Savior, lead me through life problems; not know concerns before(#3) me, hiding like(#2) hard(#1) dangerous sea. But plans, protect come from you; Jesus, Savior, lead me.

2. As mother still(#2) her child, you can hush ocean rough; large noisy waves obey your will(#2), happen you say waves, "Be(#1) still(#1)!" Wonder(#2) conquer sea, Jesus, Savior, lead me.

3. Happen last(#1) I near your protect, fearful danger between me peace place rest, then, while depend on you, may I hear you say me, "Fear not, I will(#1) lead you."

510   Come, Ye Disconsolate

1. Come you without hope, wherever you grow weak, come mercy(#1) place, earnest kneel. Here bring your wound hearts, here tell your grief; earth no sorrow that heaven cannot heal.[1]

2. Joy lonely, light stray, hope penitent, not fade pure! Here speaks Comforter, tender(#1)[2] say, "Earth no sorrow that heaven cannot heal."

3. Here see strength life; see waters
   continue onward from throne God, pure from
   above. Come feast love; come, ever(#3) know
   earth no sorrow, but heaven can remove.

[1]Heal: Sign "make," then the sign for "well"(#2).
[2]Tender: May be signed as "warm" also.

Am I a Soldier of the Cross   511

1. I soldier cross, follower Jesus,
   will I fear accept Jesus goal, blush
   speak Jesus name?

2. Must I go-to sky, easy life
   comfort, while others fought win award
   travel(#3) through trouble seas?

3. Are(#1) there no foe for me face? Must
   I not stop over-flow? Is(#1) this bad
   world friend grace(#1), help me God?

4. Sure I must fight, if I would reign;
   increase my courage, Lord. I bear(#4) toil,
   endure pain, support through your word.

5. Your angels all this glory war, shall
   conquer, although they die; they see
   triumph(#2) from afar, through faith they
   bring near.

6. Happen that famous day shall rise(#1).
   All your Christians shine robes, victory(#1)
   through sky, glory shall yours.

512 Stand by Me

1. Happen trouble life spread, stand near
   me; happen trouble life spread, stand near
   me. Happen world disturb me, like(#2) ship
   upon-sea, you who rule wind, water,
   stand near me.

2. Midst suffer, stand near me; midst
   suffer, stand near me. Happen group(#1)
   hell(#1) attack, my strength begin fail,
   you yourself never lost battle,
   stand near me.

3. Midst fault(#1), fail(#2), stand near me;
   midst fault(#1), fail(#2), stand near me.
   Happen I finish best I can, my friends
   misunderstand, you yourself know all about
   me, stand near me.

4. Midst persecution,[1] stand near me; midst
   persecution, stand near me. Happen my foes
   war show challenge stop my way, you yourself
   save Paul,[2] Silas,[3] stand near me.

5. Happen I become old, weak, stand near me;
   happen I become old, weak, stand near me.
   Happen my life becomes burden, I near chilly
   "J"-River, O you white flower valley,
   stand near me.

[1]Persecution: May be signed "persecute" with the "X" hand positions, then reverse and sign "persecute" with the opposite "X" hands.
[2]Paul: Right "P" hand position at the temple, palm facing left, tap several times, or any other name sign for Paul.
[3]Silas: Right "S" hand position at the temple, palm facing back, tap several times or any other name for Silas.

1. Christians Christ rise(#1), dress strong(#1), strength which God gives through his eternal Son; strong(#1) Lord group(#1), his mighty-power(#1), himself strength Jesus trusts more than conqueror.

2. Stand then his great(#2) might(#1), with all his strength provide(#2), but prepare for struggle, protect God; that accomplish(#1) all things, all your conflicts passed, you may overcome through Christ alone, stand entire last(#1).

3. Pray without cease, pray, (your Captain speaks word), his summon cheerful obey, call(#1) Lord, God every want short time pray display, pray always, pray never tire, pray without cease, pray.

4. From strength, strength onward, struggle, quarrel, pray, walk all power(#1) dark, win(#1) well(#1) fight day. Still(#1) let Spirit cry(#3) all to God Christians, "Come" till Christ Lord returns from high, carry(#2).

Stand Up, Stand Up for Jesus

1. Stand-up(#2), stand-up(#2) for Jesus,
   you Christians cross; rise(#3) high his
   splendid banner, must not suffer loss.
   From victory(#1) unto victory(#1) Jesus
   shall lead Christians, till every foe
   defeated, Christ Lord indeed.

2. Stand-up(#2), stand-up(#2) for Jesus,
   call(#1) obey; onward mighty(#2) conflict,
   this his glory day. You that brave now
   serve him against many foes; let courage
   rise(#3) with danger, strength more
   strength oppose.

3. Stand-up(#2), stand-up(#2) Jesus, stand
   his strength alone; man himself will(#1)
   fail you, you challenge not trust your own.
   Accept truth protect, each part take[1] time
   for pray; happen duty call(#1) maybe danger,
   never want there.

4. Stand-up(#2), stand-up(#2) for Jesus,
   struggle will(#1) not long(#1); today, noise
   conflict,[2] tomorrow victory(#1) song. People
   themselves defeat evil, crown life shall
   win(#1); they with King Glory shall
   reign eternally.

[1]Take: Should be signed as "require."
[2]Conflict: R and L hand positions, palms out, fingers pointing up at an angel, move both up
to a point the indexes cross.

Out of the Depths I Cry to You

1. Out deep I cry(#3) you; O Lord, now hear
me call(#1). Make willing(#3) your ear my
sorrow, in-spite-of my rebel. Don't look-at[1]
my sin deeds. Send[2] me grace(#1) my spirit
needs; without grace(#1) I nothing.

2. All things you send full grace(#1); you
honor our lives with kindness. All our good
work do with pride without our Lord, Savior.
We praise God himself give us faith, save us
from control death; our lives for
God care(#1).

3. True God that we shall hope, not our own
merit; we rest our fears God good word,
trust Holy Spirit, whose promise keeps us,
strong(#1), sure; we trust holy name
write-upon-our-temple.[3]

4. My soul wait for Lord as person himself
long(#2) for morning; no watcher(#1) wait
great(#2) hope as Israel Lord, himself sends
redeem(#1) through Word. Praise God for
continue mercy(#1).

[1]Look-at: Should be signed directionally.
[2]Send: Should be signed directionally.
[3]Write-upon-our-temple: Should be signed as a classifier, write across the forehead.

This ASL translation © 1995 Lutheran Book of Worship; Augsburg Fortress

517 By Gracious Powers

1. Through gracious power(#1) true
   wonderful protect, trust wait, happen,
   no matter, we know that God with us
   all-night, all-day, never fail meet us
   each new day.

2. Yet[1] this heart through old foe pain,
   still(#1) evil days bring burden hard
   bear(#4); O give our fright soul sure
   salvation for which, O Lord, you taught
   us prepare.

3. Happen this cup you give fill with
   bitter sorrow, hard understand, we accept
   thankful, without tremble,[2] because true
   good, true love hand.

4. Yet happen this same world you give
   us again joy we had, bright your sun, we
   shall remember all days we lived since,
   our whole life shall become yours alone.

[1]Yet: In ASL this meaning is signed as "but."
[2]Tremble: R and L "5" hand positions, palms facing body, fingers pointing down, shake both hands.

O Thou, in Whose Presence

1. O God whose presence my soul inspires,[1]
   whom pain I call(#1), my comfort through
   day, my song through all-night, my hope, my
   salvation, my all.

2. Where do-you,[2] precious Shepherd, go with
   your sheep, feed them field(#2) love? Say,
   why valley death should I weep(#1) or alone
   this bare land wander(#2)?

3. O why should I wander(#2), cut-off from
   you or cry(#3) in dry land[3] for bread? Your
   foes will(#1) rejoice happen my sorrow they
   see, smile tears(#2) I finish cry(#1).

4. Make new, my precious Savior, light your
   face(#1), your soul cheering comfort give;
   let pleasant word pardon grace(#1) bring joy
   my happy heart.

5. Lord looks! ten thousand angels rejoice,
   many, many wait for Lord word. He speaks!
   eternity, fill with his voice, sounds
   praise Lord.

[1]Inspires: R and L flat "O" hand positions, palms facing body at the heart, fingers pointing
up, move both hands up opening into "5" hand positions.
[2]Do-you: Should be signed as one sign, "as a question."
[3]Land: Sign for "dirt," then the sign for "spread."

Lift Every Voice and Sing

1. Rise(#3) every voice sing, till earth,
   heaven sound, ring(#2) with music for
   liberation; let our rejoice rise(#3) high as
   listen sky, let sound loud as rolling[1] sea.
   Sing full faith that dark past finish taught
   us; sing full hope that present(#3) finish
   brought us; face(#2) rising-sun our new day
   begun, let us march-on(#1) till
   victory(#2) win(#1).

2. Stone(#1) road we walk, bitter punish
   rod, felt days happen hope finish fade; yet
   with remain calm sound, true we finish
   arrive place our past fathers cry(#3)? We
   finish walk way that with tears finish water,
   we finish come, walk our path through past
   generations died, out from gloomy past, till
   now we stand last(#1) place white shine our
   bright star shine.

3. God our weary years, God our silent(#1)
   tears(#2), you yourself finish brought us
   thus-far on-way. You yourself through your
   might(#1) led us light, care(#1) us forever
   right path, we pray. Fear our feet stray
   from places, our God, place we met you;
   fear, our hearts drunk wine, world, we forget
   you; dark beneath your hand, may we forever
   stand, true our God, true our home land.

[1]Rolling: May be signed with R and L "open" hand positions, palms facing body, fingers pointing toward each other, roll hands out clockwise.

Nobody Knows the Trouble I See

Refrain:
> No person know trouble I see, no person
> knows but Jesus; oh, no person knows
> trouble I see, glory hallelujah!

1. Sometimes I happy, Sometimes I
   depressed, Oh, yes, Lord! Sometimes I
   almost low ground, Oh, yes, Lord!

Refrain

2. Although you see me go-ahead true,
   Oh, yes, Lord, I have my troubles here
   below, Oh, yes, Lord.

Refrain

3. What makes old Satan hate-me[1] true?
   Oh, yes, Lord. Because he caught me
   past let-me-go,[2] Oh, yes, Lord.

Refrain

[1]Hate-me: Should be signed directionally, back toward the body.
[2]Let-me-go: May be signed as "part from."

521   I Want Jesus to Walk with Me

1. I want Jesus walk with me. I want Jesus walk with me. All-along[1] my journey(#3), Lord, I want Jesus walk with me.

2. My trouble, Lord, walk with me. My trouble, Lord, walk with me. Happen my heart almost break, Lord, I want Jesus walk with me.

3. Happen I trouble, Lord, walk with me. Happen I trouble, Lord, walk with me. Happen my head bow sorrow, Lord, I want Jesus walk with me.

[1]All-along: May be signed as "wander"(#2).

522   Leave It There

1. If world keep money, gold from you, you need manage with little money, just(#2) remember his word how he feed little bird, carry your burden Lord, leave burdens there.

Refrain:
Leave burden there, leave burden there, carry your burden Lord, leave burden there. If you trust, never doubt, he will(#1) sure bring you out; carry your burden Lord, leave burden there.

2. If your body suffer pain, your health
   you can't receive again, your soul almost
   low loss hope, Jesus know pain you feel, he
   can save, he can heal, carry your burden
   Lord, leave burden there.

Refrain

3. Happen your enemies attack, your heart
   begins fail, don't forget that God heaven
   answers prayer; he will(#1) make way for you,
   will(#1) lead you safe through, carry your
   burden Lord, leave burden there.

Refrain

4. Happen your youth days finished, true
   become old age, your body bow beneath burden
   worry, Lord will(#1) never leave you, he
   will(#1) go with you end(#1), carry your
   burden Lord, leave burden there.

Refrain

Saranam, Saranam   523
(Refuge)

Refrain:
   Jesus, Savior, Lord, look you, I go:
   Refuge, Refuge, Refuge; you support, my
   refuge that true higher than I:
   Refuge, Refuge, Refuge.

1. Midst foes I cry(#3) you, from end(#1)
   world, no matter I go; my strength
   helpless, O answer me:
   Refuge, Refuge, Refuge.

Refrain

2. Your house give me place live,
   beneath your arms; may I find shelter
   grace(#1); O rise(#3) me sunshine your
   face: Refuge, Refuge, Refuge.

Refrain

3. O that my vow you may pay, that
   through your faithful(#2) me everyday
   may live, your love my burdens:
   Refuge, Refuge, Refuge.

Refrain

4. Yesterday, today, forever same, look,
   heritage all themselves bear(#4) your
   name; save them from sin Savior came:
   Refuge, Refuge, Refuge.

Refrain

524   Beams of Heaven as I Go

1. Light heaven as I go, through this bare
   land[1] below, guide my feet peace ways, change
   my dark become light. Happen dark I
   will(#1) look, faith always sees star hope,
   now from all life grief, danger I shall
   free future.

Refrain:
> I don't know how long wait, not what
> future happen me, but this I know; if
> Jesus leads me, I shall arrive home future.

2. Often my sky clear, joy plenty without
   tear(#1); although day true bright begun,
   clouds may hide tomorrow sun. There will(#1)
   day that always bright, day that never yield
   night, light streets glory, I shall see future.

Refrain

3. Hard(#1) possible fight; right may often
   yield might(#1); wicked may reign
   after-a-while, Satan cause may seem gain(#2).
   There God that rules above, with hand
   power(#1), heart, love; if I right, he fight
   my battle, I shall have peace future.

Refrain

4. My burdens now may heavy, disappointment
   all-around;[2] trouble speak mournful long(#2)
   sorrow through eye-tears.[3] True many world
   place pleasure reign, no mourn soul shall wander(#2)
   land, that land peace glory, I want go future.

Refrain

[1]Land: Sign for "dirt," then the sign for "spread."
[2]All-around: Should be signed as a classifier with right open hand, palm up move from left to right in an arc.
[3]Eye-tears: Should be signed all as one sign.

We'll Understand It Better By and By

1. We tossed,[1] back forth, rough sea time;
   gloomy sky, wind often succeed bright sun;
   that land perfect day, happen light rain
   finish fade, we will(#1) understand
   better future.

Refrain

   Future, happen morning sunrise, happen
   Christians God gather(#2) heaven, we
   will(#1) tell story how we finished overcome
   for we will(#1) understand better future.

2. We often poverty(#2) life demands, want
   food, want home, thirst hills, bare lands;
   we trust Lord, according-to God word, we
   will(#1) understand better future.

Refrain

3. Trouble dark all-around,[2] we cannot
   understand all way that God would lead us
   that bless promised land;[3] but he leads us
   with his eye, we follow till we die, because
   we will(#1) understand better future.

Refrain

4. Temptations, hid trap often become not known, our heart made pain for careless word or deed, we wonder(#1) reason test happen we try do our best, but we will(#1) understand better future.

Refrain

[1]Tossed: Should be signed as a classifier, both cupped hands, palms up together to form a boat, rock hands back and forth.
[2]All-around: Should be signed as a classifier, right open hand, palm up, move from left to the right in an arc.
[3]Land: Sign for "dirt," then the sign for "spread."

What a Friend We Have in Jesus 526

1. What[1] friend we have Jesus, all our sins, griefs bear(#4). What opportunity(#5) carry every thing God prayer! O what peace we often forfeit, O what not need pain we bear(#4), all because we don't carry every thing God prayer.

2. Have we worry, temptations? Is(#1) there trouble any place? We should never be discourage(#1); carry Lord prayer. Can we find friend true faithful(#2), himself will(#1) all our sorrows share? Jesus knows our every weakness; take Lord prayer.

3. Are(#1) we weak, heavy burden, hinder with burden worry? Precious Savior, still(#1) our refuge; carry Lord prayer. Do-your friends despise(#1), leave(#2) you? Carry Lord prayer. Jesus arms he accept, protect you; you will(#1) find comfort there.

[1]What: Should be signed as "where"(#2).

527 Do, Lord, Remember Me

1. Do,[1] Lord, do, Lord, do, Lord, remember me;
   do, Lord, do, Lord, do, Lord, remember me;
   do, Lord, do, Lord, do, Lord, remember me;
   do, Lord, remember me.

2. I accept Jesus my Savior, do, Lord,
   remember me; I accept Jesus my Savior,
   do Lord, remember me; I accept Jesus my
   Savior, do, Lord, remember me; do, Lord,
   remember me.

3. Happen I trouble, do, Lord, remember me;
   happen I trouble, do, Lord, remember me;
   happen I trouble, do, Lord, remember me;
   do, Lord, remember me.

4. Happen I dying, do, Lord, remember me;
   happen I dying, do, Lord, remember me;
   happen I dying, do, Lord, remember me;
   do, Lord, remember me.

5. I have home heaven shine[2] bright than sun;
   I have home heaven shine bright than sun;
   I have home heaven shine bright than sun;
   do, Lord, remember me.

[1]Do: May be signed as "yes."
[2]Shine: Should be signed as a directional sign, and signed with both hands.

This ASL translation © 1995 The United Methodist Publishing House

1. Nearer, my God, you, nearer you!
   No-matter cross that rise(#1) me, still(#1)
   all my song shall become, nearer, my God
   you; nearer, my God, you, nearer you!

2. Although like(#1) wander(#2),
   sun-gone-down, dark over me, my rest stone;
   yet my dreams I become nearer, my God, you,
   nearer, my God, you, nearer you!

3. There let way appear(#2), steps(#2) unto
   heaven; all that you send(#2)[1] me, mercy(#1)
   give; angels call(#1) me nearer, my God, you
   nearer, my God, you, nearer you!

4. Then, with my awake thought bright with
   your praise, out my hard grief Holy place I
   praise; true through my grief become nearer,
   my God, you, nearer, my God, you, nearer you!

5. Suppose joy onward[2] faithful(#2) sky, sun,
   moon, stars forgot, up I rise(#3), still(#1)
   all my song shall become, nearer, my God,
   you; nearer, my God, you, nearer you!

[1]Send: Should be signed directionally.
[2]Onward: Should be signed directionally toward the sky.
Note: "-er" words should be signed with a right "10" and lift up after the original sign.

529 How Firm a Foundation

1. How strong(#1) foundation, you Christians,
   Lord gives for your faith his excellent word!
   What[1] more can he say than you he finish said,
   you yourself for refuge Jesus finish flee?

2. "Fear not, I with you, O you not feel
   down,[2] because I your God, will(#1) still(#1)
   give you aid; I strengthen, help you, cause
   you stand support my righteous, power hand.

3. "Happen through deep waters I call(#1) you
   go, rivers sorrow shall not overflow; because
   I will(#1) with you, your troubles bless,
   make holy you, your deep sorrow.

4. "When through emotion temptation your way
   will(#1) remain, my grace(#1), all sufficient,
   shall you provide; strong passion(#2) will(#1)
   not hurt you; I only plan your waste(#1)
   consume(#2), your gold make pure.

5. "Soul that on Jesus still(#1) depends for
   rest, I will(#1) not, I will(#1) not forsake
   foes; that soul, no matter all hell(#1)
   should endeavor shake, I will(#1) never, no,
   never, no, never forsake."

[1]What: Should be signed as "where"(#2).
[2]Feel down: R and L "5" hand positions, palms facing the body at the heart, both middle fingers touching the heart, move down.

Are Ye Able

1. "Are(#1) you able," said Jesus, "true
   crucified with me?" "Yes," strong(#1) dreamer
   answer, "death we follow you."

Refrain:
   Lord, we able. Our spirits yours. Make new
   spirits, make us like you, divine. Your
   guide bright above[1] us shall light God,
   love, loyal.

2. Are(#1) you able remember, happen
   thief(#2) lifts-up-eyes[2] that his pardon
   soul worthy place heaven?

Refrain

3. Are(#1) you able happen shadow surround
   you with ground grass,[3] believe that spirit
   triumphs(#2), commend your soul God?

Refrain

4. Are(#1) you able? Still(#1) Jesus
   whispers-down[4] eternity, brave spirits answer,
   now as past "G"-country.

Refrain

[1]Above: Should be signed above the level of the head.
[2]Lift-up-eyes: The "look" sign should be signed with both hands, moving both upwards.
[3]Grass: Should be signed from the left to the right indicating all over.
[4]Whisper-down: Should be signed as a classifier moving the head and body slightly down.

Jesus, Priceless Treasure

1. Jesus, precious store(#2) wealth, begin
   pure(#2) pleasure, true friend me, long(#2)
   my heart finish breath, till almost
   faint(#1), desire follow you. I true yours.
   Jesus yourself no fault, I will(#1) suffer
   naught(#2) hide you, ask for naught(#2)
   other than you.

2. Your arms I rest; foes themselves would
   harm me cannot touch me here. No matter
   earth shake, every heart tremble,[1] Jesus calm
   our fear; sin, hell(#1) conflict[2] cruel(#2)
   with gloom rage attack us; Jesus will(#1)
   not fail us.

3. From this life, all thoughts sadness,
   for Lord glad, Jesus, enters. People
   themselves love Father, no matter rage may
   gather(#2), still(#1) have peace; yes, no
   matter we here must bear(#4), still(#1) you
   have pure(#2) pleasure, Jesus, precious
   store(#2) wealth.

[1]Tremble: R and L "5" hand positions, palms facing body, fingers point down, shake both hands.
[2]Conflict: R and L "index" hand positions, palms facing out, fingers pointing up at the angle, move both hands up to a point the indexes cross.

533 **We Shall Overcome**

1. We shall overcome, we shall overcome, we
   shall overcome future! Oh, deep my heart I
   believe we shall overcome future!

2. We walk hand-in-hand. We will walk
   hand-in-hand.[1] We walk hand-in-hand, future.
   Oh, deep my heart I believe we shall
   overcome future!

3. We shall all become free, we shall all
   become free. We shall all become free
   future. Oh, deep my heart I believe we
   shall overcome future!

4. We shall live peace, we shall live
   peace, we shall live peace future. Oh, deep
   my heart I believe we shall overcome future!

5. Lord will(#1) see us through, Lord
   will(#1) see us through, Lord will(#1) see
   us through future. Oh, deep my heart I
   believe we shall overcome future!

[1]Hand-in-hand: Should be signed as a classifier, the natural motion of walking while holding hands.

Be Still, My Soul   534

1. Still(#2), my soul: Lord support you.
   Bear(#4) patient cross grief, pain;
   leave(#2) your God; plan provide; every
   change God faithful(#2) will(#1) remain.
   Still(#2), my soul: your best, your heaven
   friend through troubled ways leads
   joy end(#3).

2. Still(#2), my soul: your God will(#1)
   accept guide future, as past. Your hope,
   your confidence let nothing shake; all now
   secrets shall become bright finally.
   Still(#2), my soul: waves, wind still(#1)
   know Christ himself rule(#1) waves, wind
   while he lived earth.

3. Still(#2), my soul: hour haste-on,
   happen we shall forever with Lord, happen
   disappointments, grief, fear fade, sorrow
   forgot, love pure(#2) joys made new.
   Still(#2), my soul: happen change, tears
   past, all safe, bless we shall meet finally.

536   Precious Name

1. Carry name Jesus with you, child sorrow,
   grief; name will(#1) joy, comfort give you;
   carry name then wherever you go.

Refrain:
   Precious name, O how pleasant! Hope earth,
   joy heaven. Precious name, O how pleasant!
   Hope earth joy heaven.

2. Carry name Jesus ever(#3), as shield(#1)
   from every trap; if temptations surround you
   gather(#2), breathe that holy name prayer.

Refrain

3. O precious name Jesus! Name thrill our
   soul with joy, happen his loving arms
   receive us, his songs our language use.

Refrain

4. Sound Jesus name, bow, fall-for,[1] his
   feet, King, King[2] heaven, we crown him,
   happen our journey(#3) finished.

Refrain

[1]Fall-for: Should be signed as a classifier, the natural motion of falling flat on one's face.
[2]King, King: May be signed with one hand, then sign the second sign with the opposite hand.

Filled with the Spirit's Power   537

1. Fill with Spirit power(#1), with one
   accord begin church confess rise(#1) Lord.
   O Holy Spirit, church today shows your
   power(#1) fellowship.

2. Now with mind Christ inspire[1] us, that
   unity may become our great(#3) desire. Give
   joy, peace; give faith hear your call(#1),
   ready each person work for all.

3. Wide our love, good Spirit, embrace your
   strong(#1) care(#1), all people every class.
   Like(#2) wind, fire with life among us move,
   till we recognize belong Christ,
   Christian prove.

[1]Inspire: R and L flat "O" hand positions, palms facing body at the heart, fingers pointing up move both hands up opening into "5" hand positions.

538 Wind Who Makes All Winds That Blow

1. Wind itself makes all winds-blow, winds
   that blow-small-tree,[1] winds that make sea,
   waves, move mind deep valley: aim your
   breath with continue power(#1) your church,
   today, now hour. Rise(#1), make new life we
   finish lost, Spirit God Pentecost.[2]

2. Fire that feeds all fires that burn, sun
   rotate around earth, light shine rough, land,
   shine truth guide our soul; come us as past
   you came; explode holy tongues-light.[3] Light,
   Power(#1), Strength, fill your
   church continue.

3. Holy Spirit, wind, emotion, inspire[4] our
   living body; make our hearts like(#1) altar
   wood; arouse them with your own Spirit.
   Breathe, heart till our lives, our deeds,
   our ways, speak language which each nation
   through your grace(#1) shall understand.

[1]Blow-small-tree: Should be signed as a classifier, the natural motion of the bending of a tree as a result of a strong wind.
[2]Pentecost: May be signed with a right "P" hand position, palm down in the open left palm, then move right hand up.
[3]Tongue-light: May be signed as "bright," then wiggle fingers after changing into "5" hand positions.
[4]Inspire: R and L flat "O" hand positions, palms facing body at the heart, fingers pointing up move both hands up opening into "5" hand positions.

1. O Spirit living God, your bright, light
   divine, come-upon your church again, make
   church true yours. Fill church with love,
   joy, power(#1), with righteousness, peace;
   till Christ shall live people hearts, sin,
   sorrow cease.

2. Blow-winds God, with wisdom blow until
   our minds free from blurry error. Become
   gloom, doubt(#1), which blind our eyes you.
   Like(#2) burn-fire, inspire[1] our lips with
   love, zeal. Preach all your great(#3) good
   news, God glory common[2] good.

3. Teach us say living words truth which
   all may hear, language all may understand
   happen love speaks loud, clear; till every
   generation, class, country, shall join(#1)
   beliefs become one, earth shall become one
   family through whom your will(#2) done(#2).

4. True shall we know power(#1) Christ
   himself came this world save; true shall we
   rise(#1) with him life which rise(#1) above
   grave; earth shall win true holy, which
   makes your children well(#2); till perfect
   through you, we arrive world's glory goal.

[1]Inspire: R and L flat "O" hand positions, palms facing body at the heart, fingers pointing up move both hands up opening into "5" hand positions.

[2]Common: May be signed with R and L "Y" hand positions, palms facing down and separated, move both hands in a counterclockwise circle simultaneously several times.

I Love Thy Kingdom, Lord

1. I love your kingdom, Lord, house you
   dwell, church our bless redeemer(#1) save
   with his own precious blood.

2. I love your church, O God! Church
   before(#3) you found precious as you adore,
   clear impress your control(#1).

3. For church my tears shall cry(#1), for
   church my prayers spoken, church my thoughts
   toils give,[1] till toils thoughts
   shall end(#1).

4. Beyond my high joy, I value church heaven
   ways, church pleasant communion,[2] earnest vow,
   church hymn love praise.

5. Sure as your truth shall last(#3), God
   shall receive bright glory earth can yield,
   brighter joy heaven.

[1]Give: Should be signed directionally.
[2]Communion: May be signed as "fellowship."

See How Great a Flame Aspires

1. See great(#3) light aspire, inspire[1]
   through little(#2) grace(#1). Jesus love
   people enthusiasm, establish kingdoms
   bear(#4). Bring excitement earth Jesus came,
   inspire some hearts true; O that all might
   become enthusiastic, all participate
   glory joy.

2. Happen his first work begun, small,
   feeble, his day; now Word quick spread,
   now Word wins(#1) way; more, more Word
   spreads, grows, ever(#3) mighty(#2)
   triumph(#2); sin strong(#1) control(#1) now
   overthrows, shakes trembling[2] gates hell(#1).

3. Christians God, your Savior praise,
   himself finish open-door; he finish give
   word grace(#1), Jesus word glory; Jesus
   mighty(#2) redeem(#1), himself along work
   finish made; worthy work Jesus himself
   talk(#2) world from naught(#2).

4. I not see confusion develop, little as
   persons hand. Now confusion spreads over
   sky, rest over all dry land. Look, promise
   rain comes from above; but Lord will(#1)
   short-time give all spirit, his love.

[1]Inspire: R and L flat "O" hand positions, palms facing body at the heart, fingers pointing up move both hands up opening into "5" hand positions.
[2]Trembling: R and L "5" hand positions, palms facing body, fingers pointing down, shake both hands.

O Breath of Life

1. O Breath Life, come clean through us,
   revive your church with life, power(#1).
   O Breath Life, come, clean, make new us,
   make right your church meet now hour.

2. O Wind God, come, change us, break us,
   till humbly we confess our need. Then your
   tender(#3)[1] make new us, revive, give back
   for this we plea.

3. O Breath Love, come, breathe within us,
   make new thoughts, will(#2), heart. Come,
   love Christ, new win us; revive your
   church every part.

[1]Tender: May be signed at "tender"(#1) or "warm."

544   Like the Murmur of the Dove's Song

1. Like(#2) soft sing little bird song,
   like(#2) challenge little bird flight,
   like(#2) power(#1) wind, like(#2) new excite
   eager might(#1): Come, Holy Spirit, come.

2. To members Jesus fellowship, group(#1)
   found, church faith assembled, to church
   midst as gift, show: Come, Holy Spirit, come.

3. With heal division, with continue voice
   prayer, with power(#1) love, witness, with
   peace beyond compare: Come, Holy Spirit, come.

1. Church one foundation Jesus Christ our
   Lord; we his new people, through water, Word;
   from heaven he came, seek us, because we
   might ever(#3) become his; living servant
   people, through his own death place free.

2. Call(#1) from every nation, yet(#1) one
   over all world; our right(#1) salvation; one
   Lord, one faith, one birth. One holy name
   proclaim, one table eat, one hope always
   urge(#1) through Christ own Spirit led.

3. Although with scorn(#1) wonder(#1),
   world sees us burden, through division(#1)
   separate, through different belief pain,
   yet angels watch(#1) keep; their cry(#3)
   spoken, "How long?" But short time night
   weep(#1) shall become morning song.

4. Mid toil, suffer, great(#2) trouble,
   noise our war, we wait fulfill peace
   forever; till with vision[1] glory our long(#2)
   eyes bless, great(#3) church victory(#1)
   shall become church rest.

5. We now earth finish join(#1) with God
   Three One, share through faith communion[2]
   with people whose rest won. Oh, happy
   people, holy, Lord, give us grace(#1), we
   like(#1) them, patient humble,
   high may live with you.

[1]Vision: R and L "S" hand positions, palms facing down at the forehead, left in front of the right, move hands to their respective sides of the body, opening into bent "5" hand positions.
[2]Communion: May be signed as "fellowship."

O Church of God, United

1. O church God cooperative serve one
   common[1] Lord, proclaim all one meaning, with
   hearts glad accord. Christ ever(#3) go
   before(#3) us; we follow every day with
   strong(#1) eager walk along-way.[2]

2. From every land,[3] people arrange
   group(#1) appear(#2); serve one brave
   leader they come from far near. They sing
   their confess, they praise one living Lord,
   place their sure depend Jesus saving word.

3. No matter belief, language may differ,
   they speak, O Christ, you; your loving
   spirit we shall become one people. Lord,
   may our faith service, only-one aim proclaim
   all power(#1) your redeem(#1) name.

4. May your great(#3) prayer true answer
   that we may all become one, close bound,
   through love cooperate you, God bless Son;
   bring only-one witness, make way bright,
   soul which search dark may find true light.

[1]Common: R and L "Y" hand positions, palms facing down and separated, move both hands simultaneously in a counterclockwise circle, several times.
[2]Along-way: Should be signed as a classifier, right "index" hand position, palm facing out, finger pointing up, move outward, not zig-zagging as much as "wander."
[3]Land: Sign "dirt," then the sign for "spread."

In Christ There Is No East or West   548

1. In Christ[1] there no east, west, him no
   south, north; but one great(#3) fellowship
   love throughout all world.

2. In Christ shall true hearts every place
   their high fellowship find; his service
   like(#1) gold cord join(#1) people together.

3. In Christ neither Jew, Greek, neither
   slave, free; both male, female generations
   true become kin me.

4. In Christ now meet both east, west, him
   meet south, north; all Christian people true
   become one him through-out all world.

[1]In Christ: Since "In Christ" is in the title, the authors suggest that interpreters drop the "In" and sign only "Christ."

This ASL translation © 1995 The United Methodist Publishing House

Where Charity and Love Prevail   549

1. Place charity love strong(#1), there God
   ever(#3) found; bring here together
   through Christ love, through love
   that way we bound.

2. With grateful joy, holy fear true charity
   we learn; let us with heart, mind, strength
   now love Christ, exchange.

3. Forgive us now each other's faults as we
   confess our faults; let us love each other
   well(#1) Christian holy.

4. Let struggle among us not happen, let
   all quarrel cease; Christ glory that
   we seek, our glory his holy peace.

5. Let us remember that our midst lives
   God own Son; as members his church
   join(#1), we in him made one.

6. Love can exclude no group(#1), belief
   if honor true God name; our
   common[1] life embrace all whose Maker same.

[1]Common: May be signed with R and L "Y" hand positions, palms facing down and separated, move both hands in a counterclockwise circle simultaneously several times.

550   Christ, from Whom All Blessings Flow

1. Christ, from whom all bless come, perfect
   Christian below, hear us, your world share,
   your secret body true.

2. Join(#1) us, one spirit join(#2), let us
   still(#1) receive you, still(#1) for more you
   we call(#1), you yourself fill all.

3. Move influence guide, different gifts
   each divide(#1); place accord your will(#2),
   let us all our work fulfill;

4. Never from your service move, need each
   other prove; use grace(#1) each give, soft
   through skill God.

5. Many we now, one, we ourselves Jesus
   accept; true many neither bond, free,
   male, female, Lord, you.

6. Love, like(#1) death, finish all destroy,
   made all difference empty; names, religion
   group(#1), participants fall; you,
   O Christ, true all.

Awake, O Sleeper 551

1. Awake, O sleeper, rise(#1) from dead,
   Christ shall give you light; true learn his
   love, wide, breath, love full,
   deep, height(#2).

2. People earth, he came bring from sin,
   fear free, give Spirit unity,
   very bond peace.

3. There one group(#1), one hope, one
   Spirit, one call(#1), one Lord, one faith,
   one baptism, one Father us all.

4. Then walk love as Christ finish love,
   himself died that he might save; with kind,
   hearts forgive as God Christ forgave.

5. For us Christ lived, for us he died,
   conquered struggle. Awake, rise(#1),
   forward faith, Christ shall give you life.

1. Here, O Lord, your servants gather(#2),
   hand we join with hand;[1] look toward(#3) our
   Savior cross, join(#2) love we stand. As we
   seek kingdom God, we unite pray; Jesus,
   Savior, guide our step(#1),
   because you guide.

2. Many languages we speak, scattered lands,[2]
   yet our hearts one God, hearts love demands.
   However(#2) dark hope appear(#2), call(#1)
   old, youth; Jesus teacher, live with us,
   because you Truth.

3. World secrets open-wide, changes never
   cease. Where, oh where, can weary souls find
   giver peace? Unto all people pain trouble,
   separate through continue struggle; Jesus,
   healer, bring you heal, because you life.

4. Give, O God, age made new, filled with
   eternity, love; help us as we work, pray,
   send us from above truth, courage, faith,
   power(#1), need our struggle; Jesus, Manager,
   become our Guide, our Truth, our Life.

[1]Hand we join with hand: Should be signed as a classifier, the natural motion of walking hand in hand.
[2]Lands: Sign "dirt," then the sign for "spread."

And Are We Yet Alive

1. Are(#1) we yet(#1) alive, see each
   other face(#1)? Glory thanks Jesus give
   for his almighty grace(#1)!

2. Preserve through power(#1) divine full
   salvation here, again Jesus praise we
   join(#1), his sight appear(#2).

3. What trouble we see, what mighty(#2)
   conflicts[1] past, fight without, fears within,
   since we assemble last(#1)!

4. Yet(#1) out-all Lord finish bring us
   through his love; still(#1) he accomplish
   his help give, hide our life above.

5. Then let us make our boast his
   redeem(#1) power(#1), which saves us very
   great(#2) limit, till we can sin no more.

6. Let us take-up cross till we obtain
   award, glad reckon all things loss true
   we may Jesus gain.

[1]Conflicts: R and L "index" hand positions, palms facing out, fingers pointing up at an angle,
move both hands up to a point the indexes cross.

This ASL translation © 1995 The United Methodist Publishing House

All Praise to Our Redeeming Lord

1. All praise our redeem(#1) Lord, himself
   join(#1) us through his grace(#1), bid us,
   each other made new, together seek his face.

2. Jesus bid us build-up each other,
   gather(#2) become one, our high call(#1)
   glory hope we hand-in-hand[1] onward.

3. Gift which he give, we all delight prove
   grace(#1) through every ability comes,
   pure(#2) change love.

4. However now we think speak same, cordial
   agree, center all, through Jesus name,
   perfect cooperation.

5. We all share joy Jesus, common[2] peace
   we feel, peace feel mind not known, joy
   not express.[3]

6. If our fellowship earth Jesus true
   pleasant, what height(#2) joy shall we know
   happen surround his throne[4] we meet.

[1]Hand-in-hand: Should be signed as a classifier, the natural motion of walking hand-in-hand.
[2]Common: R and L "Y" hand positions, palms facing down and separated, move both hands simultaneously in a counterclockwise circle several times.
[3]Express: R and L "S" hand positions at the heart, palms facing the body, move both hands up and down opening hands into "5" hand positions.
[4]Throne: R and L "C" hand positions, palms facing down and separated, move both hands back in an arc toward the body, indicating the arms of a large chair.

Forward Through the Ages

1. Forward through age(#2) not broken line,
   move faithful(#2) spirit happen call(#1)
   divine; gifts different measure, hearts one
   accord, with many service, one sure award.

Refrain:
   Forward through age(#2), not broken line
   move faithful(#2) spirit happen
   call(#1) divine.

2. Wide-grows[1] kingdom, reign love light;
   because we must work, till our faith become
   sight. Prophets finish proclaim, people
   suffer, testimony, poets sing glory,
   important people died for call(#1)

Refrain

3. Not alone we conquer, not alone we fall;
   each loss or triumph(#1), lose or
   triumph(#1) all. Bound through God purpose,
   one living whole, move forward together,
   shine goal.

Refrain

[1]Wide-grows: Should be signed as a classifier, R and L "C" hand positions, palms facing each other and separated, move both hands up to their respective sides, in a large, funnel-like motion.

557   Blest Be the Tie That Binds

1. Bless tie-binds our hearts Christian
   love; fellowship like(#2) minds same
   that above.

2. Before(#3) our Father throne[1] we say our
   eager prayers; our fears, our hopes, our
   aims one, our comforts, our care(#1).

3. We share each other's grief, our common[2]
   burdens-bear(#4); often for each other
   comes sympathetic tear(#1).

4. When we separate, give us pain; but we
   shall still(#1) join(#1) heart,
   hope meet again.

[1]Throne: R and L "C" hand positions, palms facing down and separated, move both hands back in an arc toward the body, indicating the arms of a large chair.
[2]Common: May be signed with R and L "Y" hand positions, palms facing down and separated, move both hands in a counterclockwise circle simultaneously several times.

558   We Are the Church

Refrain:
I true church! You true church! We true
church together! All themselves follow Jesus,
all around[1] world! Yes, we
true church together!

1. Church not building, church not steeple,[2]
   church not rest place, church true
   group(#1) people.

Refrain

2. We true many various people, with many
   various faces, all colors, all ages, same,
   from all generations, places.

Refrain

3. Sometimes church march(#1), sometimes
   church brave ambitious(#1), sometimes church
   control, sometimes hide, always learn.

Refrain

4. Happen people gather(#2), there singing
   there pray, there laugh, there cry(#1)
   sometimes, all people saying:

Refrain

5. Day Pentecost[3] some people receive Holy
   Spirit, told Good News through world, all
   themselves would listen.

Refrain

[1]Around: Should be signed as a classifier, the natural movement of a large globe, using R and
L cupped "C" hand positions, palms down, arc both out, down then back together.
[2]Steeple: Should be signed as a classifier, make a natural large skinny steeple with "indexes"
or "open" hands.
[3]Pentecost: May be signed with a right "P," palm down in the left open hand position, move
the right up.

559   Christ Is Made the Sure Foundation

1. Christ made sure foundation, Christ head[1]
   church; chosen Lord, precious, bind all
   church become one; holy God help forever,
   church confidence alone.

2. This temple, place we call(#1) you come,
   O Lord group(#1), today! With your
   faithful(#2) love kind, hear your people as
   they pray, your full bless shine within
   temple always.

3. Here give all your servants what they
   ask you receive; what they receive from you
   forever with bless keep, from-now-on your
   glory ever(#3) with you reign.

4. Praise, honor Father, praise, honor Son,
   Praise honor Spirit, ever(#3) three,
   ever(#3) one; one might(#1), one glory,
   while continue generations.

[1]Head: Should be signed with a right "10" hand position, lifting the hand higher than the head.

560   Help Us Accept Each Other

1. Help us accept each other like(#2)
   Christ accept us; teach us as sister,
   brother, each person embrace. Be(#1)
   present among us, Lord, help us believe we
   ourselves you accept, we need love, live.

2. Teach us, O Lord, your lessons, as our
   daily life we struggle become people, search
   for hope, faith. Teach us care(#1) people,
   for all people, not only some, love them as
   we find them, as they may become.

3. Let your accept change us, true that we
   may become inspire[1] through live situations,
   do truth, love; practice your accept, until
   we know through heart rules forgive,
   laughter heal skills.

4. Lord, for today experience with all
   themselves need, themselves hunger accept,
   for righteousness, bread, we need new eyes
   for see, new hands for hold-on; make new us
   with your Spirit; Lord, free us,
   make us become one.

[1]Inspire: R and L flat "O" hand positions, palms facing body at the heart, fingers pointing up
move both hands up opening into "5" hand positions.

Jesus, United by Thy Grace   561

1. Jesus, unite through your grace(#1) each
   make precious, with confidence we seek your
   face(#1), know our prayer heard.

2. Help us help each-other, Lord,
   each-other cross bear(#4); let all their
   friendly aid give, feel each-other care(#1).

3. Up-to-you,[1] our live God, let us all
   things grow; till you finish made us free,
   indeed clean here below.

4. Touch[2] through strong(#1) attract your
   love, let all our hearts agree, ever(#3)
   face(#2) each-other,[3] ever(#3) move
   before(#3) you.

5. You, not separate, join(#1), let all our
   spirits faithful(#2); O may we all love mind
   that you receive.

6. This bond perfect, your pure(#2) kind;
   O let us, still(#1) we pray, have mind that
   like(#2) yours.

[1]Up-to-you: Should be signed directionally.
[2]Touch: Should be signed at the heart.
[3]Each-other: Should be one sign only.

562   Jesus, Lord, We Look to Thee

1. Jesus, Lord, we look you; let us your
   name agree; show yourself, Prince Peace, bid
   our struggle forever cease.

2. Through your make friendly love, every
   barrier remove; each unite, make precious;
   come, spread your banner here.

3. Make us become one heart, mind, gentle,
   courteous, kind, humbly, thought, word,
   altogether like(#2) our Lord.

4. Let us for each-other[1] care(#1),
   each-other burden-bear(#4); your church
   example give,[2] show how true believers live.

5. Free from anger, from pride, God let us
   live that way; all depths love express,[3]
   all height(#2) holy.

6. Let us then with joy transfer(#2) family
    above; like(#2) wings angels-fly, show how
    true believers die.

[1]Each-other: Should be signed as one sign.
[2]Give: Should be signed directionally.
[3]Express: R and L "S" hand positions at the heart, palms facing the body, move both hands
up and out opening hands into "5" hand positions.

This ASL translation © 1995 The United Methodist Publishing House

Father, We Thank You   563

1. Father, we thank you, for you placed[1]
    your holy name within our hearts. Knowledge
    faith, life continue Jesus your Son, us give.

2. Lord, you finish made all for your
    pleasure, give[2] us food for all our days,
    give Christ strength eternity; your
    power(#1), your praise.

3. Watch(#1) care(#1) your church, O Lord,
    mercy(#1), save church from evil, guard
    church still(#1); make perfect church with
    your love, united church clean, make same
    become your will(#2).

4. As seed(#3), once scattered-all-over[3]
    ground, same broken bread become one, true
    from all lands[4] your church, gather(#2) your
    kingdom through your Son.

[1]Place: Should be signed at the heart.
[2]Give: Should be signed directionally.
[3]Scatter-all-over: Should be signed as one sign.
[4]Lands: Sign for "dirt," then the sign for "spread."

This ASL translation © 1995 The Church Pension Fund

Father, We Thank You

1. Father, we thank you, for you place[1] your
holy name within our hearts. Know, faith,
life eternity Jesus your Son us give.[2] Lord,
you finish made all for your pleasure, give
us food for all our days, give Christ
strength eternity; your power(#1),
become your praise.

2. Watch(#1) care(#1) your church, O Lord,
mercy(#1), save church from evil, guard
church still(#1); perfect church your love,
unite church clean, make same become your
will(#2). Like seed(#3), once
scatter-all-over[3] ground, same broken bread
become one, true from all lands[4] your church
gather(#2) your kingdom through your Son.

[1]Place: Should be signed at the heart.
[2]Give: Should be signed directionally.
[3]Scatter-all-over: Should be signed as one sign.
[4]Lands: Sign for "dirt," then the sign for "spread."

566 Blest Be the Dear Uniting Love

1. Bless precious unite love that will(#1)
not let us separate; our bodies may remove,
we still(#1) one heart.

2. Join(#1) one spirit our God, place God
show we go, still(#1) Jesus guide walk,
do Jesus work below.

3. O may we ever(#3) walk him, know nothing
   else, no other desire, no other consider,
   but Jesus crucified.

4. We all one Jesus himself receive, with
   each-other agree, him One, Truth, we live;
   bless true unity.

5. Receiver Savior grace(#1), same mind,
   heart, not joy, not grief, not time, not
   place, not life, not death can separate.

Heralds of Christ   567

1. Announce Christ himself presents King
   command, continue life inform your living
   hands, inform carry quick news you bring;
   make straight, make straight way King.

2. Through dry land-all-over,[1] dark wet land,
   deep soft ground, through forest, rough seas,
   mountain valley, build now road, not
   wander(#2), not stay; prepare across
   earth King way.

3. Lord, give us faith, strength build road,
   see promise day fulfill, happen war shall
   no more, struggle shall cease,
   way Prince Peace.

[1]Land-all-over: Sign "dirt," then the sign for "spread," then the sign for "over" all as one continuous sign.
Note: All directional verbs should be signed in the direction of the meaning in the hymn.

Christ for the World We Sing

1. Christ for world we sing, world Christ
   we bring, with love zeal; poor, them that
   faint(#1) burden, sin sick, sorrow, whom
   Jesus true heal.

2. Christ for world we sing, world Christ
   we bring, with earnest prayer; wander(#2)
   lost, through restless passions move,
   redeem(#1) much require, from dark loss hope.

3. Christ for world we sing, world Christ
   we bring, with one accord; with us work
   share, with us danger brave, with us cross
   bear(#4), for Christ our Lord.

4. Christ for world we sing, world Christ
   we bring, with joy song; newborn Christians
   whose days, return from error way, inspire[1]
   with hope, praise, Christ belong.

---

[1]Inspire: R and L flat "O" hand positions, palms facing body at the heart, fingers pointing up, move both hands up opening into "5" hand positions.

We've a Story to Tell to the Nations

1. We story tell people, that shall change
   their hearts right, story truth mercy(#1),
   story peace light, story peace light.

Refrain:

   For dark will(#1) change sunrise, sunrise
   change noonday bright; Christ great(#3)
   kingdom will(#1) come earth,
   kingdom love, light.

2. We song-sung people, that shall inspire[1]
   their hearts Lord, song that shall conquer
   evil, destroy spear, sword, destroy spear,[2]
   sword.

Refrain

3. We word, word, word, give people, that
   Lord himself reign above finish sent us his
   Son save us, show us that God true love,
   show us that God love.

Refrain

4. We Savior show people, himself path
   sorrow finish walk, that all world great(#3)
   peoples might come truth God, might
   come truth God.

Refrain

[1]Inspire: R and L flat "O" hand positions, palms facing body at the heart, fingers pointing up, move both hands up opening into "5" hand positions.
[2]Spear: Should be signed as a classifier, the natural motion of throwing a spear.

Go, Make of All Disciples

1. "Go, make all disciples." We hear call(#1),
   O Lord, that comes from you, our Father,
   your eternal Word. Inspire[1] our ways learn
   through earnest prayer, let our daily living
   show you every place.

2. "Go, make all disciples," baptize name
   Father, Son, Spirit, generation, generation
   same. We call(#1) each new disciple follow
   you, Lord, redeem(#1) soul, body
   through water, Word.

3. "Go, make all disciples." We your feet
   would stay until each life vocation
   emphasizes your holy way. We improve life
   God places every person heart, show through
   our witness direct(#1) teacher skill.

4. "Go, make all disciples." We welcome your
   command. "See, I am with you always." We
   accept your guide hand. Task appear(#2)
   large before(#3) us; we follow without fear;
   heaven, earth your power(#1) shall bring
   God kingdom here.

[1]Inspire: R and L flat "O" hand positions, palms facing body at the heart, fingers pointing up move both hands up opening into "5" hand positions.

Pass It On

572

1. Only require tiny(#1) bright start
   fire(#1)-burn, short time all those surround
   can warm-up[1] near fire. That same with God
   love once you finish experience love; you
   spread God love everyone; you want
   pass-it-on.[2]

2. What[3] wonderful time(#2) spring(#1),
   happen all trees budding;[4] birds begin sing,
   flowers start flower-bloom. That same with
   God love once you finish experience love;
   you want sing, love new like(#2) spring(#1),
   you want pass-it-on.

3. I wish(#1) for you, my friend, this
   happy that I finish found; you can depend
   him no matter place you go. I shout from
   mountain-top; I want my world know; Lord
   love finish come-me,[5] I want pass-it-on.

[1]Warm-up: Should be signed as a classifier, the natural motion of standing with both hands held out in front, palms out, fingers up, warming before a fire.
[2]Pass-it-on: Should be signed as a classifier, the natural motion of the right flat "O" hand from the left, moving around to the right, passing something along to each person.
[3]What: Should be signed as "where"(#2).
[4]Budding: Should be signed as a classifier, R and L "cupped" hands together, beginning from the left, open and close hands several times as they are moved around to the right.
[5]Come-me: Should be signed as "meet" and directionally coming from God meeting you.

O Zion, Haste

1. O God, haste your mission fulfill, tell
   all world that God light, that himself
   made all people, not willing(#3) one
   person should perish, lost dark night.

Refrain:
   Let-know(#1) glad tidings, tidings peace;
   tidings Jesus, redemption(#1) free(#2).

2. See how-many thousands still(#1) rest
   bound dark, like(#2) prison house sin, with
   none tell them Savior dying, tell life he
   died for them win(#1).

Refrain

3. Proclaim every people, language people
   that God, whom they live move, love; tell
   how he humbled himself save his lost world,
   died on-cross that we might live above.

Refrain

4. Give your own, bear(#4) word, word,
   glory; give your abundance, succeed them
   on-way; express[1] your soul for them prayer
   victory(#1); O God finish bring
   brighter day.

Refrain

[1]Express: R and L "S" hand positions at the heart, palms facing the body, move both hands
up and out opening hands into "5" hand positions.

Onward, Christian Soldiers

1. Onward Christian soldiers, march(#1) as
   war, with cross Jesus go-ahead before(#3).
   Christ King manager, leads against foe;
   forward battle see his banner-go!

Refrain:

   Onward Christian soldiers, march(#1) as war,
   with cross Jesus go-ahead before(#3).

2. First show triumph(#1), Satan class
   finish flee; Christian soldiers, onward
   victory(#1)! Hell(#1) foundations tremble,[1]
   shouts praise; brothers, rise(#3) your
   voices, loud your music sounds.

Refrain

3. Like(#2) mighty(#2) army moves church
   God; brothers, we walk place angels finish
   walk. We not divided, all one group(#1),
   one hope, belief, one charity.

Refrain

4. King, throne may perish(#2), kingdoms
   establish, kingdoms fade, but church Jesus
   will(#1) remain. Gate hell(#1) cannot
   against that church exist.

Refrain

5. Onward then, you people, join(#3) our
happy group(#1), join(#1) with ours your
voices triumph(#1) song. Glory, praise,
honor unto Christ, King, this through
continue generations men, angels sing.

Refrain

[1]Tremble: R and L "5" hand positions, palms facing body, fingers pointing down, shake
hands several times.

576   Rise Up, O Men of God

1. Rise-up(#1), O men God! Have finished
with less(#2) things. Give heart, mind,
soul, strength serve King, kings.[1]

2. Rise-up(#1), O men God! Kingdom remain
long. Bright day fellowship, end(#1)
all-night wrong.

3. Rise-up(#1) O men God! Church for you
wait, church strength not equal, church
task; rise-up(#1), make church great(#3)!

4. Rise(#3) high cross Christ! Walk place
his feet finish walk. As brothers, Son Man,
rise-up(#1), O men God!

[1]King, kings: May be signed with one hand, then sign the second sign with the opposite
hand.

God of Grace and God of Glory

1. God-grace(#1), God glory, your people
   give your power(#1); honor your long-ago
   church story bring church tiny(#1) begin
   to glory. Give us wisdom, give us courage,
   for face(#2) now hour, for face(#2) now hour.

2. Look! group(#1) evil surround us,
   scorn(#2) your Christ, attack his ways!
   Fears, doubts, long(#2) finish bound us; free
   our hearts, work, praise. Give us wisdom,
   give us courage, for live now days,
   for live now days.

3. Heal your children conflict[1] great(#2)
   rage, yield our pride your control; shame
   our reckless, selfish glad, value thing,
   poor soul. Give us wisdom, give us courage,
   else we miss your kingdom goal, else we
   miss your kingdom goal.

4. Save us from weak accept, evils we hate;
   let search for your salvation become our
   glory ever(#3). Give us wisdom, give us
   courage serve you whom we adore, serving
   you whom we adore.

[1]Conflict: R and L "index" hand positions, palms facing out, fingers pointing up at an angle, move both up to a point the indexes cross.

578   God of Love and God of Power

1. God love, God power(#1), give us
   present(#3) excite hour, grace(#1) ask these
   gifts from you, brave hearts, spirits free.
   God love, God power(#1), you finish call(#1)
   us for present(#3) hour.

2. We not first banish through fears from
   you; give us courage, let us see heaven
   proclaim clear. God love, God power(#1),
   you finish call(#1) us for present(#3) hour.

3. All our lives belong-to you, you our
   final loyal; we slaves happen we share that
   faithful(#2) every place. God love, God
   power(#1), you finish call(#1) us for
   present(#3) hour.,

4. God love, God power(#1), make us worthy
   present(#3) hour; offer lives if your
   will(#2), keep free our spirits still(#1).
   God love, God power(#1), you finish call(#1)
   us for present(#3) hour.

579   Lord God, Your Love Has Called Us Here

1. Lord God, your love finish call(#1) us,
   through love, for love made your living
   like(#2) continue we share, no matter
   mar(#1), not honor, disobey; we come, with
   all our heart, mind, your call(#1) see,
   your love find.

2. We come ourselves pains, broken trust,
   choose wrong, part free, part bound through
   habits, through live forces move onward
   through power(#1), systems close keep, yet
   seek hope for people.

3. Lord God, Christ you call(#1) our name,
   then receive us as your own; not through
   some merit, right(#1), demand, but through
   your gracious love alone; we try catch short
   look your mercy(#1) place, find you
   kneel our feet.

4. Then accept towel, break bread, humble
   us, call(#1) us friends; suffer, serve till
   all satisfy, show how grand(#1) love intend
   work till all world sings, fill all worlds,
   honor all things.

5. Lord God, Christ you free us live your
   life, your joy share; give us your Spirit
   liberation change from guilt, loss hope,
   offer all that faith can do, while love
   make all things news.

Lead On, O King Eternal 580

1. Lead onward, O King eternity, day
   march(#1) arrive; as areas conquer tent
   shall become our home. Through days
   prepare, your grace(#1) finish made us
   strong(#1); now, O King eternity, we
   rise(#3) our battle song.

2. Lead onward, O King eternity, till sin
   rage war shall cease, holy shall whisper
   pleasant amen, peace. For not with swords
   loud conflict,[1] not continue excite sound,
   with deeds love, mercy(#1) heaven
   kingdom comes.

3. Lead onward, O King eternity, we follow,
   not with fears, for glad begin like(#2)
   morning, place your face(#1) appears(#2).
   Your cross rise(#3) over us, we journey(#3)
   light cross; honor(#1) waits conquer;
   lead onward, O God might(#1).

[1]Conflict: R and L "index" hand positions, palms facing out, fingers pointing up at an angle,
move both up to a point the indexes cross.

581   Lord, Whose Love Through Humble Service

1. Lord, your love through humble service
   bear(#4) weight people need, yourself
   on-cross, abandon(#1) offer mercy(#1)
   perfect deed: we your servants bring worship
   not voice alone, but heart, make holy your
   purpose every gift that you give.

2. Still(#1) your children wander(#2) no(#1)
   home; still(#1) hungry cry(#3) for bread;
   still(#1) grief we mourn our dead. As, O Lord,
   your real pity heal sick free soul, use love
   your spirit arouse still(#1) save make us whole.

3. As we worship, give us vision(#2) till
   your love display light height depth
   great(#3) begin upon our quick sight, make

known needs burdens your compassion bids us
bear(#4) inspire[1] us never cease struggle
your abundant life share.

4. Call(#1) through worship unto service,
   forward your precious name we meet child,
   youth, aged(#1), love deeds show; hope
   health, good will(#2) comfort, counsel, aid,
   peace we give, that your servants, Lord,
   with free may your mercy(#1) know, live.

[1]Inspire: R and L flat "O" hand positions, palms facing body at the heart, fingers pointing
up, move both hands up opening into "5" hand positions.

Whom Shall I Send? 582

1. Whom will(#1) I send? our Maker cry(#3);
   many happen hear God voice, sure need their
   vocation do; but many avoid that choice.

2. For who can serve God true pure, require,
   speak same name, while doubt makes every
   step(#1) not sure, self confuses every aim?

3. Yet, believe God himself call(#1), knows
   what we are(#1), what still(#1) may become,
   our past defeat, our future arrive we brave
   answer: Lord, send me!

4. People themselves God call(#1), God
   pure(#2), daily give us strength
   pay-attention our thoughts, our skills, our
   power(#1), life itself this end(#1).

Sois la Semilla
(You Are the Seed)

1. You person that will(#1) grow new
Christian; you star that will(#1) shine
through all-night; you yeast[1] tiny(#1) salt,
bright shine dark. You begin that will(#1)
bring new day; you wheat[2] that will(#1) grow
gold grain; you pain, soft gently touch,
my witness wherever you go.

Refrain:

Go, my friends, go world, proclaim love all,
bring word my forgive peace, eternity love.
Be(#1) my friends, loyal witness, from dead I rise(#1);
"See, I with you forever, till end(#1) world."

2. You bright that will(#1) light dark,
send[3] shine hope, faith, love; you shepherds
lead whole world through valley, field(#2)
peace. You friends that I chose for myself,
word that I want proclaim. You new kingdom
built on-rock place justice(#1), truth always reign.

Refrain

3. You life that will(#1) care(#1) grow;
you wave(#1) rough sea; yesterday yeast
begin rise,[4] new loaf[5] will(#1) bake. There no
place for city hide, not mountain can cover
might(#1); may your good deeds show world
loss hope path that will(#1) lead all God.

Refrain

[1]Yeast: Should be signed as a classifier, natural swelling of the bread.
[2]Wheat: The sign for "grain" may be signed.
[3]Send: Should be signed directionally.
[4]Rise: Should be signed as a classifier, the natural rising of the bread.
[5]Loaf: Should be signed as a classifier, the R and L "C" hand positions, palms facing down, move to the respective sides, indicating a loaf of bread.

Lord, You Give the Great Commission

1. Lord, you give great(#3) command: "heal[1]
   sick, preach word." Else church neglect
   mission(#1), gospel(#2) not heard, help us
   witness your purpose with make new honest.

Refrain:
   With Spirit gifts power(#1) us
   for work ministry.[2]

2. Lord, you call(#1) us your service: "In
   my name baptize, teach." That world may
   trust your promise, life abundance meant for
   each, give us all new zeal, draw(#2) us
   closer community(#2).

Refrain

3. Lord, you make common[3] holy: "This my
   body, this my blood." Let us all for world
   true glory, daily rise(#3) life heaven, ask
   that world surround us share your
   children liberation.

Refrain

4. Lord, you show us love true measure:
   "Father what people do, forgive." Yet we
   save(#2) as private wealth all that you free
   give. May your care(#1), mercy(#1) lead us
   just(#1) group(#1) people.

Refrain

5. Lord, you bless with words make certain:
   "I true with you end(#1)." Faith, hope, love
   make new, may we serve as you intend, amid
   worry that require us, keep mind eternity.

Refrain

[1]Heal: Sign "make" then the sign for "well"(#2).
[2]Ministry: May be signed with a right "M," palm down over the back of the left wrist, move
right up and down several times as in sign for "work."
[3]Common: R and L "Y" hand positions, palms facing down and separated, move both hands
simultaneously in a counterclockwise circle several times.

585   This Little Light of Mine

1. This[1] little(#1) light[2] mine, I let shine,[3]
   this little(#1) light mine, I let shine;
   this little(#1) light mine, I let shine,
   let shine, let shine, let shine.

2. Every place I go, I let shine,
   every place I go, I let shine,
   every place I go, I let shine,
   let shine, let shine, let shine.

3. All through all-night, I let shine,
   all through all-night, I let shine,
   all through all-night, I let shine,
   let shine, let shine, let shine.

[1]This: Should be signed as a classifier, left "index," palm facing right, finger pointing up,
right "Y," palm down, move toward left index, indicating that particular one.
[2]Light: Left "5" hand position, palm facing right, fingers pointing up and wiggling. Right
"index" hand position, palm down, finger touching the heel of the left hand.
[3]Let shine: Should be first signed to the left, then the second time in front, and the third time
sign to the right, indicating shining all over, move the body slightly to the left, turn, then to
the right.

1. "Let my people seek their freedom,
   wilderness[1] while, from slave Egypt,[2] from
   poor houses near "N"-river": God spoke from
   "S"-mountain, God spoke, done(#2), people
   cross Red Sea waters toward rising sun.

2. "Let my people seek their freedom,
   wilderness while, from age(#1) holy place,
   building, from quiet places close world":
   same Son God finish speak, rage, suspect(#1),
   spread-out, for God people must scatter,
   become servant through world.

3. Happen we continue sound on-mountains
   for old Egyptian plains,[3] happen we miss our
   old bondage, hope, promise, decrease
   power(#1), then rock shall yield water, bread
   fall[4] through all-night, with vision(#2)
   future we shall march(#1) toward light.

4. Confusion world, journey(#3) into-space,
   conflict generations, hunger for grace(#1),
   our agony, glory, we call(#1), new ways
   through Lord our tomorrow, God our today.

[1]Wilderness: May be signed using the sign for "bare"(#2), with the exception of using both hands moving respectively to their sides, then sign "spread."
[2]Egypt: May also be signed with a right "X," palm facing out at the forehead.
[3]Plains: May be signed as "spread," indicating flat all over.
[4]Fall: Should be signed as "fall"(#4), but sign with both hands, repeating the movements several times, starting from above the head, then moving down.

587   Bless Thou the Gifts

Bless your gifts our hands
finish brought; bless your work
our hearts finish plan.
Our true faith, will(#2), thought;
all, O God, in your hand.

588   All Things Come of Thee

All things come from you,
O Lord; from your own we
finish give you.

589   The Church of Christ, in Every Age

1. Church Jesus every generation, surround
   through change, but Spirit led, must demand,
   examine heritage, keep rise(#1) from dead.

2. Around[1] world, across street, people
   themselves injustice, cry(#3) for shelter,
   for bread eat, never live until they die.

3. Then let servant church rise(#1),
   care(#1) church that long(#2) share Christ
   sacrifice, surround church Christ humanity.

4. For he alone, himself blood spread, can heal our sin, teach us share our bread, feed starve people.

5. We have no mission but serve full obedience our Lord, care(#1) all, without reserve(#3), spread his liberation word.

[1]Around: Should be signed as a classifier, the natural motion of making a globe with the R and L "C" hand positions.

Christ Loves the Church   590

1. Christ love church, with grace(#1) above all expect. We bear(#4) his name, for all world see. He will(#1) not let us go, not let us be(#1), but choose clay vessels[1] for his worth.

2. Christ bear(#4) church, corrupt, act like(#2) obsess[2] with little(#2) things, bless greedy, war. Jesus love more cleaver for us, change bad become good, through angels, prophets, praying, become better.

3. Christ satisfy church, fills us with vision,[3] through praise, preach, wine, broken bread, share people, doing what people said, themselves win(#1) world respect, opposite.

4. Christ needs church, live, tell his
    story, praise his love, marvel his trust,
    till church shine bright, awake from earth,
    we walk with God alive grace(#1), glory.

[1]Vessels: Should be signed as a classifier, may be signed like "form," or right "Y," palm facing the body, twist wrist down to the left, or any other signs representing a container.
[2]Obsess: Sign "think" then change the right to the "feel" hand position, with the middle finger on the back of the left, move both hands in a clockwise circle several times, indicating mind dwelling on something.
[3]Vision: R and L "S" hand positions, palms facing down at the forehead, left in front of the right, move hands to their respective sides of the body, opening into bent "5" hand positions.

591   Rescue the Perishing

1. Rescue perishing,[1] care(#1) for dying,
    seize them pity from sin, grace; weep over
    sinner rise-up(#1) fall(#4), tell them
    Jesus, mighty(#2) save.

Refrain:
    Rescue perishing, care(#1) for dying;
    Jesus mercy(#1), Jesus will(#1) save.

2. No matter they neglect him, still(#1)
    he wait, wait penitent child receive; plea
    with them earnest, plea with them gentle;
    he will(#1) forgive if they only believe.

Refrain

3. Down-in[2] person heart, subdue through
    devil, feel rest bury that grace(#1) can
    inspire;[3] touch through love heart, awake
    through kind, music that was silence(#1)
    will(#1) sound again.

Refrain

4. Rescue perishing, duty demands; strength
   for your labor Lord will(#1) provide; back
   narrow way patiently win(#1) them; tell
   poor(#3) wander(#2) Savior finish died.

Refrain

[1]Perishing: R and L "A" hand positions, palms facing body, separated about shoulder height, move both down simultaneously, indicating a person declining in health.
[2]Down-in: Should be signed at the heart.
[3]Inspire: R and L flat "O" hand positions, palms facing body at the heart, fingers pointing up, move both hands up opening into "5" hand positions.

When the Church of Jesus   592

1. Happen church Jesus shut out(#1)
   unless loud traffic fade voice prayer, may
   our prayers, Lord, make us ten times more
   aware that world we banish, our
   Christian care(#1).

2. If our heart rise(#3), place devotion
   aspire high above this hungry suffer world,
   unless our hymns should effect us forget
   needs, shape(#1) our Christian worship
   become Christian deeds.

3. Unless gifts we offer, money, skills,
   time, serve heal our conscience, our secret
   shame, Lord reprove, inspire us through way
   you give; teach us, dying Savior, how true
   Christians live.

Here I Am, Lord

1. I, Lord sea, sky, I finish heard my
   people cry(#3). All themselves dwell dark,
   sin, my hand will(#1) save. I myself made
   stars, all-night, I will(#1) make their dark
   bright. Who will(#1) bear(#4) my light,
   people? Whom will I send?

Refrain:
   Here I true, Lord. Is(#1) I, Lord? I finish
   heard you call(#1) all-night. I will(#1) go,
   Lord, if you lead me. I will(#1) care(#1)
   your people my heart.

2. I, Lord snow, rain, I finish bear(#4) my
   people pain. I finish weep for love them.
   They turn away. I will(#1) break their heart
   stone,[1] give them hearts for love alone. I
   will(#1) speak my word them.
   Whom shall I send?

Refrain

3. I, Lord wind, flame, I will(#1) care(#1)
   poor(#1), lame, I will(#1) found feast for
   them. My hand will(#1) save. Finest bread
   I will(#1) provide, till their hearts become
   satisfy. I will(#1) give my life them.
   Whom shall I send?

Refrain

[1]Stone: Should be signed at the heart.

1. Bless Jesus, your word we gather(#2) see
   you; let our heart, soul become inspire,[1]
   now seek, love, fear you, through your holy
   teach, attract from world, love you sole.

2. All our know, sense(#2), sight rest real
   dark cover(#1), till your spirit makes known
   our night with light truth clear. You alone,
   God can win us; you must work all
   good within us.

3. Glory Lord, yourself give light of light,
   from God proceed, open our ears,[2] open heart;[3]
   help us through your spirit plea; hear
   cry(#3) your people rise(#3); hear, bless
   our prayers, praise.

[1]Inspire: R and L flat "O" hand positions, palms facing body at the heart, fingers pointing up, move both hands up opening into "5" hand positions.
[2]Open our ears: Should be signed at the ear.
[3]Open heart: Should be signed at the heart.

598   O Word of God Incarnate

1. O Word God humanity form, O wisdom from
   high, O truth not changed, O light our dark sky:
   we praise you for inspire[1] Holy Bible, light our
   step(#1), shines[2] from generation, generation.

2. Church from you, our Savior, receive
   gift divine, still(#1) that light rise(#3)
   over all world shine. This holy vessel[3]
   place value truth store(#2); this heaven
   picture Christ, living word.

3. Scripture like(#2) banner before(#3) God
   group(#1) spread-out; that shine-light above
   dark world. That map, show direction(#1)
   over life, up, down, amid not clear,
   struggle, soft, you, O Christ will guide.

4. O make your church, precious Savior,
   light pure gold, bear(#4) before(#3) world
   your true light as past. O teach your wander(#2)
   people through their path follow, till, gloom,
   dark end(#1), they see you face-to-face(#2).

[1]Inspire: R and L flat "O" hand positions, palms facing body at the heart, fingers pointing up move both hands up opening into "5" hand positions.
[2]Shine: Should be signed with both hands.
[3]Vessel: Should be signed as a classifier, may be signed like "form," or fight "Y," palm facing body, twist wrist down to the left, or any other signs representing a container.

This ASL translation © 1995 The United Methodist Publishing House

599   Break Thou the Bread of Life

1. Break your bread life, precious Lord,
   to-me[1] as you finish break bread near sea;
   beyond holy page, I seek you Lord; my spirit
   wants you O Living Word.

2. Bless your truth, precious Lord, to-me,
   to-me, happen you finish bless bread near
   "G"-country; then shall all bondage cease,
   all chains detach; I shall find
   my peace, my all.

[1]To-me: Should be signed the whole person, R and L "cupped" hand positions, palms facing the body, move fingertips down the body.

Wonderful Words of Life   600

1. Sing words again me,[1] wonderful(#2) words
   life; let me see beauty words, wonderful(#2)
   words life; words life beauty teach me faith, duty.

Refrain:
   Beautiful words, wonderful(#2) words,
   wonderful(#2) words life. Beautiful words,
   wonderful(#2) words, wonderful(#2) words life.

2. Christ bless person, gives all
   wonderful(#2) words life; sinner, listen
   love call(#1), wonderful(#2) words life; all
   true free give, seek win(#1) us heaven.

Refrain

3. Pleasant sound again gospel call(#2),
   wonderful(#2) words life; offer pardon,
   peace all, wonderful(#2) words life; Jesus,
   only Savior, make holy forever.

Refrain

[1]Me: Should be signed as the whole person, both hands cupped, move down the body.

601   Thy Word Is a Lamp

1. Your word light[1] my feet, light unto my
   path. Happen I feel afraid, think I lost my
   way, still(#1) you there near me,[2] I will(#1)
   fear nothing as long you near. Please stay
   near me, end(#1).

2. Your word light unto my feet, light unto
   my path. Now I will(#1) not forget your
   love for me, yet my heart forever wander(#2).
   Jesus, true guide, keep me close you,
   I will(#1) love you, end(#1).

[1]Light: Should be signed directionally.
[2]Me: Should be signed the whole person.

This ASL translation © 1995 Meadowgreen Music Co./Bug and Bear Music

603   Come, Holy Ghost, Our Hearts Inspire

1. Come, Holy Spirit, our hearts inspire,[1]
   let us your influence prove; begin old
   prophet inspire begin life, love.

2. Come, Holy Spirit, inspire through you,
   prophets wrote, spoke, make known truth
   yourself key, open Holy Bible.

3. Expand your arms[2] heaven Spirit, protect
   our world through all-night; our sick
   spirits inspire, let there now true light.

4. God, through Spirit we shall know if
   you shine[3] through us, sound with all
   your angels below, real love divine.

[1]Inspire: R and L flat "O" hand positions, palms facing body at the heart, fingers pointing up
move both hands up opening into "5" hand positions.
[2]Arms: Should be signed the natural opening of the arms.
[3]Shine: Should be signed directionally.

Praise and Thanksgiving Be to God   604

1. Praise, thanksgiving, give[1] God our maker,
   begin all bless, generous creator. Baptize,
   made your own, now we come before(#3) you,
   while we adore you.

2. Not our own holy, not that we finish
   struggle, bring us peace which you, Christ,
   finish give. Baptize separate, strength us,
   O Savior, with grace(#1), favor.

3. Come, Holy Spirit, come visit; you
   truth, our hope, our salvation. Baptize
   with joy, power(#1), give, O Spirit come,
   life never end(#1).

4. Praise Father, Son, Holy Spirit; one
   Lord, one faith, one begin every merit.
   Here now make new your church through this
   water give; give peace from heaven.

[1]Give: Should be signed directionally.

605   Wash, O God, Our Sons and Daughters

1. Wash, O God, our sons, daughters, place
   your clean water come. Number them among
   your people; bless as Christ bless long-ago.
   Weave them clothes bright, shine surround
   them with love, light. Fill, anoint(#1)
   them; send your Spirit, Holy Spirit, heart delight.

2. We ourselves bring them long(#2) for
   care(#1); through your Spirit, may we become
   fill. Let us join(#3) your celebration,
   participate your bless, live strength. God
   make new us, guide our steps(#1); free from
   sin, all temptations, one with Christ live,
   dying, through your Spirit, children, heritage.

3. O how real your holy wisdom! Not
   imagined, all your ways. Your name glory,
   honor. With our lives we worship, praise.
   We your people stand before(#3) you, baptize,
   Spirit fill. Through your grace(#1), our
   lives we offer. Create new us, God, change.

606   Come, Let Us Use the Grace Divine

1. Come, let us use grace(#1) divine, all
   with one accord, lasting(#3) agree, join(#1)
   ourselves Christ Lord; give-up ourselves
   through Jesus power, his name glory; promise,
   present(#3) holy hour, for God live, dies.

2. Earnest agree we make ever(#3) keep mind;
   we will(#1) no more our God give-up, cast-out
   these words behind. We never will(#1)
   cast-off fear God himself hears our promise;
   if you please hear, come-down meet us now.

3. You Father, Son, Holy Spirit, let all
   our hearts receive, present(#3) with your
   heavenly group(#1) peace answer give; each
   agree, use blood which takes-away our sins,
   register-our names high, keep us that day.[1]

[1]Register-our: Should be signed as "write," the natural writing in the air above head height.
Names-high: Should be signed "very high."
Keep us: Should be signed as "care"(#1).
That day: Should be signed as "future."

This Is the Spirit's Entry Now   608

1. This Spirit entry now: water,
   word, cross Jesus your head, seal(#1)
   both felt, heard.

2. Let water holy show that we must
   die each day, rise(#1) again through his
   plan as follower his way.

3. Make new Spirit, hear our praise for
   your baptize power(#1) that washes us
   through all our days. Lord,
   cleanse again present(#3) hour.

609   You Have Put On Christ

You finish show Christ,
Christ you finish baptize,
Alleluia! Alleluia!

610   We Know That Christ Is Raised

1. We know that Christ rise(#1), dies no more.
   Embrace through death, he conquer fear death,
   our loss hope, he change, inspire[1] joy. Alleluia!

2. We share through water his save death.
   Begin new, we share with him Easter(#2) life
   as live members live Christ. Alleluia!

3. New creation comes life grows as Christ
   new body, accept flesh, blood. World made
   new, whole will(#1) sing: Alleluia!

[1]Inspire: R and L flat "O" hand positions, palms facing body at the heart, fingers pointing up move both hands up opening into "5" hand positions.

611   Child of Blessing, Child of Promise

1. Child bless, child promise, baptize with
   Spirit show; with this water God finish
   promise you love, grace(#1) divine.

2. Child love, our love express,[1] love
   creation, love indeed! New from God, make
   new our spirits, joy, laugh lead(#1).

3. Child joy, our precious value, you true
   God, from God you came. Back God we humbly
   give you; live as person himself bear(#4) Christ name.

4. Child God your love Parent, learn know
   whose child you are(#1). Grow, laugh, sing
   worship, trust, love God more than all.

[1]Express: R and L "S" hand positions at the heart, palms facing the body, move both hands
up and out opening hands into "5" hand positions.

Deck Thyself, My Soul, with Gladness   612

1. Cover yourself, my soul, with glad,
   leave(#2) gloom feel sad. Come day bright,
   there with joy your praises give, Christ,
   whose grace(#1) not limit, finish this
   wonderful(#2) banquet found. High over
   all heavens he reigns, yet lives
   with you he plans.

2. Sun, itself all my life true bright;
   Light, itself true my soul make clear; Joy,
   best that any person knows; Since my
   life began; your feet I cry(#3), my Maker,
   let me right participant this bless food
   from heaven, for our good, your glory, give.

3. Jesus, strength life, I pray you, let me
   glad now obey you, never my hurt tempt,
   become your love with love revenge. From
   this banquet let me measure, Lord, how large
   real worth; through gifts you now finish
   give me, as your angels heaven receive me.

O Thou Who This Mysterious Bread

1. O You yourself this secret bread you
   finish share, "E"-town, return here inspire[1]
   our soul, your follower speak.

2. Open-volume[2] your grace(#1), apply(#2)
   gospel word; open-our-eyes[3] see your face(#1),
   our hearts know Lord.

3. You talk still(#1), we mourn
   til you take-away-cover,[4] talk with
   us, our hearts shall inspire with
   warm earnest love.

4. Excite now heaven zeal, make
   your mercy(#1) known, give our pardon
   souls, feel that God, love, true one.

[1]Inspire: R and L flat "O" hand positions, palms facing body at the heart, fingers pointing up move both hands up opening into "5" hand positions.
[2]Open-volume: Should be signed as a classifier, the natural opening of a large book.
[3]Open-our-eyes: Should be signed as one sign at the eyes as "awake."
[4]Take-away-cover: Should be signed as a classifier, the natural removing of a mask.

For the Bread Which You Have Broken   614, 615

1. For bread which you finish break, for
   wine which you finish pour,[1] for words which
   you finish speak, now we give you
   thanks, O Lord.

2. Through this pledge, you true love us,
   through your gift peace made new, through
   your call(#1) heaven above us, holy all
   our lives, O Lord.

3. With our angels glory seated heaven
   board, may church that wait for you,
   keep love connect continue, Lord.

4. Your service, Lord, defend us, our
   hearts keep watch(#1), protect; world place
   you finish send us, let your kingdom
   come, O Lord.

[1]Pour: May be signed with a right "10," palm facing left, twist wrist to the left, turning
thumb into left "C," or may use right "Y," palm facing body, the natural motion of pouring
from a pitcher toward the left "C."

616   Come, Sinners, to the Gospel Feast

1. Come, sinners, gospel(#2) feast, let every
   person become Jesus visitor. You not need left
   behind, because God finish call(#1) all people.

2. Don't begin make excuses; don't refuse
   Jesus grace(#1); your world trouble, pleasures
   leave(#1), accept what Jesus finish give.

3. Come participate gospel(#2) feast,
   become saved from sin, Jesus rest; O
   experience good our God, eat bread represent
   his body, drink wine represent his blood.

4. See Jesus onward before(#3) your eyes;
   see bleed sacrifice; his offer love, haste embrace,
   free now become saved through grace(#1).

5. You yourself believe his record true
   shall eat with him, he eat with you; come
   feast, become saved from sin, because
   Jesus waits accept you.

617   I Come with Joy

1. I come with joy meet my Lord, forgiven,
   loved, free, great(#2) fear, wonder(#2),
   recall(#2) his life sacrifice for me,
   his life sacrifice for me.

2. I come with Christians far, near find,
   as all fed, new community love Christ
   communion(#2), Christ communion(#2).

3. As Christ breaks bread, bid us share,
   each proud division ends(#3). Love that
   made us become one, strangers[1] now become
   friends, strangers now become friends.

4. That way with joy we meet our Lord. His
   presence, always near, true same friend
   better known; we see, praise him now, we see
   praise him now.

5. Together met, together bound, we
   will(#1) go different ways, as his people
   world, we will(#1) live, speak his praise,
   we will(#1) live, speak his praise.

[1]Strangers: May be signed as "new persons" or "strange" persons.

Let Us Break Bread Together   618

1. Let us break bread together we kneel,
   let us break bread together we kneel.
   Happen I kneel with my face rise-sun,
   O Lord, have mercy(#1) me.[1]

2. Let us drink wine together we kneel,
   let us drink wine together we kneel.
   Happen I kneel with my face rise-sun,
   O Lord, have mercy(#1) me.

3. Let us praise God together we kneel,
   let us praise God together we kneel.
   Happen I kneel with my face rise-run,
   O Lord, have mercy(#1) me.

[1]Me: Should be signed the whole person, with both "cupped" hands moving down the body.

619 Now the Silence

Now silence(#2) Now peace Now empty
hands rise(#3) Now kneel Now plea,
Now Father arms welcome now
hearing Now power(#1) Now vessel[1]
fill for pour[2] Now body Now blood
Now joy celebration Now wedding
Now songs Now heart forgive leap
Now Spirit visit Now Son epiphany
Now Father bless Now Now Now.

[1]Vessel: Should be signed as a classifier, any natural form of a container, like a pitcher, right "Y" representing the handle, or the sign for vase, signed like form, etc.
[2]Pour: May be signed with a right "10," palm facing left, twist wrist to the left, turning thumb into left "C," or may use right "Y," palm facing body, the natural motion of pouring from a pitcher toward the left "C."

620 One Bread, One Body

Refrain:
One bread, one body, one Lord all, one cup
bless which we bless. We, no matter many
through-out world, we one body this one Lord.

1. None Jew, Jew, servant, free,
woman, man, no more.

Refrain

2. Many gifts, many works,
one Lord all.

Refrain

3. Grain for field(#2), scatter, grown,
   gather(#1) one, for all.

Refrain

Be Present at Our Table, Lord 621

Be(#1) here our table,[1] Lord;
be(#1) here, every place adore;
your mercy(#1) bless, give
that we may feast,
fellowship with you.

[1]Table: May be signed with right "open" hand position, palm down over the left forearm, move right hand up and down several times.

There Is a Fountain Filled with Blood 622

1. There fountain fill with blood come
   from Jesus blood; sinner haste beneath
   overflow take-away all their guilty
   wrongdoing. Take-away all their guilty
   wrongdoing; sinner haste beneath overflow
   take-away all their guilty wrongdoing.

2. Dying thief rejoice see, new begin his
   day; may I, however(#2) bad as he, wash(#1)
   all my sins. Wash(#1) all my sins, wash(#1)
   all my sins; may I, however(#2) bad as he,
   wash(#2) all my sins.

3. Precious dying Jesus, your precious
   blood shall never lose power(#1), till all
   redeem(#1) church God become save, sin no
   more. Become saved, sin no more, become
   saved, sin no more; till all redeem(#1)
   church God become saved, sin no more.

4. Ever since, through faith, I saw your
   continue hurts provide, redeem(#1) love
   since my theme, shall be(#1) till I die.
   Shall be(#1) till I die, shall be(#1) till
   I die; redeem(#1) love since my theme,
   shall be(#1) till I die.

5. Then noble pleasant song, I sing your
   power(#1) save, happen my poor speech(#1)
   not perfect, repeat language keep silent
   grave. Keep silent grave, keep silent grave;
   happen my poor speech(#1) not perfect,
   repeat language keep silent grave.

623   Here, O My Lord, I See Thee

1. Now, O my Lord, I see your face(#2); now
   would I touch, manage things not seen; now
   control with strong(#1) hand eternity
   grace(#1), all my weary, you depend.

2. This hour banquet song; this heaven
   table spread for me; now let me feast,
   still(#1) last(#3) holy hour
   fellowship with you.

3. Now would I feed upon bread God, now
   drink with you, king wine heaven; now would
   I lay aside[1] each world burden, now
   experience new calm, sin, forgive.

4. Short time we rise(#1); idol disappear;
   feast, although not love, finish, gone.
   Bread, wine remove; but you here, nearer
   than ever(#3), still(#1) my shield, sun.

5. After many feast finish; yet, finish go
   glad feast above, give pleasant experience
   before(#3) feast joy, Jesus great(#3)
   wedding feast joy, love.

[1]Lay aside: R and L "open" hand positions, both palms facing right, fingers pointing out,
move both hands to the right.

This ASL translation © 1995 The United Methodist Publishing House

Bread of the World   624

1. Bread world, mercy(#1) broke, wine
   soul mercy(#1) scatter, through whom words
   life speak, whose death our sins forgive.

2. Look[1] heart through sorrow broke,
   look tears through sinner eye; become
   your feast us, mark[2] that through your
   grace(#1) our souls satisfied.

[1]Look: Should be signed directionally.
[2]Mark: Should be signed as "show."

This ASL translation © 1995 The United Methodist Publishing House

625   Come, Let Us Eat

1. Come, let us eat, because now food
   spread. Come, let us eat, because now food
   spread. Our Lord meal, bread, wine let us
   eat together. Our Lord meal, bread, wine,
   let us eat together.

2. Come, let us drink, because now wine
   pour.[1] Come, let us drink, because now wine
   pour. Jesus finish pour, let us drink
   together. Jesus finish pour, let us
   drink together.

3. His presence we meet rest now,
   his presence we meet and rest now.
   His presence our Lord we gather(#2).
   His presence our Lord we gather(#2).

4. Rise(#1), spread far God mighty(#2) word.
   Rise(#1) spread far God mighty(#2) word.
   Jesus finish rise(#1), will(#1) bring
   kingdom. Jesus finish rise(#1), will(#1)
   bring kingdom.

[1]Pour: May be signed with a right "10," palm facing left, twist wrist to the left, turning thumb into left "C," or may use right "Y," palm facing body, the natural motion of pouring from a pitcher toward the left "C."

This ASL translation © 1995 Augsburg Fortress

626   Let All Mortal Flesh Keep Silence

1. Let all living people keep silent(#1),
   with fear, tremble[1] stand; ponder nothing
   world, for with bless his hand, Christ our
   God came-down world, our full respect demand.

2. King, kings, yet born Virgin-Mary, as
   past earth he stood, Lord, lords, same form
   person, body, blood; he will(#1) give all
   Christians his own self for heaven food.

3. Many row² group(#1) heaven spreads leader
   positions on-way, as light-light, come-down
   from kingdom continue day, that power(#1)
   hell(#1) may fade, as dark clears-away.

4. Jesus feet six wing lower angels, high
   angels with restless eyes, cover faces
   presence, as with continue voice, they
   cry(#3); Alleluia, Alleluia
   Alleluia, Lord Most High!

¹Tremble: R and L "5" hand positions, palms facing body, fingers pointing down, shake hands several times.
²Row: R and L bent "5" hand positions, palms facing down and separated, move both hands out.

O the Depth of Love Divine 627

1. O real love divine, cannot measure
   grace(#1)! Who shall say how bread, wine
   God convey us! How bread his flesh give,
   how wine represent his blood, fill his faith
   people hearts with all life God!

2. Let wise people show how we receive
   grace(#1); feeble parts bestow power(#1) not
   theirs give. Who explain wonder(#2) way,
   how through these good came? These good
   finish convey, still(#1) remain same.

3. How can spirits heaven rise(#1), through
   world issues influence, drink with this
   divine provide, eat eternity bread? Ask
   Father wise how: Christ himself finish
   appoint angels surround our altars kneel
   search, without success.

4. Sure true grace(#1), manner(#2) not
   known; only meet us your ways, perfect us
   one. Let us experience heaven power(#1),
   Lord, we ask for nothing more. You bless,
   this only ours wonder(#1), adore.

628   Eat This Bread

Eat this[1] bread, drink this cup,
come me,[2] never become hungry.
Eat this bread, drink this cup,
trust me, you will(#1) not thirst.

[1]This: Left "index" hand position, palm facing right, finger up, right "Y" hand position, palm down, move right toward left index.
[2]Me: Should be signed the whole person, R and L "cupped" hands, move down the body.

629   You Satisfy the Hungry Heart

Refrain:
You satisfy hungry heart, with gift finest
wheat. Come, give us, O saving Lord,
bread life eat.

1. As happen shepherd call(#2) his sheep,
   they know, listen his voice, true happen you
   call(#1) your family, Lord,
   we follow, rejoice.

Refrain

2. With joy speech we sing you, our praise,
   grateful, that you should count us worthy,
   Lord, share this heaven bread.

Refrain

3. Is(#1) not cup we bless, share, blood
   Christ expressed?[1] Is(#1) not one cup, one
   bread, declare our one Lord?

Refrain

4. Secret your presence, Lord, no person
   voice can tell; whom all world cannot keep,
   comes our hearts live.

Refrain

5. You give yourself us, O Lord; then
   without self you let us become, serve each
   other your name, truth, charity.

Refrain

[1]Expressed: R and L "S" hand positions at the heart, palms facing the body, move both hands up and out opening hands into "5" hand positions.

630   Become to Us the Living Bread

1. Become us living bread through which
   Christian life fed, make new,
   great(#2) comfort:

Refrain:
    Alleluia! Alleluia! Alleluia!

2. Become never fail wine, begin joy
   that shall incline our hearts bear(#4)
   agree show.

Refrain

3. May Christians all with one accord
   unite surround holy table[1] praise your
   holy name, O Lord.

Refrain

[1]Table: May be signed with a right "open" hand, palm facing down over the left forearm, move right hand up and down several times.

This ASL translation © 1995 Westminster Press

631   O Food to Pilgrims Given

1. O food people journey(#3) holy place
   given, O bread life from heaven, O bread
   from high! We hunger; Lord, provide(#2)
   us, not your delight deny us, whose
   heart you come near.

2. O continue love past tell, O pure begin,
   continue from Jesus side! We faint(#1) with
   thirst; renew[1] us, from your abundance give
   us, all we need provide(#1)

3. O Jesus, through your bid, we here adore
   you, hid form bread, wine. Promise happen
   cover rise(#3), we may see, heaven, your
   face(#1) divine.

[1]Renew: May be signed as "make" then the sign for " new."

Draw Us in the Spirit's Tether 632

1. Draw(#2) us Spirit connect, for happen
   humbly your name, two or three met together,
   you midst them. Alleluia! Alleluia! We
   now touch bottom your garment.

2. As disciples past gather(#2) name Christ
   eat, then with thanks God Father break bread
   bless cup: Alleluia! Alleluia! True
   now bind us together as friends.

3. All our meals all our living make as
   sacrament you, that through care(#1), help,
   give, we may become true disciples.
   Alleluia! Alleluia! We will(#1) serve
   you faithful(#2).

633   The Bread of Life for All Is Broken

1. Bread life for all broke! Christ
drink cup on-Calvary. God grace(#1) we
trust, spread with much respect this holy
feast, this way remember.

2. With holy fear we seek your presence,
our hearts sorrow through people grief.
Your holy face(#1) stain with bitter tears;
our personal pain still(#1) bear(#4)
you with us.

3. O Lord, we pray, you come among us,
bright our eyes, bright appear(#2)! Jesus,
heaven joy continue, our life with you
forever join(#2).

634   Now Let Us from This Table Rise

1. Let us rise(#1) from table now made new
body, mind, soul; with Christ we die live
again, his generous love finish make us whole.

2. With minds awake, support through
grace(#1) spread word through speech deed we
follow step(#1) Christ, one with hope, need.

3. Fill each home with love, sacrament
care(#1); work Christ began do, we humbly
pledge ourselves share.

4. Give[1] us courage, Father God, choose
   again travel holy way, help us accept
   with joy challenge tomorrow.

[1]Give: Should be signed directionally.

Because Thou Hast Said   635

1. Because you finish said: "Do this for
   me," secret bread we glad eat; we thirst for
   Spirit that comes from above, long(#2)
   receive your full love.

2. True here we look-up, grasp your mind,
   true here that we hope your image find;
   way bestow your gifts we embrace; but all
   things owe Jesus grace(#1).

Christian People, Raise Your song   636

1. Christian people rise(#3) your song,
   fade all grief. Sing your joy, become
   strong(#1), our Lord life receive. Nature
   gifts bread, wine now found before(#3) us;
   as we offer bread, wine, Christ
   comes renew[1] us.

2. Come welcome Christ today, God great(#3)
   make known, himself finish first find way
   new world. Meet Christ, our rise(#1) King,
   glad recognize, as with joy we meet spring
   follow winter.

[1]Renew: May be signed as "make" then sign "new."

637

Una Espiga
(Sheaves of Summer)

1. Wheat gather(#1) bundle[1] summer change
   gold through sun, grapes bunches[2] removed
   happen full grown, red, changed become bread,
   wine God love body, blood our precious Lord.

2. We share same bread, wine meal, we true
   bread through same great(#3) Maker; like(#2)
   stone grind(#1), life depress with sorrow,
   pain, but God makes us new people join(#1)
   through love.

3. Like(#2) grains which become one same
   whole bread, like(#2) sounds that blend[3]
   become song, like(#2) rain water that
   become sea, we, as Christians,
   one body shall become.

4. God table together we shall sit around.
   As God children, Christ body we will(#1)
   share. One same hope we will(#1) sing
   together as we walk along. Brothers,
   sisters, life, love, we will(#1) become.

[1]Bundle: Should be signed as a classifier, the natural motion of making a sheave with both the "C" hand shapes.
[2]Bunch: Should be signed as a classifier, the natural motion of making a bunch of grapes, as "class," etc.
[3]Blend: R and L "5" hand positions, palms down, fingers pointing out at angles, move both toward each other, right overlaps left, then move both out in front.

Antiphon (Unison)
This feast, victory(#1) for our God.
Alleluia! Alleluia! Alleluia!

1. Worthy Christ, himself killed,
   whose blood, free us become people God.

Antiphon
2. Power, riches, wisdom, strength, honor,
   bless, glory his.

Antiphon
3. Sing with all people God, join(#3) hymn
   all world.

Antiphon
4. Bless, honor, glory, might(#1) belong-to
   God, Jesus forever. A-men.

5. For Jesus himself killed
   finish began his reign. Allelujah!

Final Antiphon
This feast, victory(#1) for our God.
Alleluia! Alleluia! Alleluia!

640 Take Our Bread

Refrain:
> Accept our bread, we ask you; accept our
> hearts, we love you. Accept our lives,
> O Father, we true yours, we true yours.

1. Yours as we stand near table you
   prepare; yours as we eat bread our hearts
   can't forget. We true show your life with
   us yet(#1), we true yours, we true yours.

Refrain

2. Your holy people stand wash(#1) your
   blood, Spirit fill yet(#1) hungry we wait
   your food. We poor, but we finish bring
   ourselves best we could; we true yours,
   we true yours.

Refrain

This ASL translation © 1995 G. I. A.

641 Fill My Cup, Lord

> Fill my cup, Lord, I rise(#3) cup, Lord.
> Come, satisfy thirst my soul. Bread
> heaven, feed me[1] till I want no more,
> fill my cup, fill cup, make me whole.[2]

[1]Me: Should be signed the whole person, R and L "cupped" hand positions, palms facing body, fingertips move down the body.
[2]Whole: Should be signed as "well"(#2).

This ASL translation © 1995 Sacred Songs

As Man and Woman We Were Made

1. As man, woman, we made that love found,
   life begun, true praise Lord himself made us
   two, praise Lord happen two become one;
   praise for love that comes life through
   child, parent,[1] husband, wife.

2. Now Jesus lived, gave his love make
   our life, loving new; true celebrate with
   him today, accept joy he offers you, that
   makes simple(#2) moment shine, changes
   water become wine(#1).

3. Jesus died live again, true praise love
   that, always, can bring sunrise, clear sky,
   wait dry-away all tears; let us hope for
   what[2] will(#1) become, believe place
   we cannot see.

4. Then spread table, clear room, celebrate
   till day done(#2); let peace strong(#1)
   between us all, joy share through every one;
   laugh, make merry with your friends, praise
   love that continue!

[1]Parent: Should be signed as "mother/father."
[2]What: Should be signed as "where"(#2).

643   When Love Is Found

1. Happen love found, hope comes home, sing,
   become glad that two become one. Happen love
   spreads, fill sky, praise God, share our Maker joy.

2. Happen love grow with trust care(#1), build
   both each day, that love may challenge, reach
   beyond home warm, light, serve, work hard for truth, right.

3. Happen love prove, as love people change,
   keep still(#1) hope, no matter all seems
   strange, till comfort return, love grows
   wise, through listen-ears, open-eyes.

4. Happen love divide, trust deceive, pray
   strength love, till torment fade, till
   lovers keep no list(#1) wrong, but hear
   through pain love Easter(#2) song.

5. Praise God for love, praise God for life,
   children, youth, husband, wife. Rise(#3)
   your hearts, let love true fed, through
   death, life, through broke bread.

644   Jesus, Joy of Our Desiring

1. Jesus, joy our desire, holy wisdom, love
   most bright; attract through you, our souls
   aspire toward light. Word God, our body that
   form, with excite life emotion(#2) work hard,
   still(#1) truth not known, aspire dying
   around your throne.[1]

2. Through way hope guide, listen, peace
   music sounds; place crowd you trust, drink
   joy from eternity water. Theirs beauty
   fair(#1) pleasure; theirs wisdom holy
   possess. You ever(#3) lead your own, love
   joys not known.

[1]Throne: R and L "C" hand positions, palms facing down and separated, arc both hands back toward the body, indicating the arms of a large chair.

O Perfect Love   645

1. O perfect Love, all persons thoughts
   above, humble we kneel prayer before(#3)
   your throne,[1] that theirs may become love
   which knows no end(#1), whom you
   forever become one.

2. O perfect Life, you become their full
   confidence, tender(#3) charity, continue
   faith, patient hope, quiet, brave endure(#2),
   with child-like(#2) trust that fears
   no pain, no death.

3. Give them joy which bright world sorrow;
   give them peace which calms all world
   struggle, life day glory not known tomorrow,
   that begin, eternity love, life.

[1]Throne: R and L "C" hand positions, palms facing down and separated, arc both hands back toward the body, indicating the arms of a large chair.

647   Your Love, O God, Has Called Us Here

1. Your love, O God, finish call(#1) us
   here, for all love finds begin you, perfect
   love that cast-out fear, love that Christ
   makes ever(#3) new.

2. O gracious God, you make holy all that
   beautiful, good, true. Bless those
   themselves your presence wait, everyday
   their love made new.

3. O God love, inspire our life, make known
   your will all we do; join(#1) every husband,
   every wife mutual(#1) love, love for you.

648   God the Spirit, Guide and Guardian

1. God Spirit, guide care(#1), wind quick
   flame, flying little bird, breath life voice
   prophets, show bless, power(#1) love: give
   those themselves lead your people new
   anoint(#1) your grace(#1); send them onward
   as bold followers your church every place.

2. Christ our Savior, king, shepherd, word
   made new, love crucified, teacher, healer,
   suffer servant, friend sinner, foe pride;
   your care(#1) may all pastors learn live
   shepherd care(#1); give them courage
   compassion shown through word, deed, prayer.

3. Great(#3) Creator, life giver, truth
   beyond all thoughts recall(#2), begin wisdom,
   begin mercy(#1), give forgive all; as you
   know our strength weak, may those church
   honor, watch(#1) church life continue,
   yet(#1) not over-look[1] church faults.

4. Trinity God, secret person, not divided
   diverse, more deep than our minds can
   understand, more great(#2) than our belief
   practice; help us our varied call(#1) your
   full image to proclaim, that our ministry[2]
   unite may give glory your name.

[1]Over-look: Right "open" hand position at side of the head, palm facing back, arc right hand to the left in front of the face.
[2]Ministry: Should be signed with a right "M," palm facing down, tap wrist of the right hand on the back of the left hand several times.

How Shall They Hear the Word of God   649

1. How will(#1) people hear word God except
   truth told? How will(#1) sinner become free,
   sorrow console? All themselves speak truth
   today, give your Spirit, Lord, we pray.

2. How will(#1) people call(#1) God for help
   except people finish believed? How will(#1)
   poor(#1) receive hope, prisoner forgiven?
   People themselves help blind see, give light,
   love, clear.

3. How will(#1) gospel proclaim that sinner
   may repent? How will(#1) world find peace,
   last(#1) if announce not sent? Send us, Lord,
   for we rejoice speak, Christ with life, voice.

650   Give Me the Faith Which Can Remove

1. Give me faith which can remove, low
   mountain become plain;[1] give me like(#2)
   child pray love, which long(#2) build your
   house again; let your love, over-come my
   heart, all my simple soul consume(#2).

2. I would precious time redeem(#1),
   long(#2) live for this alone, use my time
   for people themselves not yet known my
   Savior; full on these my mission prove,
   only breathe, breathe your love.

3. My skill, gifts, grace(#1), Lord, into
   your bless hands receive; let me live preach
   your word, let me your glory live; my
   ever(#3) holy moment use proclaim
   sinner Friend.

4. Expand, arouse desire, fill my heart
   with no limit charity divine, true I shall
   use all my strength, love people with zeal
   like(#2) you, lead them your open position,
   people for whom Jesus died.

[1]Plain: Should sign "spread" with much larger arc.
[2]Over-come: Should be signed directionally.

This ASL translation © 1995 The United Methodist Publishing House

651   Come, Holy Ghost, Our Souls Inspire

1. Come, Holy Spirit, our soul inspire,[1]
   bright with heaven excite; your anoint(#1)
   Spirit true, yourself finish give
   gifts seven times.

2. Your bless sympathy(#1) from above
   comfort, life, excite love; help with
   last(#3) light slow understand
   our blind sight.

3. Anoint(#1) cheer our soil(#2) face with
   abundance your grace(#1); keep far our foe;
   give peace home; place you true guide,
   no bad can come.

4. Teach us know Father, Son, you, both
   become but One; that through generations
   ever-since, this may become our continue
   song. Praise your eternity worth, Father,
   Son, Holy Spirit. Amen.

[1]Inspire: R and L flat "O" hand positions, palms facing body at the heart, fingers pointing
up, move both hands up opening into "5" hand positions.

Christ the Victorious   653

1. Christ Victory(#1) give[1] your servants
   rest with your angels area light. Grief,
   pain end(#3), sad no more, there may people
   find everlasting life.

2. Only Eternity God, mighty(#2) Creator!
   We your people, children world. From earth
   you form us, both glory sure die, earth
   shall we all return.

3. God spoken prophecy, word from creation:
   "You came from dirt, dirt you return."
   Yet(#1) grave shall we sing our glad sounds,
   "Alleluia! Alleluia!"

4 Christ Victory(#1), give your servants
   rest with your angels area light. Grief,
   pain end(#3), sad no more, there may people
   find everlasting life.

¹Give: Should be signed directionally.

654   How Blest Are They Who Trust in Christ

1. True very bless people themselves trust
   Christ happen those we love must die; we
   yield people we love, for they must
   go-heaven, but not lose them from our heart.

2. Older people finish bring home award,
   gone from us youth first, Christ they finish
   eternity life, free from all connect time.

3. Christ himself experience death for us,
   we rise(#1) above our natural grief, witness
   trouble world, strength, glory belief.

655   Fix Me, Jesus

Refrain:
   Oh, prepare me, Oh, prepare me, Oh, prepare
   me; prepare me, Jesus, prepare me.

1. Prepare me for my long white robe,¹
   prepare me, Jesus, prepare me. Prepare me
   for my starry crown, prepare me, Jesus
   prepare me.

2. Prepare me for my journey(#3) home,
   prepare me, Jesus, prepare me. Prepare me
   for my dying bed, prepare me, Jesus,
   prepare me.

Refrain

[1]Robe: R and L "cupped" hand positions, palms facing up, backs of fingers on chest, move
both hands down body.

This ASL translation © 1995 The United Methodist Publishing House

This Is the Day   657

Now true day, now true day that Lord
finish made, that Lord finish made.
Let us rejoice, let us rejoice
true glad now day, true glad now day.
Now true day that Lord finish made;
let us rejoice true glad now day.
Now true day, now true day that Lord
finish made.

This ASL translation © 1995 Scripture in Song

This Is the Day the Lord Hath Made   658

Now true day Lord finish made;
Lord call(#1) time his own. Let
heaven rejoice, let earth true
glad, praise surround throne.[1]

[1]Throne: R and L "C" hand positions, palms facing down and separated, arc both hands back
toward the body, indicating the arms of a large chair.

This ASL translation © 1995 The United Methodist Publishing House

659   Jesus Our Friend and Brother

Jesus our friend, brother,
Jesus our friend, brother,
He invites us, he invites us,
meet together, meet together;
Jesus call(#1) us together, come now.

This ASL translation © 1995 Mennonite Leaders' Council

660   God Is Here

1. God here! As we your people meet
   offer praise, prayer, may we find-out full
   what[1] we share Christ. Here,
   as world surround us, all our various skills,
   arts wait come Spirit open minds, hearts.

2. Here represent, remind us our life need
   grace(#1); here table, basin,[2] pulpit;[3] here
   cross finish center place. Here honest
   preach, here silence(#1), as speech, here,
   new, make new, God Spirit comes each.

3. Here our children find welcome Jesus
   crowd, church; here as bread,
   wine accept, Christ aid us as past.
   Here servants Jesus seek worship examine
   what means daily living, believe, adore.

4. Lord all, church, kingdom, generation,
   change, doubt, keep us faithful(#2)
   gospel; help us work your purpose. Here,
   this day duty, all we finish give, receive;
   we, ourselves cannot live without you, we love you!
   We believe!

[1]What: Should be signed as "where"(#2).
[2]Basin: Should be signed as a classifier, natural motion of a large bowl with "cupped" hands. May also be signed as "holy water" after bowl.
[3]Pulpit: Should be signed as a classifier, "wood" then flat top, then the sides or any classifier representing a platform.

Jesus, We Want to Meet 661

1. Jesus, we want meet now your holy day;
   we gather(#2) surround your throne[1] now your
   holy day. You true our heaven Friend; hear
   our prayers as prayers true spoken; look our
   hearts, minds today, now your holy day.

2. We kneel wonder(#1), fear, now your holy
   day; pray God teach us here now your holy
   day. Save us, clean our hearts, lead, guide
   our acts praise; let our faith from begin
   grow, now your holy day.

3. Your bless, Lord, we seek, now your holy
   day; give joy your victory(#1) now your holy
   day. Through grace alone we saved; your
   crowd may we there; let mind Christ live us
   now your holy day.

4. Our minds we give you now your holy day;
   heart, soul consecration now your holy day.
   Holy Spirit, make us whole; bless sermon
   this place; as we leave(#1), lead us, Lord;
   we shall become your ever(#3).

[1]Throne: R and L "C" hand positions, palms facing down and separated, arc both hands back toward the body, indicating the arms of a large chair.

662   Stand Up and Bless the Lord

1. Stand-up(#2), bless Lord, you people his
   choice; stand-up(#2), bless Lord your God
   with heart, soul, voice.

2. No matter high above all praise, above
   all bless high, who will not fear his holy
   name, praise, glory?

3. O for live shine bright from his own
   altar(#1) brought, touch-our-lips, our minds
   inspire, onward heaven our thought!

4. God our strength, song, his salvation
   ours; then his love Christ proclaim with all
   our save power(#1).

5. Stand-up(#2), bless Lord; Lord your God
   adore; Stand-up(#2), bless Jesus glory name,
   from-then-on, forever.

663   Savior, Again to Thy Dear Name

1. Savior, again your precious name we
   rise(#3) with one accord our leave(#1) hymn
   praise; guard your speak from sin, hearts
   from shame, that house have
   call(#1) your name.

2. Give us your peace our going home; with
   you began, with you will end(#3) day. From
   harm danger keep your children free, for
   dark, light both like(#2) you.

3. Give us your peace through our earth
   life; peace your church from error, from
   struggle; peace our land, plenty truth, love;
   peace each heart, your spirit from above.

4. Your peace life, heal every pain; your
   peace death, hope rise(#3) again; then,
   happen your voice shall bid our conflict[1]
   cease, call(#1) us, O Lord,
   your eternity peace.

[1]Conflict: R and L "index" hand positions, palms out, fingers pointing up at an angle, move
both up to a point the indexes cross.

Sent Forth by God's Blessing   664

1. Send forward through God bless, our true
   faith confess, people God from this house
   leave(#1). Service finish, O now true
   extend, success our worship all ourself
   believe. Begin teach, receive souls reach,
   shall grow action for God, for all. God
   grace(#1) invited us, love shall unite us
   work for God kingdom, answer call(#1).

2. With praise thanks-giving God ever(#3)
   living, task our every day life we will(#1)
   face(#2). Our faith ever(#3) share, love
   ever(#3) care(#1), embrace God children each
   group(#1), people. With your grace(#1) you
   feed us, with your light now lead us; unite
   us as one this life that we share. Then may
   all live with praise thanks-giving give
   honor Christ, that name which we bear(#4).

665   Go Now in Peace

Go now peace, go now peace, may
love God surround you every place,
every place you may go.

666   Shalom to You

Peace you now, peace, my friends.
May God full mercy(#1) bless you,
my friends. All your live,
through your loving, Christ your
peace, Christ your peace.

667   Shalom

Peace, precious friends, stay(#1)
safe, precious friends, have peace, have
peace. We shall see you again, we shall
see you again, have peace, have peace.

668   Let Us Now Depart in Thy Peace

Let us now depart your peace, bless
Jesus. Send us, your homes with God
love, our hearts. Let not busy world
demand all our faithful(#2). Keep us
ever(#3) think, precious Lord, you. Amen.

Go Forth for God

1. Go-onward for God, go-to world with
   peace; be(#1) good courage, prepare with
   heaven grace(#1), God good Spirit daily
   increase, till kingdom we see face(#2).
   Go-onward for God, go-to world with peace.

2. Go-onward for God, go-to world with love;
   strengthen faith(#1), give courage weak;
   help trouble; abundance from above God love
   provide grace(#1), power(#1) we seek.
   Go-onward for God, go-to world with love.,

3. Go-onward for God, go-to world with
   strength; keep good, demand pay-attention
   right; give no person evil; Christ shall
   overcome all dark with his light. Go-onward
   for God, go-to world with strength.

4. Go-onward for God, go-to world with joy,
   serve God people every day, every hour,
   serving Christ, our every gift use, rejoice
   Holy Spirit power(#1). Go-onward for God,
   go-to world with joy.

This ASL translation © 1995 Mildred E. Peacey

Lord, Dismiss Us with Thy Blessing

1. Lord, dismiss[1] us with your bless; fill
   our hearts with joy peace; Let each
   possess(#2) your love, triumph(#2)
   redeem(#1) grace(#1). O make new us, O make
   new us, journey(#3) through this world.

2. We give thanks worship for your gospel
   joy sounds. May grow your salvation our
   heart live plenty; ever(#3) faithful(#2);
   ever(#3) faithful(#2) truth may we find.

¹Dismiss: Should be signed as "scatter."

672   God Be with You till We Meet Again

1. God with you till we meet again; through
   his counsel guide, support you, with his
   people strong(#1) embrace you; God with you
   till we meet again.

Refrain:
   Till we meet, till we meet, till we meet
   Jesus feet; till we meet, till we meet,
   God with you till we meet again.

2. God with you till we meet again; beneath
   his arms safe hide you, daily strength
   still(#1) provide you; God with you
   till we meet again.

Refrain

3. God with you till we meet again; happen
   life peril plenty confuse you, God place his
   arms never fail around you; God with you
   till we meet again.

Refrain

4. God with you till we meet again; keep
love banner-wave over you, strike(#1) life
death harm before(#3) you; God with you
till we meet again.

Refrain

God Be with You till We Meet Again   673

1. God with you till we meet again; through
God counsel guide, support you, with his
people feel care(#1) you; God with you
till we meet again.

2. God with you till we meet again; beneath
his arms safe hide you, daily strength
still(#1) provide you; God with you
till we meet again.

3. God with you till we meet again; happen
life peril plenty confuse you, God place his
arms never fail around you; God with you
till we meet again.

4. God with you till we meet again; keep
love banner-wave over you, strike(#1) death
harm before(#3) you; God with you
till we meet again.

Refrain

674   See the Morning Sun Ascending

1. See morning sun-rise, bright east sky;
   pay-attention angel voice sing praise God,
   high! Alleluia! Alleluia!
   Glory God high!

2. True may we, humble position, join(#3)
   sing above; sing with whole world, praise
   you for your great(#3) love. Alleluia!
   Alleluia! Glory God above!

3. Because your love kind ever(#3), show
   our earth way; because your mercy(#1), never
   cease, because your bless every day:
   Alleluia! Alleluia! Glory God always!

4. "Wisdom, honor, power(#1), bless!" with
   angels group(#1) we cry(#3); surround your
   throne,[1] your name confess, Lord, we would
   you come near. Alleluia! Alleluia!
   Glory God high!

[1]Throne: R and L "C" hand positions, palms facing down and separated, arc both hands back toward the body, indicating the arms of a large chair.

675   As the Sun Doth Daily Rise

1. As sun-rise daily, bright all morning
   sky, true you with one-accord, we rise(#3)
   our hearts, O Lord.

2. Every-day you provide us food, because
   from you come all good things; strength you
   give our hearts from your living
   bread, O Lord.

3. Become our guard, sin, struggle; become
   leader our life; for fear we stray far from
   you, prevent our wander(#2), O Lord.

4. Haste through Spirit grace(#1) all your
   holy will(#2), follow, while we daily search
   your Word, wisdom true give, O Lord.

5. Praise we, with heaven group(#1), Father,
   Son, Holy Spirit; you would we with
   one-accord, praise, glory, O Lord.

Rise to Greet the Sun   678

1. Rise(#1) welcome sun, red across-sky
   like(#2) warrior, strong, please face
   as man servant; birds fly high above, smell
   flower now bloom; with gracious light,
   my toil I resume.

2. Father, I implore, safe keep this child;
   make my conduct good, action calm, mild;
   respect age, humbly teach youth, always
   serving you, share your worthy truth.

3. May now day receive bless; trust Jesus
   love, my heart free from evil; clear blue
   sky above. Glad for cotton coat, plain food
   satisfy; all my many needs your
   kind hand provide.

[1]Across-sky: Should be signed with a sweeping motion across sky after signing "red."

679   O Splendor of God's Glory Bright

1. O bright God glory shine, O you that
   bring light[1] from light; O Light light, light
   living begin,[2] O day, all days make bright.

2. O you true Son, look-on-us,[3] same(#2)
   king great(#2) bright, Spirit make holy
   shine-on[4] our earth, sense(#1), continue.

3. Father, too, our prayers implore, Father
   glory ever(#3); Father all grace(#1),
   might(#1), banish sin from our delight.

4. Guide no matter we noble do, with love
   all envy subdue; make evil success change
   honest, give us grace(#1) our wrongs bear(#4).

[1]Light from light, light of light, etc.: Should be signed with both hands, directionally, first "light" with one hand, then switch and sign "light" with the other hand.
[2]Light living begin: Should be signed directionally, coming from the heart.
[3]Look-on-us: Should be signed directionally, from above to person.
[4]Shine-on: Should be signed directionally.

680   Father, We Praise Thee

1. Father, we praise you, now all-night
   end(#3); active, watch(#1), we all stand(#1)
   before(#3) you; sing, we offer prayer,
   meditation; that way we adore you.

2. Ruler(#1) all things, prepare us for
   your large-house;[1] banish our weak,
   health-whole send; bring us heaven, with
   your angels union; joy continue

3. All Holy Father, Son, equal Spirit,
   bless Trinity, send us your salvation; you
   glory, glisten, sound through all world.

[1]Large-house: Should be signed as a classifier, sign "house" very large up high.

This ASL translation © 1995 Oxford University Press

All Praise to Thee, My God, This Night   682

1. All praise you, my God, now night, for
   All bless light! Keep me, O keep me, King,
   kings[1], beneath your own almighty arms.

2. Forgive me Lord, for your precious Son,
   evil I finish done(#2) today, that with
   world, myself, you, before(#3) I sleep
   I may become peace.

3. Teach me live, that I may dread grave(#1)
   as little as my bed. Teach me die, that
   true I may rise(#1) glory on judgment day.

4. O may my soul rest on you, with pleasant
   sleep, my eyes-close,[2] sleep that may become
   more health, make serve my God
   happen I awake.

5. Praise God, from whom all bless come;
   praise him, all people here below; praise
   him above, you[3] heaven group(#1); praise
   Father, Son, Holy Spirit

[1]King, kings: Should be signed with one hand, then sign with the other hand.
[2]Eye-close: Should be signed with G" hand positions at the eyes then close the "G" hands.
[3]You: Should be signed as the plural sign.

This ASL translation © 1995 The United Methodist Publishing House

683   The Day Is Past and Over

1. Day past, and(#3); all thanks, O Lord,
   you! We pray you that hours sin may not
   become dark, O Jesus, keep us your sight,[1]
   guard us through coming night.

2. Joy day end(#3); we rise(#3) our hearts
   you, call(#1) you that hours dark may be
   without sin. O Jesus, make their dark
   become light, guard us through coming night.

3. Toil day end(#3); we rise(#3) our song
   you, ask that hour dark may free from peril.
   O Jesus, keep us in your sight, guard us
   through coming night.

4. You become our soul preserver, O God,
   because you know how-many peril through
   which we must travel(#3). Lord Jesus Christ,
   O hear our call(#1), guard save us from them all.

[1]Sight: Should be signed directionally.

684   Christ, Mighty Savior

1. Christ mighty(#2) Savior, Light all
   World, you make day bright with sunlight,
   all-night give glisten adorn, stars heaven.

2. Now come day end(#3) as sun-go-down,
   look(#2) same(#2) sunrise, pledge
   resurrection; while heaven, many
   stars appear(#2) hallowed night dark.

3. Therefore(#3) we come now evening act
   worship offer, joy sing holy song praise you,
   with all world join(#1) hearts, voices
   sing your glory.

4. Give pay-attention, we pray you, our
   earnest request(#1), that you may give us
   pardon for sin, strength for our weak heart,
   rest for hurt body, comfort weary.

5. No matter people sleep, heart shall keep
   watch(#1), forever rest peace, Jesus, light,
   dark worship our Savior now, forever.

Now, on Land and Sea Descending   685

1. Now, land,[1] sea descend, bright night
   peace very great(#2); let our evening song
   mix with holy calm surround. Alleluia!
   Alleluia! Alleluia! Amen! Let our
   evening song mix with holy calm around.

2. Short time sunset glory, stars heaven
   shine above, still(#1) tell old story, God
   continue love. Alleluia! Alleluia!
   Alleluia! Amen! Still(#1) tell old
   story, God continue love.

3. Now, our wants, burdens leave(#2) God
   care(#1), himself care(#1) all, we cease
   fear, we cease grieve; touch[2] through God our
   burden fade. Alleluia! Alleluia!
   Alleluia! Amen! We cease fear, we cease
   grieve, touch through God our burdens fade.

4. As night dark surround us, look! eternity
   stars shine; hope, faith, love show glory,
   shine Spirit sky. Alleluia! Alleluia!
   Alleluia! Amen! Hope, faith, love show
   glory, shining Spirit sky.

[1]Land: Sign "dirt," then the sign for "spread."
[2]Touch: Should be signed at the heart, not on the left wrist.

686   O Gladsome Light

1. O glad light, O grace(#1) our Creator
   face(#1), eternity glory fade, heaven, holy
   bless, our Savior Jesus Christ,
   joy your appear(#2)!

2. As light fade become dark, we see light
   all-night,[1] our common[2] song-sing. O God
   might(#1), not know you, Son form person,
   Spirit bless adore.

3. You, right belongs all praise holy song,
   O Son God, life giver.[3] You, no matter, O
   Most High, world true glory, shall
   praise forever.

[1]Lights all-night: Should be signed as "moon light" or "stars," etc.
[2]Common: R and L "Y" hand positions, palms down and separated, move both hands in a
simultaneous counterclockwise circle several times.
[3]Giver: Should be signed directionally.

Day Is Dying in the West

1. Day fade west; heaven touch earth with
   rest; wait, worship while night begin stars
   shine, through-out sky.

Refrain:
   Holy, holy, holy, Lord God group(#1)!
   Heaven, earth full you! Heaven,
   earth praise you, O Lord most high!

2. Lord life, beneath area heaven, your
   home, gather(#2) us ourself seek your face
   in your embrace, for you true near.

Refrain

3. While all-night become dark, heart love
   surround all, through glory, grace(#1) stars
   that cover your face(#1), our hearts ascend.

Refrain

4. Happen forever from our sight stars fade
   become day, become night, Lord angels, let
   our eyes see eternity morning sunrise,
   dark night.

Refrain

688   God, That Madest Earth and Heaven

1. God, himself made earth, heaven, dark,
   light, himself day for toil finish given, for
   rest night: may your angels guard-defend us,
   sleep pleasant your mercy(#1) send[1] us; holy
   dreams, hopes presence us, this long night.

2. Happen continue sunrise return
   opens-our-eyes,[2] may we begin new like(#2)
   morning, labor rise(#1). Become ready for
   task that call(#1) us, let not comfort, self
   fascinate(#2) us, strong(#1) through you
   no matter happen us, O God most wise!

[1]Send: Should be signed directionally.
[2]Opens-our-eyes: Should be signed with both closed "G" hand positions at the eyes, open
both "G" hand positions slowly.

690   The Day Thou Gavest, Lord, is Ended

1. Day you gave,[1] Lord end(#3); night
   becomes dark your command: you our morning
   song ascend; your praise shall hallow
   now our rest.

2. We thank you that your church, awake
   while earth turns onward into light,
   through all world, church keep watch(#1),
   rest not through day, not through night.

3. As over(#1) each land,[2] island(#2),
   sunrise begin another new day, voice prayer
   never silent(#1), never die, speak
   praise continue.

4. This will(#1) be done(#2), Lord; your
   throne shall never, like(#2) earth proud
   power(#1), fade. Your kingdom endures(#2),
   grows forever, till all your people own
   your control(#1).

¹Gave: Should be signed directionally.
²Land: Sign "dirt," then the sign for "spread."

This ASL translation © 1995 The United Methodist Publishing House

Creator of the Stars of Night   692

1. Creator stars all-night, your people
   eternity light, O Christ, you Savior all
   us, we pray you, hear us happen we call(#1).

2. Happen great(#3) name Jesus now all
   kneel must bow, all hearts must honor;
   things heaven you shall own, things earth
   Lord alone. Amen.

This ASL translation © 1995 The Church Pension Fund

Come, Ye Thankful People, Come   694

1. Come, you thank people, come rise(#3)
   song harvest home; all safe gather(#1)-in,
   before(#1) winter storms begin. God, our
   Maker, finish provide for our wants come God
   own temple, come, rise(#3) song harvest home.

2. All world God own kingdom, grow as
   praise God we yield; good bad together
   spread, same as joy sorrow grow; first green
   grow, then ear, then full corn shall
   appear(#1); Lord harvest, grant(#1) that we
   health pure may become.

3. For Lord our God shall come, shall bring
harvest home; from field(#2) shall that day
all sin clean-away, give angels control(#1)
last(#1) cast-out bad fire; but good keep
store(#2) house ever(#3).

4. Nevertheless Lord, quick come, bring
your final harvest home; gather(#2) your
people, free from sorrow, free from sin,
there, forever pure, presence remain; come,
with all your angels, come, bring glory
harvest home.

695 O Lord, May Church and Home Combine

1. O Lord, may church, home join(#1) teach
your perfect way, with gentle(#1), love
like(#2) you, that none will ever(#3) stray.

2. Let all not worthy aims depart, inspire[1]
us with your grace(#1); within home, let
every person become your dwell place.

3. Shine, Light divine; show your face(#1)
place might(#2) dark. Grant(#1), Love
divine, every place glad fellowship with you.

4. May continue faith, earnest prayer keep
holy vow safe; build your hallowed dwell
place true joy, peace endure(#2).

[1]Inspire: R and L flat "O" hand positions, palms facing body at the heart, fingers pointing
up, move both hands up opening into "5" hand positions.

America the Beautiful

1. O beautiful for space sky, for yellow waves[1] grain;
   for purple mountain very strong(#1) above
   green[2] plain! America! America! God scatter
   his grace(#1) you, crown you good with
   common[3] aim from sea, shine sea.

2. O beautiful for brave persons prove liberation
   struggle, themselves more than self they love
   country, mercy(#1) more than life! America! America!
   May God your gold make pure, till all success
   become noble, every gain(#2) divine.

3. O beautiful for people dream that see beyond years,
   your white like(#2) cities glisten, not fade
   through people tears! America! America!
   God correct your every fault, make certain
   your soul self control(#1), your liberation law.

[1]Waves: Should be signed as a classifier, R and L "4" hand positions, palms facing each other, fingers pointing up, natural motion of wheat blowing in the wind.
[2]Green: Should be signed from the left all the way to the right.
[3]Common: R and L "Y" hand positions, palms down and separated, move both hands in a simultaneous counterclockwise circle several times.

This ASL translation © 1995 The United Methodist Publishing House

America

1. My country, true you, pleasant land[1]
   liberation, you I sing; land place my
   fathers died, land traveler(#3) pride, from
   every mountain let free ring(#2)!

2. My native[2] country, you, land noble free,
   your name I love; I love your rock, small
   river, your woods flat hills;[3] my heart with
   joy thrills, like(#2) that above.

3. Let music fill breeze, ring(#2) from
   all trees pleasant free song; let people
   languages awake; let all that breathe
   participate; let rocks their silence(#1)
   break, sound continue.

4. Our father God, you, Creator liberation,
   you we sing, long(#2) may our land bright
   with free holy light; protect us through
   your might(#1), great(#3) God, our King.

[1]Land: Sign "dirt," then the sign for "spread."
[2]Native: Should be signed as "natural."
[3]Hills: Should be signed as a classifier, the natural motion of making hills from the left to the right, with "cupped" hand positions.

698   God of the Ages

1. God generations, himself almighty hand
   leads onward beauty, all star group(#1) shine[1]
   world glory through sky, our grateful songs
   before(#3) your throne[2] sing.

2. Your love divine finish led us past; now
   free land with you we join(#3); become our
   ruler(#1), protect, guide, support, your Word
   become our law, your path become our
   chosen way.

3. From conflict[3] warn, from spread evil,
   become your strong(#1) arm our ever(#3) sure
   defense, your true religion our hearts
   increase; your plenty good care(#1) us, peace.

4. Make new your people as people require
   hard work way; lead us from night continue
   day; fill all our lives with love, grace(#1)
   divine, glory, praise ever(#3) become yours.

[1]Shine: Should be signed directionally.
[2]Throne: R and L "C" hand positions, palms facing down and separated, arc both hands back toward the body, indicating the arms of a large chair.
[3]Conflict: R and L "index" hand positions, palms out, fingers pointing up at an angle, move both up to a point the indexes cross.

Come, and Let Us Sweetly Join 699

1. Come, let us pleasant join(#3), Christ
   praise hymns divine; give[1] us all with
   one-accord glory our common[2] Lord.

2. Hands, hearts, voices rise(#3), sing as
   long-ago; happen before(#3) joys above,
   celebrate feast love.

3. Jesus, precious expect visitor, you true
   bid feast; our hearts prepare for you; come,
   sit-around[3] table there.

4. Make us holy, Lord, bless, breathe your
   Spirit, give your peace; you yourself within
   us inspire,[4] make our feast become feast love.

[1]Give: Should be signed directionally.
[2]Common: May be signed with R and L "Y" hand positions, palms facing down and separated, move both hands simultaneously in counterclockwise circle several times.
[3]Sit-around: R and L bent "V" hand positions, palms facing down, fingers pointing out in front of the body, twisting both wrists respectively out in an arc motion, ending with fingers pointing toward body.
[4]Inspire: R and L flat "O" hand positions, palms facing body at the heart, fingers pointing up, move both hands up opening into "5" hand positions.

Abide with Me

1. Dwell with me; sundown comes fast;
   become dark; Lord, with me dwell.
   Happen other helpers fail, comforts flee,
   help for without help, O dwell with me.

2. Fast finish life quick day; world
   joy become dark; glory fade; change, decay I
   see all around; O God yourself never change,
   dwell with me.

3. I need your presence every hour. What
   but your grace(#1) only can prevent devil
   power(#1)? Who, like(#2) yourself, can become
   my guide, support? Through cloud, sunshine,
   dwell with me.

4. I fear no foe, with you near bless; evil
   no power(#1) conquer me, tears not bitter.
   Where death heartache?[1] Where, grave, your
   victory(#1)? I triumph(#1) still(#1),
   if you dwell with me.

5. You hold your cross before(#3) my
   close-eyes;[2] shine[3] through gloom, show me blue[4]
   sky. Heaven morning bright, world dark fade
   life, death, O Lord, dwell with me.

[1]Heartache: Should be signed at the heart.
[2]Close-eyes: Should be signed with both "G" hand positions at the eyes, then close both "G" hand positions.
[3]Shine: Should be signed directionally.
[4]Blue: Should be signed starting from the left and move all the way across to the right.

When We All Get to Heaven

1. Sing wonderful(#1) love Jesus; sing his mercy(#1) his grace(#1). Large house bright bless Jesus will(#1) prepare for us place.

Refrain:

Happen we all arrive heaven, what day rejoice that will(#1) be(#1)! Happen we all see Jesus, we sing shout victory(#1)!

2. While we walk traveler(#3) path, clouds will(#1) spread over sky; but happen travel(#3) days end(#3), not shadow, not sad.

Refrain

3. Let us then true faithful(#2), trust serving every day; only one look him glory will(#1) value toil life.

Refrain

4. Onward gift before(#3) us! Now his beauty we will(#1) see; now heaven gates will(#1) open; we shall walk streets gold.

Refrain

Sing with All the Saints in Glory

1. Sing with all angels glory, sing resurrection
   song! Death, sorrow, earth dark story,
   past days belong. All around clouds true fade,
   now storms time will(#1) cease; God like(#2) we,
   awake, know ever(#3) last(#3) peace.

2. O what glory, far-beyond all that eye finish see!
   Most holy hearts, since generation plea,
   never that full joy conceive(#2).
   God finish promise, Christ prepare, there high
   our welcome wait. Every humble spirit share;
   Christ finish pass through eternity gates.

3. Life eternity! heaven rejoice: Jesus lives,
   himself past dead. Join(#1) we now continue voices;
   child God, lift-up[1] your head! Fathers
   from long-ago, saints all long(#2) for their
   heaven, prophets, psalmists, star watch(#1),
   wise men, all await glory give.

4. Life eternity! O what[2] wonders(#2) crowd faith:
   what joy not known, happen, amid earth
   closing thunders, angels shall stand before(#3)
   throne![3] O enter that bright door, see that glow
   sky; know, with you, O God live forever,
   "Jesus Christ whom you finish sent!"

[1]Lift-up: Should be signed as a classifier, Right "S" hand position, arm is up with wrist bent so that palm is facing down, fingers facing out, bend wrist up, the natural motion of lifting up the head.
[2]What: Should be signed as "where"(#2).
[3]Throne: R and L "C" hand positions, palms facing down and separated, arc both hands back toward the body, indicating the arms of a large chair.

Swing Low, Sweet Chariot

Refrain:
Ride, pleasant chariot, coming carry me
heaven; ride, pleasant chariot, coming
carry me heaven.

1. I look-over[1] "J"-country, what[2] I see,
coming carry me heaven? Group(#1) angels
coming carry me, coming carry me heaven.

Refrain

2. If you arrive before I arrive, coming
carry me heaven; tell[3] all my friends, I
coming too, coming carry me heaven.

Refrain

3. Sometimes I inspire,[4] sometimes I depress,
coming carry me heaven; but still(#1) my
soul feels arrive heaven, coming
carry me heaven.

Refrain

4. Bright day that I can say, coming carry
me heaven; happen Jesus wash-away my sins,
coming carry me heaven.

Refrain

[1]Look-over: Should be signed as a classifier, as the sign "look" is moved out and up, slowly bend wrist to move down.
[2]What: Should be signed as "where" (#2).
[3]Tell: Should sign "announce."
[4]Inspire: R and L flat "O" hand positions, palms facing body at the heart, fingers pointing up, move both hands up opening into "5" hand positions.

Steal Away to Jesus

Refrain:
> Go quiet, go quiet; go quiet Jesus. Go quiet, go quiet home. I not long(#2) stay here.

1. My Lord he call(#1) me, he call(#1) me through thunder; trumpet[1] sounds within my heart. I not long(#2) stay here.

Refrain

2. Green trees bend,[2] poor sinner stand trembling;[3] trumpet sounds within my heart. I not long(#2) stay here.

Refrain

3. My Lord he call(#1) me, he call(#1) me through lightning; trumpet sounds within my heart. I not long(#2) stay here.

Refrain

[1]Trumpet: Same sign as "trombone" with the exception the right does not move out and back, but held steady, and the left fingers tap up and down.
[2]Bend: Should be signed as the natural motion of the tree bending over as a result of a strong wind.
[3]Trembling: R and L "5" hand positions, palms facing body, fingers pointing down, shake hands several times.

Soon and Very Soon

1. Short time, very short time, we go-to
   see King; (Hallelujah!) short time, very
   short time, we go-to see King: (Hallelujah!)
   short time, very short time, we go-to see
   King. Hallelujah! Hallelujah!
   We go-to see King.

2. No more dying there, we go-to see King;
   (Hallelujah!) no more dying there, we go-to
   see King: (Hallelujah!) no more dying there,
   we go-to see King. Hallelujah! Hallelujah!
   We go-to see King.

3. No more crying there, we go-to see King;
   (Hallelujah!) no more crying there, we go-to
   see King; (Hallelujah!) no more crying there,
   we go-to see King. Hallelujah! Hallelujah!
   We go-to see King.

707   Hymn of Promise

1. Bulb[1] there true flower; seed(#3), apple
   tree; cocoon,[2] hid promise: butterfly
   will(#1) short time free! In cold snow
   winter find spring that wait begin, not made
   known till time, something God alone can see.

2. True song every silence(#1), seek word
   song; true many sunrise every dark, bring
   hope you me.[3] From past become future; what
   future holds, secret not made known till
   time, something God alone can see.

3. Our end(#1) our begin; our time,
   continue; in our doubt our believe our life,
   eternity. In our death, resurrection;
   last(#1), victory(#1), not made known till
   time, something God alone can see.

[1]Bulb: Should be signed as a classifier, both "cupped" hands together, fingers pointing up, open, close.
[2]Cocoon: Should be signed as a classifier, both "cupped" hands together, right on top, fingers pointing out, then right index finger makes winding motions around the left hand several times.
[3]You me: Right "V" hand position, palm up, point out with the index, then bend wrist back toward body with the middle finger pointing to the body, repeat several times.

708   Rejoice in God's Saints

1. Rejoice God saints, today, everyday;
   world without saints forgets how praise.
   Their faith become habit prayer, their
   center adore, Lord, help us share.

2. Some march(#1) with events change them
   God way; some need withdraw(#1), better pray.
   Some tell gospel through excite, through inform;
   our world true their area; their purpose true God.

3. Rejoice with saints, not praised, not
   known, themselves bear(#4) other cross,
   burden their cross. They shame our complain,
   our comforts, our worry, what patience
   care(#1), what courage, true theirs!

4. Rejoice God saints, today, everyday;
   world without saints forget how praise.
   Love, live, they prove true; way self give, Lord, lead us you.

Come, Let Us Join Our Friends Above   709

1. Come, let us join(#3) our friends above
   themselves obtain gift, eagle wings love joy
   heaven rise(#3). Let Christians on-earth
   unite sing with those gone past, for all
   servants our King on-earth heaven one.

2. One family we dwell him, one church
   above, beneath, although now divide through
   death, narrow continue death; one group(#1)
   live God, his command we bow; part his
   group(#1) finish arrive, part arrive now.

3. Ten thousand their continue home this
   real earnest moment, we different come, we
   expect die. Even now through faith we join(#1)
   our hands with those that gone before,
   welcome offspring spread group(#1) eternity heaven.

4. Our spirit shall quick join(#1),
   like(#2) theirs with glory crown, shout see
   our Captain show, hear his trumpet[1] sound.
   O that we now might(#1) grasp our guide! O
   that word give! Come, Lord group(#1), more
   divide, all us arrive heaven.

[1]Trumpet: Same sign as "trombone" with the exception the right does not move out and back, but held steady, and the left fingers tap up and down, the natural motions of playing a trumpet.

710   Faith of Our Fathers

1. Faith our fathers, live still(#1),
   no-matter dark enter, fire, sword; O how our
   heart beat high with joy happen we
   pay-attention that glory word! Faith our
   fathers, holy faith! We will(#1) true you
   till death.

2. Faith our fathers, we will(#1) struggle
   win all world you; no matter truth that
   comes from God, we shall then become truly
   free. Faith our fathers, holy faith! We
   will(#1) true you till death.

3. Faith our fathers, we will(#1) love both
   friend, foe all our struggle; preach you,
   too, as love knows how, through kind word,
   good life. Faith our fathers, holy faith!
   we will(#1) true you till death.

For All the Saints

1. For all saints, themselves rest from
   labor, themselves you through faith
   before(#3) world confess, your name, O Jesus,
   forever bless. Alleluia, Alleluia!

2. You past their support, their protect,
   their might(#1); you Lord, their captain
   well(#1) fought battle; you dark gloom,
   their one true light. Alleluia, Alleluia!

3. O may your Christians, faithful(#2),
   true, brave, struggle as saints themselves
   nobly succeed long-ago, win(#1) victory(#1)
   crown gold. Alleluia, Alleluia!

4. O bless communion, fellowship divine!
   We feeble struggle, they glory shine; yet
   all become-one you, for all yours.
   Alleluia, Alleluia!

5. Happen struggle strong(#1), battle long,
   sounds far victory(#1) song, hearts true
   brave again, arms strong(#1).
   Alleluia, Alleluia!

6. From around world, from far ocean,
   through gates white, comes crowd people,
   sing Father, Son, Holy Spirit.
   Alleluia, Alleluia!

I Sing a Song of the Saints of God

1. I sing, saints, God, patient, brave,
   true, themselves toil, fought, live, died for
   Lord they love, knew. One was doctor, one
   was queen, one was shepherd on-green; they
   were all saints God, I mean, God help,
   become-one too.

2. They love Lord much, true worthy, true
   precious his love made them strong; they
   follow right for Jesus, all their good lives
   long(#2). One was soldier, one was priest,
   one was kill strong animal; there not reason,
   no, not one reason I should not become-one too.

3. They lived not only generations past;
   there hundred thousand living still(#1).
   World bright with joy saints themselves
   love do Jesus will(#2). You can meet them
   school, street, meet store, meet church,
   meet near sea, meet neighbor house; they
   saints God, whether rich, poor, I mean
   become-one too.

1. I know not reason God wonder(#2)
   grace(#1) me he finish made known, not
   reason, not worthy, Christ love redeem(#1)
   me for his own.

Refrain:
   But I know whom I finish believe, I persuade
   that he able keep that which I pledge him
   against that day.

2. I know not how this save faith me he
   finish give, I know not how believe his word
   made peace my heart.

Refrain

3. I know not how Spirit moves, convince us
   sin, make known Jesus through word,
   create faith him.

Refrain

4. I know not happen my Lord may come,
   night, noon, I know not if I walk valley
   with him, meet him Spirit.

Refrain

715 Rejoice, the Lord Is King

1. Rejoice, Lord King! Your Lord King adore;
   people, give thanks sing, triumph(#1)
   ever(#3). Rise(#3) your heart, rise(#3)
   your voice! rejoice, again I say, rejoice!

2. Jesus, Savior, reigns, God truth love;
   happen he finish clean our sins he take-up
   his seat above. Rise(#3) your heart,
   rise(#3) your voice! rejoice,
   again I say, rejoice!

3. His kingdom cannot fail; he rule(#1)
   over(#1) earth heaven; answer death hell(#1)
   comfort our Jesus. Rise(#3) your heart,
   rise(#3) your voice! rejoice,
   again I say, rejoice!

4. Rejoice glory hope! Jesus Judge shall
   come, carry his servants their eternity home.
   Rise(#3) your heart, rise(#3) your voice!
   rejoice, again I say, rejoice! Amen.

716 Rejoice, the Lord Is King

1. Rejoice, Lord King! Your Lord, King
   adore; people give thanks, sing,
   triumph(#1) ever(#3).

Refrain 1, 2, 3:
   Rise(#3) your heart, rise(#3) your voice;
   rejoice; again I say, rejoice.

Refrain 4:
> We short time will(#1) hear angels voice;
> trumpet[1] God shall sound, rejoice!

2. Jesus Savior reign, God truth, love;
   happen he finish clean our sin, he
   take-up his seat above.

Refrain

3. His kingdom cannot fail; he rule(#1)
   over(#1) world, heaven; answer world, hell
   come from our Jesus.
Refrain

4. Rejoice glory hope! Jesus Judge shall
   come, carry his servants their eternity
   home heaven.

Refrain 4

[1]Trumpet: Same sign as "trombone" with the exception the right does not move out and back, but held steady, and the left fingers tap up and down.

The Battle Hymn of the Republic   717

1. Mine eyes finish see glory coming Lord:
   He trampling[1]-out gather(#1) grapes(#1) place
   grapes(#1) rage store(#1); he finish free
   determine lightning his great(#2) fear quick
   fight power(#1); his truth march(#1) onward.

Refrain:
> Glory, glory, hallelujah! Glory, glory,
> hallelujah! Glory, glory, hallelujah!
> His truth march(#1) onward.

2. I finish see him watch(#1) excite hundred circle camps, they have build him altar evening dews;[2] I can read his righteous decision through dim[3] burn light; his day march(#1) onward.

Refrain

3. He finish sound trumpet[4] that shall never call(#3) fall-behind; he screen[5] hearts men before(#3) his judgment(#1) seat; O quick, my soul, answer him; rejoice, my feet! Our God march(#1) onward.

Refrain

4. Beauty white flower Christ was born across sea, with glory his heart that change you me;[6] as he died make men holy, let us die make men free, while God march(#1) onward.

Refrain

5. He come like(#2) glory morning wave(#1), he wise mighty(#2), he honor brave; true on world rest his feet, soul wrong his slave. Our God march(#1) onward.

Refrain

[1]Trampling: Should be signed as a classifier, the natural motion of walking in place, move "S" hands up and down.
[2]Dews: Should be signed, "water," then "wet" from the left to the right.
[3]Dim: R and L "5" hand positions, palms facing before the eyes, move both hands down to about the mouth level, bending all fingers.
[4]Trumpet: Same sign as "trombone" with the exception the right does not move out and back, but held steady, and the left fingers tap up and down.
[5]Screen: R and L "5" hand positions, palms facing up, move right hand down across the left, then reverse the right hand position and move out, natural motion of screening something.
[6]You me: Should be signed as one sign, Right "V," palm up, point out with the index finger, then bend wrist back toward the body, point to the body with the middle finger, repeat several times.

Lo, He Comes with Clouds Descending

1. Look, he comes with clouds descent(#2),
   past because favor sinners kill; many
   thousand saints gather(#2), increase
   triumph(#1) his group(#1) followers.
   Hallelujah! Hallelujah! Hallelujah! God
   appear(#2) on-earth reign.

2. Every eye shall now see him, dress dread
   noble; those themselves anger sold him,
   crucified him on-Cross, now deep cry(#1),
   deep cry(#1), deep cry(#1), shall
   true Jesus see.

3. Precious show his passion(#2) still(#1)
   his dazzle body bear(#4); cause continue
   exultation his save worshipers; with what[1]
   joy, with what joy, with what joy, we look
   Jesus glory wound!

4. True, Amen! Let all adore you, high your
   eternity throne;[2] Savior, accept power(#1),
   glory, demand kingdom for your own.
   Hallelujah! Hallelujah! Hallelujah!
   Everlasting God, come down.

[1]What: Should be signed as "where"(#2).
[2]Throne: R and L "C" hand positions, palms facing down and separated, move both hands back in an arc toward the body, representing the arms of a large chair.

My Lord, What a Morning

Refrain:
> My Lord what[1] morning; my Lord, what
> morning, oh, my Lord, what morning, happen
> stars begin fall.

1. You will(#1) hear trumpet[2] sound, awake
   nation beneath, look my God right hand,
   happen stars begin fall.

Refrain

2. You will(#1) hear sinner grieve, awake
   nation beneath, look my God right hand,
   happen stars begin fall.

Refrain

3. You will(#1) hear Christian shout, awake
   nation beneath, look my God right hand,
   happen stars began fall.

Refrain

[1]What: Should be signed as "where"(#2).
[2]Trumpet: Same sign as "trombone" with the exception the right does not move out and back, but held steady, and the left fingers tap up and down.

1. Awake, awake, because night fade;
   watch-men(#1) above cry(#3): Awake,
   Jerusalem,[1] last(#1)! Midnight hears welcome
   voices, thrill cry(#3) rejoices; come onward,
   you pure, night past; man come, awake; your
   glad bring your light; Alleluia! For his
   marriage feast prepare, for you must go, meet
   him there.

2. Israel hears watch-men(#1) sing, all her
   heart with joy begin; she awakes, she
   rise(#1) from gloom; for her Lord come all
   glory, strong(#1) grace(#1), truth
   victory(#1). Her Son rise(#1); her light
   true come. Joy come, you bless one, God own
   love Son; Alleluia! We follow till room
   we see place you finish bid us eat with you.

3. Now let all heaven adore you, saints
   angels sing before(#3) you, with harp, cymbal[2]
   clear sounds; one very fine(#1) white shine
   gate, place we with sing group(#1)
   everlasting angel, sit-around[3] your dazzle
   throne;[4] not eye finish see, not ear finish
   pay-attention what there become ours; but we
   rejoice, sing you our hymn(#1) joy eternity.

[1]Jerusalem: May be signed as "J"-town or "old town."
[2]Cymbal: Should be signed as a classifier, R and L "A" hand positions the natural motion of clashing the cymbals together.
[3]Sit-around: R and L bent "V" hand positions fingers point out, palms face down in front of the body, twist both wrists respectively out in arc motions, ending with fingers pointing toward body.
[4]Throne: R and L "C" hand positions, palms facing down and separated, move both hands back in an arc toward the body, representing the arms of a large chair.
[5]What: Should be signed as "where"(#2).

I Want to Be Ready

Refrain:
> I want ready, I want ready, I want ready
> walk Jerusalem[1] exact like(#2) John.[2]

1. O John, O John, what you say? Walk
   Jerusalem exact like(#2) John! That you
   would before(#3) us judgment day. Walk
   Jerusalem exact like(#2) John!

Refrain

2. John said city just(#1) beyond there.
   Walk Jerusalem exact like(#2) John! He
   declare he meet me there. Walk Jerusalem
   exact like(#2) John.

Refrain

3. Now sinners, watch(#1) how you
   step-on(#1) cross. Walk Jerusalem exact
   like(#2) John! Your foot might(#2) slip,[3]
   your soul become lost. Walk Jerusalem exact
   like(#2) John.

[1]Jerusalem: May be signed as "J"-town or "old town."
[2]John: Inscribe a "J" on the back of the left wrist with the right "J" hand position, or any other name sign for this disciple.
[3]Slip: Should be signed as a classifier, the natural motion of someone slipping, the left open hand, palm facing up, right "V" hand position.

Shall We Gather at the River

1. Shall we gather(#2) river, place bright
   angels finish walk, with clear rise(#1)
   forever come near throne[1] God?

Refrain:
   Yes, we gather(#2) river, beautiful,
   beautiful river; gather(#2) with angels river
   that comes near throne God.

2. Land[2] surround river, wash(#1) white water
   wave(#1), we will(#1) walk worship ever(#3),
   all happy very good day.

Refrain

3. Before(#3) we reach shine river, give up
   our every burden; grace(#1) our spirits
   will(#1) deliver, provide robe,[3] crown.

Refrain

4. Short time we will(#1) reach shine river,
   short time our journey(#3) will(#1) cease;
   short time our happy hearts will(#1) tremble[4]
   with music peace.

Refrain

[1]Throne: R and L "C" hand positions, palms facing down and separated, move both hands back in an arc toward the body, representing the arms of a large chair.
[2]Land: Sign for "dirt," then the sign for "spread."
[3]Robe: R and L "cupped" hands, palms up, fingers at the chest, move both hands down.
[4]Tremble: R and L "5" hand positions, palms facing body, fingers pointing down, shake hands several times.

724 On Jordan's Stormy Banks I Stand

1. "J"-country(#1) storm bank¹ I stand,
   look-foward "C"-country(#1) fair(#1)
   happy land(#1), place my possess(#2) remain.

Refrain:
   I go(#1) for promise land(#1), I go(#1) for
   promise land(#1); Oh, who will(#1) come,
   go(#1) with me? I go(#1) for promise land(#1).

2. Over(#2) all wide spread shine one
   forever day; there God, Son forever reign,
   night become day.

Refrain

3. No cold wind, harm breath can
   reach health support; sick, sorrow,
   pain, death, feel, fear no more.

Refrain

4. Happen I reach that happy place,
   I forever bless, because I shall see
   my Father face(#1), his arm, I rest(#1).

Refrain

¹Bank: Should be signed as a classifier, the natural motion of a mound of dirt, with the "cupped" hands, palms facing down.

This ASL translation © 1995 The United Methodist Publishing House

Arise, Shine Out, Your Light Has Come 725

1. Rise(#1), shine-out,[1] your light finish
   come, open city our dreams. On far hill[2]
   glory glisten; new world finish begun.

2. Above earth valley, dark with night,
   high on your walls(#2) level[3] sunrise
   appear(#2), history shall dry tears, as
   nations march(#2) onward your light.

3. From walls(#2) exceed time, space not
   counted gates, like(#2) open hands, shall
   gather(#1) gifts from all country(#1),
   welcome all people world.

4. Sounds destruction will cease, as house
   salvation build shine forever sky from
   street praise, peace.

5. Dance music will(#1) shine with light,
   sun, moon, fade, happen love shine from
   every face(#1), our good, our
   glory, delight.

[1]Shine-out: Should be signed directionally.
[2]Hill: Should be signed as a classifier, the natural motion of making a hill with "cupped" hand positions from the left to the right.
[3]Level: Should be signed as a classifier, the natural line of sun appearing on the wall.

O Holy City, Seen of John

1. O holy city, see John,[1] place Christ, Lord
   true reigns, within whose area wall(#1) shall
   come no night, no need, no pain, place tears
   dry from eyes that shall not weep(#1) again.

2. Pay-attention, how from men whose lives
   true more cheap than things, from women
   struggle hard for bread, from little
   children cry(#1), there increase grief people
   complaint that bid your defense appear(#2).

3. O shame us ourself rest(#1) content
   while desire, greedy for profit street,
   store, homes force-out gold from people pain,
   bitter talk, blind loss hope cry(#3), "Christ
   finish die vain!"

4. Give us, O God, strength build city that
   finish stood too long dream, whose laws love,
   whose crown servant, place sun that shine
   God grace(#1) for people good.

5. Finish mind God, that city rise(#3)
   fair(#1): see, how city great(#2)
   bright challenges soul that brave; yes, bid us
   grasp whole life, build glory there.

[1]John: Inscribe a "J" on the back of the left wrist with the right "J" hand position, or any other name sign for this disciple.

1. O what their joy, their glory must become,
   those continue Sundays bless people see;
   crown for brave, weary people rest(#1);
   God shall become all, ever(#3) bless.

2. True, "J"-old-town name we support,
   city peace that bring joy ever(#3);
   wish(#1), promise not separate there,
   not thing pray for come short prayer.

3. There, place no trouble disturb can bring,
   we pleasant song heaven shall sing; while for
   your grace(#1), Lord, their voice praise your
   bless people forever inspire.[1]

4. Now, while with heart inspire, we for
   that country(#2) must desire, must grieve(#2),
   seek "J"-old town, precious native land(#1)
   through our long(#2) escape "B"-country(#1)
   abandon(#2).

5. Humble before(#3) him with our praise
   we kneel, whom, through whom all; whom
   Father(#1);[2] whom Son, through Spirit, with
   them ever(#3) one.

[1]Inspire: R and L flat "O" hand positions, palms facing body at the heart, fingers pointing up, move both hands up opening into "5" hand positions.
[2]Father: Should be signed as "our heavenly Father."

728   Come Sunday

Oo, Oo, Come Sunday, oh, come Sunday that day.

Refrain:
> Lord, precious Lord above, God almighty,
> God love, please look-down, see my
> people through.

1. I believe that God put sun, moon, up-sky.
   I don't-care(#2) gray(#4) sky, because only
   clouds that pass-by.

Refrain

2. Heaven good time, bright light high.
   "Do unto others as you want others do unto
   you," have bright future.

Refrain

3. I believe God now, past, always future,
   with God bless, we can make through eternity.

729   O Day of Peace That Dimly Shines

1. O day peace that everyday shine through
   all our hopes, prayers, dreams, guide us
   justice(#1), truth, love, deliver from our
   selfish plans. May hate fade from our minds,
   our hearts from envy find free, till
   through God grace(#1) our world shall see
   Christ promise reign peace.

2. Then shall greedy dwell with innocent,
   not shall angry destroy small; like(#2)
   animals, cows calm eat together, little
   child shall lead them. Then enemies shall
   learn love, all people find their true
   accord; hope peace shall satisfy, for all
   world shall know Lord.

O Day of God, Draw Nigh   730

1. O day God, come near with beauty,
   power(#1); come with your continue
   judgment now, equal our present hour.

2. Bring our trouble mind, not certain,
   afraid, quiet continue faith,
   calm call(#1) obey.

3. Bring justice(#1) our country(#1)
   that all may dwell safe, fine(#1) build
   for future foundation that endure(#2).

4. Bring our world struggle your great(#2)
   world peace, that war may no more annoy
   world, sorrow cease.

5. O day God, come near as world begin;
   let there light again, found your
   judgments on-earth.

Glorious Things of Thee Are Spoken

1. Glory things spoken about you,
   "J-old-town," city our God; God himself
   word cannot broken, form you for his own
   dwell. On strong(#1) support found, what
   can shake your sure peace? With salvation
   wall(#1) surround, you may smile
   all your foes.

2. See, river living water, begin from
   eternity love, well(#2) provide for your sons,
   daughters, all fear want remove. Who can
   faint(#1) while same river ever(#3) will(#1)
   their thirst satisfy? Grace(#1) which
   like(#2) Lord, give, never fails from
   generation, generation.

3. Around each house not certain, see cloud,
   excite appear(#2) for glory all over, show
   that Lord near! That way get from our leader
   light through all-night, cool wind through
   all-day, safe we eat bread which God gives
   us happen we pray.

4. Bless people Israel, wash(#1) with our
   Redeemer(#1) blood; Jesus, himself our souls
   depend, make us ruler(#1), priests for God.
   Us, through his great(#3) love, he rise(#1)
   rule(#1) over self reign, as priests his
   earnest praise we bring thank offer.

Come, We That Love the Lord

1. Come, we ourselves love Lord,
   let our joys become known; join(#3)
   song with pleasant accord, that
   way surround throne.[1]

2. Let those themselves refuse sing,
   themselves never knew our God; but
   children heaven King may speak
   their joys far.

3. Hill "J-old-town" yield thousand
   holy pleasant before(#3) we reach
   heaven field(#2), walk gold streets.

4. Then let our songs plenty, every
   tear become dry; we march(#1) through
   Christ land(#1) fair(#1) world on-high.

[2]Throne: R and L "C" hand positions, palms facing down and separated, move both hands
back in an arc toward the body, representing the arms of a large chair.

Marching to Zion

1. Come, we that love Lord, let our joys
become known; join(#3) song with pleasant
accord, join(#3) song with pleasant accord,
that way surround throne, that way
surround throne.

Refrain:
We march(#1) Heaven City, beautiful,
beautiful Heaven City; we march(#1)
upward Heaven City, beautiful city God.

2. Let people themselves refuse sing,
themselves never knew our God; but children
heaven King, but children heaven King may
speak their joys far, make speak
their joys far.

Refrain

3. Hill "J-old-town" yield thousand holy
pleasant before(#3) we reach heaven field(#2),
before(#3) we reach heaven field(#2), walk
gold streets, walk gold streets.

Refrain

4. Then let our songs plenty, every tear
become dry; we march(#1) through Christ
land(#1), we march(#1) through Christ
land(#1), fair(#1) worlds high, fair(#1)
worlds high.

Refrain

INDEX OF FIRST LINES AND COMMON TITLES

478